THE LORD IS
MY SHEPHERD

**TOUCHSTONE
TEXTS**

Stephen B. Chapman, Series Editor

*The Lord Is My Shepherd: Psalm 23 for the Life of
the Church* by Richard S. Briggs

THE LORD IS MY SHEPHERD

Psalm 23 for the Life of the Church

RICHARD S. BRIGGS

Baker Academic

a division of Baker Publishing Group
Grand Rapids, Michigan

© 2021 by Richard S. Briggs

Published by Baker Academic
a division of Baker Publishing Group
PO Box 6287, Grand Rapids, MI 49516-6287
www.bakeracademic.com

Printed in the United States of America

Library of Congress Cataloging-in-Publication Data
Names: Briggs, Richard S., 1966– author.
Title: The Lord is my shepherd : Psalm 23 for the life of the church / Richard S. Briggs.
Description: Grand Rapids, Michigan : Baker Academic, a division of Baker Publishing Group, [2021] | Series: Touchstone texts | Includes bibliographical references and indexes.
Identifiers: LCCN 2021006697 | ISBN 9781540961853 (cloth) | ISBN 9781493432127 (ebook)
Subjects: LCSH: Bible. Psalms, XXIII—Criticism, interpretation, etc.
Classification: LCC BS1450 23d .B75 2021 | DDC 223/.206—dc23
LC record available at https://lccn.loc.gov/2021006697

Baker Publishing Group publications use paper produced from sustainable forestry practices and post-consumer waste whenever possible.

21 22 23 24 25 26 27   7 6 5 4 3 2 1

To Hugh and Barbara Mason
and to Melinda, Dustin, and the ever-growing circle
of Melody's family

with thanks for happy days on the farm
and for welcoming me into your lives

Contents

Series Preface   ix

Preface   xi

Abbreviations   xv

1. Introduction: *On Attending to Psalm 23*   1

2. The World behind Psalm 23: *Background*   21

3. The World in Psalm 23: *Exegesis*   65

4. The World in Front of Psalm 23: *Ministry*   131

5. Conclusion: *Hearing and Preaching Psalm 23 Today*   171

Appendix: *Notes on Psalm 23 in Hebrew*   179

Bibliography   183

Scripture Index   195

Subject Index   199

Series Preface

In writing workshops, "touchstone texts" are high quality writing samples chosen to illustrate teaching points about compositional techniques, genre conventions, and literary style. Touchstone texts are models that continually repay close analysis. The Christian church likewise possesses core scriptural texts to which it returns, again and again, for illumination and guidance.

In this series, leading biblical scholars explore a selection of biblical touchstone texts from both the Old Testament and the New Testament. Individual volumes feature theological *exposition*. To exposit a biblical text means to set forth the sense of the text in an insightful and compelling fashion while remaining sensitive to its interpretive challenges, potential misunderstandings, and practical difficulties. An expository approach interprets the biblical text as a word of God to the church and prioritizes its applicability for preaching, instruction, and the life of faith. It maintains a focus primarily on the biblical text in its received canonical form, rather than engaging in historical reconstruction as an end in itself (whether of the events behind the text or the text's literary formation). It listens to individual texts in concert with the rest of the biblical canon.

Each volume in this series seeks to articulate the plain sense of a well-known biblical text by what Aquinas called "attending to the way the words go" (*salva litterae circumstantia*). Careful exegesis is pursued either phrase by phrase or section by section (depending on the biblical text's length and genre). Authors discuss exegetical, theological, and pastoral concerns in combination rather than as discrete moves or units. They offer constructive interpretations that aim to transcend denominational boundaries. They consider the use of these biblical texts in current church practice (including the lectionary) as well as church history. The goal of the series is to model expositional interpretation and thereby equip Christian pastors and teachers to employ biblical texts knowledgeably and effectively within an ecclesial setting.

Texts were chosen for inclusion partly in consultation with the authors of the series. An effort was made to select texts that are representative of various biblical genres and address different facets of the Christian life (e.g., faith, blessing, morality, worship, prayer, mission, hope). These touchstone texts are all widely used in homiletics and catechesis. They are deserving of fresh expositions that enable them to speak anew to the contemporary church and its leaders.

Stephen B. Chapman
Series Editor

Preface

In this book I seek to resource the reader to understand Psalm 23 well—in and for the life of the church. This involves cultivating several practices, including developing the necessary tools of exegesis and interpretation and accessing the necessary reserves of theological and spiritual wisdom. For better or for worse I think of the first of these as drawing mostly upon my scholarly training and the second of these as drawing mostly upon my ministerial training, although each also strengthens and refines the other. One result is a book that seeks to speak with both scholarly and ministerial integrity about multiple aspects of reading Psalm 23. I have written for students and parishioners; essay writers and worshipers; scholars and ministers. I like to think that some readers—like myself—may fit all these labels at once.

Psalm 23 is a familiar text to many, and some of the interpretive ground we will be covering may seem familiar too. But how and why we read the Bible the way we do is not always well understood. Thus I try to explain the interpretive moves we can and do make when we handle this particular "touchstone text." One result is that the book might serve as a primer on questions that are helpful to explore in the task of reading any scriptural passage wisely, even while the main focus throughout is on Psalm 23.

It has been an immense privilege to write this book. I grew up in London and had a happy childhood, though not one that involved Christian faith. I am at home in large cities, riding metro systems—of which the London Underground tube network is still my favorite—shopping at large supermarkets, writing in urban coffee shops, and mixing in large crowds. By background I am therefore possibly one of the least qualified people to write a book about Psalm 23 in the life of the church. But it turns out that it is not where you come from that matters most in reading a scriptural text but where your heart dwells, and my heart (and mind and soul) has been seeking to live in the world of the biblical text for many years now.

I owe much to my wife, Melody, and her family for my sympathy toward a vision of rural life. Melody grew up on a farm in West Virginia and prefers to live a long way from crowds and metro systems. What wisdom there may be about shepherds and farming in this book comes from her and her family, and so it is my pleasure to dedicate this book to them, with many thanks for happy rural adventures that I did not imagine when growing up.

As always, writing is not a solo achievement. I am grateful to Stephen Chapman for inviting me to contribute to this series and offering wise editorial oversight. Likewise it has once again been a pleasure to work with Jim Kinney and the wonderful staff at Baker Academic. Walter Moberly has been a good friend and dialogue partner throughout, providing encouragement and insight in equal measure. I am also indebted to Philip Plyming for his life-giving leadership of Cranmer Hall, Durham, where I work, and for facilitating the study leave that enabled the writing of this book.

I began writing three days after Matthew, our youngest child, went to college. The house was mysteriously quiet—a very mixed blessing. It has since been filled with Psalm 23, which is a very real blessing. I must also acknowledge the presence of our dog, Charlie, who would make absolutely the worst sheep dog ever because he would be scared of the sheep. Normally I need to say that all errors are mine alone. But on this occasion I would like to share responsibility for any remaining errors with Charlie, since his gift for barking mainly while I'm editing tricky details is remarkable.

A Note on Presentation

There are a lot of minor technical issues that beset writing about the Psalms. These include decisions about which numbering system to use for each psalm and its verses and what versions (ancient and modern) to discuss when reading the text—all matters that are taken up at various points in the book. I have simplified these here and always give the psalm number according to the NRSV, and usually the verse number too, which makes no difference in the case of Psalm 23. Exceptions are clearly stated. I restrict key translations, for the purpose of reviewing options, to the KJV, NIV, NRSV, ESV, and NJPS. Others make appearances when interesting, especially *The Message* (MSG) and Robert Alter's *The Hebrew Bible* translation with commentary (Alter). In general, when I say "modern versions," I mean those just noted after the KJV. The Greek version of the Old Testament (known generally as the Septuagint [LXX]) is available in English as NETS. Jerome's Vulgate Latin text of the Psalms is explained as necessary. I have made a small attempt to stem the flood of endless referencing and footnotes by restricting myself to noting only sources that I have actually read on the point being discussed, with a couple of exceptions (noted) where it is appropriate to reference someone being discussed by another author.

Abbreviations

Old Testament

Gen.	Genesis	Eccles.	Ecclesiastes
Exod.	Exodus	Song	Song of Songs
Lev.	Leviticus	Isa.	Isaiah
Num.	Numbers	Jer.	Jeremiah
Deut.	Deuteronomy	Lam.	Lamentations
Josh.	Joshua	Ezek.	Ezekiel
Judg.	Judges	Dan.	Daniel
Ruth	Ruth	Hosea	Hosea
1 Sam.	1 Samuel	Joel	Joel
2 Sam.	2 Samuel	Amos	Amos
1 Kings	1 Kings	Obad.	Obadiah
2 Kings	2 Kings	Jon.	Jonah
1 Chron.	1 Chronicles	Mic.	Micah
2 Chron.	2 Chronicles	Nah.	Nahum
Ezra	Ezra	Hab.	Habakkuk
Neh.	Nehemiah	Zeph.	Zephaniah
Esther	Esther	Hag.	Haggai
Job	Job	Zech.	Zechariah
Ps(s).	Psalm(s)	Mal.	Malachi
Prov.	Proverbs		

New Testament

Matt.	Matthew	1 Cor.	1 Corinthians
Mark	Mark	2 Cor.	2 Corinthians
Luke	Luke	Gal.	Galatians
John	John	Eph.	Ephesians
Acts	Acts	Phil.	Philippians
Rom.	Romans	Col.	Colossians

1 Thess.	1 Thessalonians	1 Pet.	1 Peter
2 Thess.	2 Thessalonians	2 Pet.	2 Peter
1 Tim.	1 Timothy	1 John	1 John
2 Tim.	2 Timothy	2 John	2 John
Titus	Titus	3 John	3 John
Philem.	Philemon	Jude	Jude
Heb.	Hebrews	Rev.	Revelation
James	James		

Apostolic Fathers

1 Clem.   1 Clement

Bible Versions

Alter   Alter, Robert. *The Hebrew Bible: A Translation with Commentary*. 3 vols. New York: Norton, 2019

BHS   *Biblia Hebraica Stuttgartensia*. Edited by K. Elliger and W. Rudolph. Rev. ed. Stuttgart: Deutsche Bibelgesellschaft, 1997

ESV   English Standard Version

KJV   King James Version

LXX   Rahlfs, Alfred, ed. *Septuagint*. 2nd rev. ed. Edited by Robert Hanhart. Stuttgart: Deutsche Bibelgesellschaft, 2006

MSG   *The Message*

MT   Masoretic Text

NA28   Eberhard Nestle et al., eds. *Novum Testamentum Graece*. 28th rev. ed. Stuttgart: Deutsche Bibelgesellschaft, 2012

NEB   New English Bible

NETS   *A New English Translation of the Septuagint and the Other Greek Translations Traditionally Included under That Title*. Edited by Albert Pietersma and Benjamin G. Wright. New York: Oxford University Press, 2007

NIV   New International Version

NJPS   New Jewish Publication Society Version

NRSV   New Revised Standard Version

REB   Revised English Bible

RSV   Revised Standard Version

Grammar Terms

1cs   first-person common singular

2ms   second-person masculine singular

3ms   third-person masculine singular

3mp	third-person masculine plural
fem	feminine
impf	imperfect
inf	infinitive
masc	masculine
perf	perfect

Secondary Resources

BCP	*1662 Book of Common Prayer.* Cambridge: Cambridge University Press, 2004
BDB	Brown, Francis, S. R. Driver, and Charles A. Briggs. *A Hebrew and English Lexicon of the Old Testament.* Peabody, MA: Hendrickson, 1996
DCH	*Dictionary of Classical Hebrew.* Edited by David J. A. Clines. 9 vols. Sheffield: Sheffield Phoenix, 1993–2014
FIOTL	Formation and Interpretation of Old Testament Literature
GKC	*Gesenius' Hebrew Grammar.* Edited by Emil Kautzsch. Translated by Arther E. Crowley. 2nd ed. Oxford: Clarendon: 1910
JSOT	*Journal for the Study of the Old Testament*
JSOTSup	Journal for the Study of the Old Testament Supplement Series
LHBOTS	Library of Hebrew Bible/Old Testament Studies
NICOT	New International Commentary on the Old Testament
NICOT, *Psalms*	deClaissé-Walford, Nancy L., Rolf A. Jacobson, and Beth LaNeel Tanner. *The Book of Psalms.* NICOT. Grand Rapids: Eerdmans, 2014
SHS	Scripture and Hermeneutics Series
VTSup	Supplements to Vetus Testamentum

1

Introduction

On Attending to Psalm 23

■ **"The Lord Is My Shepherd; I Shall Not Want"**

The opening verse of the Twenty-Third Psalm is a famous statement of confidence and trust. Cited here in its familiar King James idiom, the declaration resounds that the Lord God is concerned with me personally, as *my* shepherd, and that my needs will therefore be met. Questions of technical complexity—history, hermeneutics, scholarly commentary—take a back seat in the first flowering of the joy of a plain reading: the Lord is my shepherd. Only professional biblical scholars would have thought otherwise. For multitudes of readers and hearers over many centuries, it is the emotive uplift of this great opening verse that rings loud and clear. All is well and all shall be well. God is good . . . even specifically to me.

Students and ministers trained by long years of hard engagement with the works of biblical studies may be expecting a "but . . ." You may anticipate, dear reader, that after this heartwarming opening focus I shall immediately cut across your desires for spiritual edification and theological encouragement with some such statement as "But such simple reading fails to take into account all the interpretive complexities with which one must wrestle." Then this deflationary moment would be followed by page after page of slowly removing the text from the realms of joy or reassurance and leaving it stranded millennia ago under layers of reconstructed history or learned discussions of shepherding practices in the ancient Near East. There would perhaps be opportunity, too, for those most disheartening of scholarly observations: that our familiar and much-loved translations are mistaken, that the text never really said *that*, and so forth.

As the apostle Paul might have said, By no means! The purpose of this book is not to lose that first joyful plain-sense reading. Instead I affirm: the basic contours of the traditional understanding of Psalm 23 have not led us astray. I have no new discoveries that will show that everyone before me was wrong about this text—which would in any case be a problematic thing to claim in many ways, including theologically. More to the point, I also have no new, grand theories of historical reconstruction that will not so much *discover* the text anew as *invent* a framework for reading it. One of the points I want to make in this book is that a great deal of scholarly reflection on Psalm 23, especially in the twentieth century, is best filed under "speculation" rather than "serious historical research." Speculation can be useful, as when, for instance, it provokes us to look afresh for different kinds of supporting evidence that open up new lines of inquiry. But in my judgment, to be defended as we go, the multiple scholarly hypotheses about the setting and purpose of Psalm 23 have been supported by almost no evidence at all. Reflecting on these so-called advancements, I have felt that one purpose of this book is to set the study of Psalm 23 *back* about one hundred to one hundred fifty years, which is when it began to go off the rails. Of course there was insight and progress in that time. But as we will see, there was also a lot of unsupported conjecture, and I want to scrape much of that away.

By way of contrast, the purpose of the kind of biblical scholarship I pursue here is to allow the picture that Psalm 23 actually paints to shine forth more clearly and constructively. We will seek a full, imaginative, and serious engagement with the psalm's words and phrases, its images and its own imaginative vision, in order that we might hear it in all its widescreen wonder.[1] Let me introduce a spoiler of sorts: I will argue that Psalm 23 encourages us to rejoice that the Lord is our shepherd, who accompanies us both beside quiet waters and through the valley of the shadow of death. We will reflect on paths of righteousness, or perhaps rightness, and on goodness and mercy. In some cases, such as with the "valley of the shadow of death," I will work hardest at the scholarship of what these words mean precisely because I think that the traditional understanding has merit in spite of what several scholars have said in the intervening centuries. Overall this book will provide encouragement to those who wonder if the interpretive paths on which readers have trodden over the centuries are the right ones. The short answer is yes, they are. A longer answer would add, "more or less."

Perhaps, though, the paths have become so well worn that their full impact is sometimes missed. One aspect of our task is therefore to refresh our grasp of what Psalm 23 says and to hear it anew, and perhaps more clearly. This is *not* to hear it "as if for the first time," since as with all good poetry a first hearing is rarely the most significant one. Nor is it necessarily to hear it as having a different intent, although obviously that will depend on how any given person has heard it before. Images that get close to what we are seeking here include the renewed freshness of hearing after one has had an ear blockage removed and the ears are syringed clean, the clarity of sight that follows a new prescription of correctly specified glasses, or the joy of hearing a remastered Beatles album that reveals notes and nuances missed on a scratched and much-loved old copy. Young readers may find all these examples mystifying. So it is also like seeing an Avengers film in the movie theater when you have only seen it previously on your phone or meeting a good friend face-to-face whom you have only been able to engage with online. In none of these cases is

---

1. The language of "full imaginative seriousness" as foundational to the constructive reading of Scripture is indebted to the many works of Walter Moberly. For a clear statement, see his *Theology of the Book of Genesis*, 197; and *Old Testament Theology*, 285.

the project one of suddenly realizing that one had it all wrong, but in each case there is learning and recalibration of the insights that made the experience valuable in the first place and a deeper entry into the joy and wonder of the whole experience.

The process I have been describing is a hermeneutical engagement with Scripture that seeks a so-called second naivete—that sense of coming fresh ("naively") to the text with eyes alert and with critical insight harnessed to know what to look for and what to appreciate in an imaginative and serious reading *of what the text says*. The contrast is with all those other fascinating approaches that major on what the text does not say, or why it says what it says, and so forth. Those approaches do indeed have their place, but I seek to prioritize this critically refreshed ("second") naivete.[2]

If I labor the point, it is because modern biblical studies has often majored on critical reconstruction of much-loved texts with scant regard for its resultant trampling over much-loved understandings. Of course, this is sometimes necessary, and for some texts there have indeed been major shifts in knowledge and understanding that render former readings untenable. In my opinion, this has happened rather less than one might think from the tenor of a lot of academic biblical studies, and indeed a lot of teaching of biblical studies even in faith-based contexts. As a result, there is real work to be done in reconnecting the scholarly bricks and mortar of critical study with the living and breathing faith of thoughtful readers (Christian and Jewish) down through the ages.

Whether we are therefore engaging in "theological interpretation," "spiritual reading," or pursuing the "plain (or literal) sense of the text" is a matter of how useful such labels are for whatever purposes are at hand. What really does matter is that the integrative work is done that brings together critical attention to the details of the text, on the one hand, with thoughtful reflection on life and faith on the

---

2. The phrase "second naivete" comes from the work of Paul Ricoeur, but it is an idea better experienced than described theoretically. In my view, the most helpful account of it in theory is still Wallace, *Second Naiveté*.

other. Theological preunderstanding need not trump exegesis, nor vice versa. Holding this balance in a productive dialogue turns out to be a challenging but life-giving task. As I have sometimes expressed it to students nearing the end of taking classes in Old Testament: the task is "simply" to pay attention to what the text says, but it turns out that few tasks are as difficult to do well as paying attention to what the text says. This is in part because of the wide range of questions that immediately rush in once one takes seriously the ancient horizon of the text, the present horizon of the reader, and the intervening centuries with all their own views of what the "simple/plain understanding" might be. But all of this is recognizably different from spending our time guessing about how and when and why our featured text came to be written.

Attending to Psalm 23 in this way, with intellectual-spiritual-theological-historical-critical seriousness, requires the best of us with regard to thinking about the psalm then and now, and also at times in between then and now. As a result, understandings of the psalm through history, and uses of it in liturgy and hymnody, can all make a positive contribution to our appreciation of the text and its function(s). All such receptions of the psalm need weighing, of course, and we will be doing that in the pages that follow. Likewise, detailed focus on the original context, meaning(s), and original function of the psalm are also important to weigh, even though the extent to which we can be sure about these proves to be rather limited.

There will be plenty of focus on the text itself in what follows. I have written the book to presuppose no knowledge of Hebrew. However, detailed study of a text originally written in Hebrew does require discussion of features of the language and how it works. I do try to explain what you need to know as we go along, and I am mindful, too, that readers with awareness of Hebrew will benefit from seeing the details explored. I even hope that readers with some dim and distant memory of studying Hebrew might be encouraged to refresh their skills. However, technical Hebrew classifications and issues are reserved in a brief appendix, for those with critically trained ears to hear.

Does detailed scholarly work turn any of our cherished readings of Psalm 23 upside down? Does it do so in practice, and could it do so in theory? My third chapter will engage in a careful critical reading of the text under the broad rubric sketched above—so this will be "critical" as in "attentive to detail." But of course we read with awareness that traditional understandings may have been unhelpful or inadequate, and no matter how established a traditional reading might be, that should not exempt it from critical weighing. Now in theory I can conceive of a well-established reading being overturned, although it is worth reflecting on what such an overturning would say about centuries of earnest and already attentively critical reading.

Probably the clearest and least controversial example of such a scholarly shift has been with regard to authorship, since for reasons to be discussed in chapter 2 we should almost certainly say that King David was not the "author" of Psalm 23, in the modern sense of the term. This does make some degree of difference to various resonances set up by the psalm, although of course it is not a point about the psalm's meaning as such (except with regard to its title). However, with the poetry of Psalm 23 I find it to be the case that no established reading has become established without reason. That falls short of saying that any such reading is the best we can do, but even where I might want to change or nuance a reading, I do not think we approach such interpretation in the spirit of knocking out other contenders until one's own preferred approach is the last one standing. Texts (and especially poetic texts) simply do not work like that.

In practice, to forewarn the reader regarding chapter 3, I think there are nuances aplenty to learn in our reading, but in only one case do I think that there is a serious interpretive option that is especially clouded by a poor tradition. This is with the force of the verb traditionally interpreted "to follow" in the last verse. A lot of the details of Psalm 23:6 are difficult to handle well, but in this one instance I would urge a stronger translation than "goodness and mercy will *follow* me." Details can await the full discussion. But I hope this indicates the scale of the reliability of our traditional translations and understandings.

A Crowd of Witnesses: Cultural, Scholarly, and Popular

Psalm 23 has not suffered neglect over the years in the life of God's people, nor indeed in the academy. Here I note briefly three traditions of witnessing to the text that all have their part to play in our own engagement with the psalm. Specific points about the psalm will be harnessed for later readings of the text in subsequent chapters. Here the goal is to get a sense of the territory that lies before a reader of Psalm 23 in terms of the psalm's influence. First we note the cultural impact of the text, initially in and through worship and ministry, and now also more widely. Since this has now become itself the focus of some academic study, it is appropriate then to note various academic treatments of the psalm's reception. As a result, another category, which in some ways belongs more with the cultural impact examples, is deferred to third place: what I call "popular" readings of the psalm in devotional literature.

Cultural Impact: From Church to World

Psalm 23's setting as a Scottish hymn is well known, sung to the tune of "Crimond."[3] Arguably this is the most famous English-language version of the psalm, and it is hard for most who have sung the hymn to do anything other than read Psalm 23 through its lens. This has some interesting implications, as we will see in our exegesis in chapter 3. A more recent musical version by Stuart Townend has also become popular across a range of church traditions, testifying perhaps to the power of the familiar imagery to win over churches

---

3. For a regal version see, for example, "Psalm 23: The Lord Is My Shepherd ('Crimond')," Martin Baker, posted November 7, 2014, YouTube video, 3:06, https://www.youtube.com/watch?v=yHQoRfFr1rE. Many other versions are available.

less inclined to sing more modern worship songs. At the same time, Townend's repeated chorus line "I will trust in you alone" uses a slightly more familiar idiom for churches inclined to prefer affective choruses and songs that emphasize self-expression.[4] There are plenty of other examples of Psalm 23 set to music down through the centuries, and I am not qualified to discuss their musical merits. Susan Gillingham notes that "almost every composer interested in sacred music has had a hand in arranging this psalm as a motet or anthem," and she surveys multiple examples. Such examples extend as far as Howard Goodall's choral arrangement of the psalm used in the UK as the theme song for *The Vicar of Dibley*, a well-known 1990s TV comedy series set in the life of the Church of England.[5]

More recent examples of Psalm 23 in musical settings strike out across the waters of wide-ranging cultural and artistic receptions, perhaps sometimes in parody, but often take the psalm's promise of comfort in dark times at face value. I do not wish to do more than point to the kinds of examples relevant here, since time would fail us to tell of Coolio's 1995 "Gangsta's Paradise," beginning "As I walk through the valley of the shadow of death"; or Kanye West's 2004 "Jesus Walks," which samples the gospel longing of the Harlem Addicts Rehabilitation Center Choir singing "Jesus walks with me" while reimagining urban decay in the Midwest as the valley of the shadow ("I walk through the valley of Chi where death is").[6] Whereas rap seems to have read the psalm's trust and longing at something close to face value, even if not necessarily aspiring to it, rock music sometimes appropriates it in order to deem its comfort a failure. Pink Floyd's

---

4. See Stuart Townend, "The Lord's My Shepherd," accessed October 21, 2019, https://www.stuarttownend.co.uk/song/the-lords-my-shepherd/.

5. Gillingham, *Psalms through the Centuries*, 2:151–52.

6. "Chi" = Chicago. Both these songs are readily available on the internet in various versions. The first was written by Coolio, Stevie Wonder (whose "Pastime Paradise" is sampled in it), L. V. (Larry Sanders), and Doug Rasheed and was originally on Coolio's *Gangsta's Paradise* album in 1995 (Tommy Boy/Warner Bros records). The second was written by Che Smith, Miri Ben-Ari, Kanye West, and Curtis Leon Lundy for West's debut album *The College Dropout* in 2004 (Def Jam/Roc-A-Fella).

"Sheep," part of the Orwellian parable of their 1977 *Animals* album, transfers the sheep imagery into a symbol for culpable passivity, and Psalm 23 is transmuted into arrival not in the house of the Lord but into the slaughterhouse. Similarly, U2's "Love Rescue Me" curses the rod and staff because "they no longer comfort me" and seems to turn to love as an alternative to divine aid.[7] If one were to begin cataloging the uses of the psalm in film, the list of contemporary uses could become very long, though it would surely include reference to the priest reading it as the ship goes down in James Cameron's *Titanic*.[8] Spreading the net wider, the literary reception of Psalm 23 could be another study again, ranging over a much longer time period.[9]

What is the significance of looking at such reception? This is a much-contested question at present, and views range from seeing it as an interesting afterthought to interpretation, to being one interpretive key among others to unlock a text's significance, right through to those who defend reception theory as an essential element of taking seriously a text that has been interpreted over many centuries of changing horizons (perhaps even arguing that the text as such has no significance until it is received wherever it has landed).[10] I wonder if a blanket answer to this question may be inadvisable. Each example could be worth exploring for its (various different kinds of) significance, and there is no need to be more programmatic than that. However, it does seem clear that all these examples point to the substantive iconic and totemic status of Scripture—or at least some

7. "Sheep" is written by Roger Waters and is on Pink Floyd's 1977 *Animals* album (Harvest/Columbia records). "Love Rescue Me" is written by U2 and Bob Dylan, no less, and is on U2's 1988 *Rattle and Hum* album (Island records), an album that stands a little outside of U2's normal stance on Christian faith.

8. James Cameron, dir., *Titanic* (Los Angeles: 20th Century Fox/Paramount, 1997). Examples of the psalm's use in film include *Pale Rider*, *Full Metal Jacket*, and others.

9. For an interesting start consider Hamlin, *Psalm Culture*, 147–72, a chapter titled "'Happy Me! O Happy Sheep!': Renaissance Pastoral and Psalm 23," as a "case study in Psalm translation."

10. Useful orientation to all these issues and more may be found in Parris, *Reading the Bible with Giants*. Parris is somewhere in the middle of the spectrum of views outlined here.

of its famous selections, including Psalm 23—in wider culture. That is certainly an area worth exploring, though it is not quite the focus of this book.[11] It does bring us, however, to reception history as a live area in contemporary biblical studies.

Academic Engagement: From Origins to Reception

Modern biblical studies has poured forth its never-ending torrent of critical studies on the Psalms more widely, and on Psalm 23 in particular, for well over a hundred years now. We will be sampling many such studies in the chapters to come, and in particular in chapter 2 I will say a little about trends in Psalms scholarship that have had an impact on how Psalm 23 (among others) has been interpreted in academic circles. Such commentaries and critical studies are typically excellent at "analysis": a word that signifies the breaking apart of an object of study into components. These historical-critical approaches to the text offer key insights into how Psalm 23 works. At the same time, they seem to have short memories and often rehearse scholarship only from within their own (relatively modern) horizon, so that Erasmus's lengthy reading of the psalm, for instance, which overlaps at various points with modern exegetical concerns, is conspicuously absent in modern commentaries.[12] I will also seek to explore some of these older readings in the discussions that follow.[13]

The days of such critical amnesia are passing, however. With the Psalms in particular, looking at the history of their interpretation seems to tap into something close to the essence of the Psalter: a

11. The best discussion of the refracted nature of these cultural Psalm 23 references is Jacobson, "Through the Pistol Smoke." See also Roncace, "Psalm 23 and Modern Worldviews," 205–6, commenting in particular on Coolio's *Gangsta's Paradise*, and also his own "Psalm 23 as Cultural Icon" on SBL's *Bible Odyssey* website: https://www.bibleodyssey.org/en/passages/related-articles/psalm-23-as-cultural-icon (accessed October 21, 2019).

12. See Erasmus, "Threefold Exposition of Psalm 22," 119–99, and discussed in chap. 4 below.

13. The task is eased by the remarkable compendium of material found in Neale and Littledale, *Commentary on the Psalms*; 1:307–16 is on Psalm 23.

compilation arguably designed as a prayer book and certainly used as a prayer book. The magisterial study of William Holladay, *The Psalms through Three Thousand Years*, sets the pace and is helpful to us not least because he uses Psalm 23 as his initial case study in considering what may be gained and lost through the history of interpretation.[14] Earlier examinations of usage and reception were also particularly interesting. I have benefitted from W. O. E. Oesterley's *The Psalms in the Jewish Church*, which is an assessment of Jewish interpretation and use of the Psalms from origins to the present, including in synagogue and private spiritual life.[15] John Alexander Lamb's comparable volume from 1962, *The Psalms in Christian Worship*, offers a wide-ranging review of the liturgical use of the Psalms in the Eucharist and in daily and occasional offices across a broad spectrum of Christian traditions. There is also an earlier and unique volume by Rowland E. Prothero called *The Psalms in Human Life*, which is a fund of stories accumulated by a former fellow of All Souls, Oxford, who was already en route to a career in British politics. The book is discursive, anecdotal, and consistently illuminating.[16] Prothero's book also seems to be the source of the thought that Psalm 23 "was fitly chosen by Augustine as the hymn of martyrs," which has been much cited since, though without evidence of Augustine actually saying it.[17]

The flowering of academic interest in the reception of the biblical text since Holladay's book in 1993 has borne fruit in various ways,

14. Holladay, *Psalms through Three Thousand Years*, 6–14.

15. Oesterley (1866–1950) would go on to be Professor of Hebrew and Old Testament at King's College London, and was the author of many well-respected books. This 1910 study was one of his earliest and appears to have left little trace—it is absent from the works of Gillingham and Holladay, for instance.

16. Prothero was not a biblical commentator but a "learned Victorian," and the resultant eclectic nature of his musings is pointed out by Dawes, *Psalms*, 184–85. (Dawes also provides a fascinating biographical note on Prothero in Dawes, *Psalms*, 206n8.)

17. Prothero, *Psalms in Human Life*, 12. There is no footnote, and scholars have been unable to trace this claim in Augustine's work. Augustine offered only the briefest of comments on Psalm 23 in his lengthy Psalms writings (see Augustine, *Expositions of the Psalms*, 1:244–45), and nothing in it accords with Prothero's remark. It may be an error or perhaps an overly free recasting of some other thought of Augustine's. Prothero offers no further context for the reference.

among the most notable of which is the (Wiley) Blackwell Bible Commentary series.[18] In my view these volumes have been always fascinating but sometimes frustrating, since the accumulation of instances of reception can provoke the question, To what end? What exactly is the benefit of seeing multiple interpretations amassed, especially if there are no evaluative criteria of any kind in play? However, the Psalms commentary in this series, by Susan Gillingham, is a significant exception to this judgment, not least because how the Psalms have been used in worship and art and wider cultural circles chimes with their purpose: to be sung or prayed in dialogue with God and in the midst of God's world. Her three-volume work is an indispensable guide to the living power of the Psalms as it has been experienced in Jewish, Christian, and wider cultural circles.[19] Her study of Psalm 23 takes the reader from King David all the way to George W. Bush, with wide-ranging coverage of options in between.[20] With respect to this particular text, she has also offered an earlier exemplary study of a range of historical and literary interpretations up to the end of the last century in a thoughtful discussion of how best to evaluate competing and complementary interpretations.[21] Part of her agenda there is to flag the importance of the reader in interpretation and the interdependence of historical and literary categories for interpretation. The framing argument of the book involves an appeal for openness to a postmodern sensibility within the confines of an academic discipline more naturally "modern," though the implications of such an interpretive shift are left largely open.[22]

In certain respects, the present study builds upon Gillingham's approach in her various studies of Psalm 23 and considers further developments in the early twenty-first century, as the nature and pos-

18. See the series website at http://bbibcomm.info/ (accessed October 22, 2019).
19. Gillingham, *Psalms through the Centuries*. Vol. 1 (2008) is an overview of the issues, vol. 2 (2018) covers Pss. 1–72, while vol. 3 will complete the project.
20. Gillingham, *Psalms through the Centuries*, 2:144–53.
21. Gillingham, *Image, the Depths and the Surface*, 45–78. The chapter is entitled "In and Out of the Sheepfold: Multivalent Readings in Psalm 23."
22. Gillingham, *Image, the Depths and the Surface*, 122–27.

sibilities (and problems) of "postmodern" interpretation have become gradually more clearly drawn. The core issue, in my view, is how to balance openness to text-oriented *and* reader-oriented approaches, much as Gillingham advocates herself, and perhaps also to let one's (critical) reading be part of the ongoing conversation of interpretation that extends back to before the arrival of modern critical categories. This was sketched in principle at the beginning of this chapter and will be explored in practice throughout the book.

The challenges of such an approach may be seen with reference to another project that is similarly interested in historical (and spiritual) reception of the Psalms while simultaneously assigning priority to historical reconstruction of the original intent. This is the fascinating multivolume historical commentary study by Bruce Waltke and James Houston, which includes Psalm 23 as one of its extended examples in *The Psalms as Christian Worship* volume.[23] Unlike the reception approach of Gillingham's work, what we have here is a two-author defense of a two-step approach: meaning, which can be (largely) determined, and then significance, which may be appreciated but must ultimately be measured against "the textual or doctrinal meaning of the psalm."[24] Despite many helpful insights, their work's adherence to such a two-step approach is problematic, as we will see shortly.

Popular Devotion: From the Text to the Life of a Shepherd

One could amass a bookshelf of popular readings of Psalm 23 alone. On that shelf would be much encouragement and devotional wisdom. Yet not all of it would have much to do with the psalm itself. Despite my own intention to remain positive with respect to received spiritual wisdom about the psalm, it is true that much of

---

23. See Waltke and Houston, *Psalms as Christian Worship*, 416–45, on Ps. 23. Other volumes in the series are *Psalms as Christian Lament* (2014) and *Psalms as Christian Praise* (2019).

24. Waltke and Houston, *Psalms as Christian Worship*, 433.

what passes for devotional reading of "the LORD is my shepherd" tells us more about life in general than the impress of the text. In particular, it can tell us a remarkable amount about shepherding. Why this happens is worth pondering, and part of chapter 2 will be given over to reflecting on the interest in (ancient) shepherding that particularly characterizes popular readings of the psalm while also lurking in the middle-distance of critical study.

In preparing for this project, I took on vacation with me an old study of *The Twenty-Third Psalm* by a well-known Scottish preacher, which I will refrain from identifying further. It was a startling read: a spirit-stirring mix of personal experience, doctrinal reflection, sideways references to other Scriptures, and a loose arrangement of six chapters, ostensibly one per verse of the psalm. Not only did it end with an evangelistic (Christian) altar call to come to Christ the Shepherd, but at one point it offered something of a pastoral rebuke to the reader: "So, dear friends, when the minister calls, let him hear less of that weary tale of your doubts and fears."[25] The tone of the book, if nothing else, was rather a long way from the tone of Psalm 23. My perusal of more recent popular accounts suggests that this is not a problem unique to this one older book.

But in fact the problem here is not just one of tone. Amid all the encouragement of this opening chapter, for us to construe positively the history of the church's reception of Psalm 23 and to seek theological and spiritual insight therein really does not mean that anything goes. Specifically, it does not mean that you can say what you like in loose connection with Psalm 23 and count it as a good interpretation. Sometimes it is not even an interpretation at all. Ironically, although the mode of the problem is different, the issue here is actually similar to that of critical study that spends its time on historical reconstruction: something has been substituted in place of reading the text. In this case, what has been substituted is spiritual edification rather than critical conjecture, but the distance from the text can be similar. Of

25. The book is almost a hundred years old.

course, spiritual edification is not in itself a problem, and we live in a world where vaguely aspirational preaching is hardly among the greatest of evils, so a certain degree of perspective is in order. But such approaches to Psalm 23, which I label "popular readings," are running on empty, making little of the text, and often relying instead on randomly sourced Gospel verses or (surprisingly often) on quotations from hymns.

My suspicion is that readings like this, and preaching like this, persist in part because people are not well trained in the art of reading the text. Scholars who make this point (like myself) typically prefer not to dwell on the thought that it is the guild of biblical scholars who might be as much at fault here as the readers and preachers making their way through the valley of the shadow of academic biblical studies. What are often lacking in readerly formation are sustained examples of attending to the text rather than allowing it to be eclipsed by critical, historical, and literary examination. No more need be said in general terms on this issue. In chapter 2 we will look at the specific issues raised by enthusiasm about studying shepherding as a way into Psalm 23. But the overarching task before us is to set out beyond this, to just the kind of attentive reading of the text that I have been advocating in this introduction.

Living in the World of Psalm 23

Let us draw together the threads of this review of other readers by way of outlining a hermeneutical focus for our work with the text. The goal of a theologically and ministerially relevant reading is not first to exegete the text and then, secondly and separately, to apply its insights to today's world. There are many who would say that this is precisely what Christians are doing when they preach, for example. I think one can honor such sermons and their wisdom without necessarily thinking that the hermeneutical model in play is actually "exegesis + application."

The problems with this model are well known. Firstly, objective exegesis is always an approximation at best, since we read as embodied people from certain sociocultural (and theological) horizons, foregrounding certain types of questions and living largely unaware of others—at least until such time as we mix with those of profoundly different perspectives. Secondly, it is a model overly focused on abstracting principles from texts that, all unawares, were often not designed to be in the business of offering principles, let alone "doctrinal meaning."[26] Thirdly, as the great hermeneutical theorist Hans-Georg Gadamer once magisterially defended, all worthwhile interpretation already includes aspects of "application" anyway, in that the text is approached from within a particular horizon (or interpretive framework) that factors into how the text is being perceived in the first place.[27] As a result, the two-stage nature of such reading is a heuristic simplification at best, useful—in my opinion—for reflecting on what sorts of moves we have made in offering an interpretation, but not particularly useful as a method with which to set out and generate interpretations in the first place.

This is one reason why students of Scripture are often puzzled by the challenge to "go and do likewise" in exegesis after watching a favorite professor demystify a text and show how it works, thinking that they have thereby learned a method for so doing. Far more likely they have watched a wise reader deploy some wisdom and will be unable to "go and do likewise" unless they have some comparable wisdom with which to read a new and different text. Biblical studies is only slowly catching on to the probability that this is key for reading: good character is part of what shapes having eyes to see what is at stake in the biblical text.[28]

One could go on—since theoretical hermeneutical discussion has a way of extending itself almost indefinitely, sometimes with a curi-

26. Cf. Waltke and Houston, *Psalms as Christian Worship*, 433 (cited above).
27. Gadamer, *Truth and Method*.
28. I offer an account of how one might match up biblical study with cultivation of character in *Virtuous Reader*; and I discuss the implications for how we learn Bible reading in "Biblical Hermeneutics and Practical Theology," 201–17.

ous disregard for actually reading any biblical texts. For us, all our hermeneutical thinking will be tethered to working on the specific example of Psalm 23. I want to suggest just one overarching rubric for how the hermeneutical task will play out as we engage in this interpretive practice.

As noted, the "exegesis + application" model seems to suggest that we need first to isolate the original communicative intent as the key to our understanding, subsequent to which we will then deploy our broader hermeneutical and theological thinking. However, in practice all sorts of hermeneutical and theological judgments are inevitably involved along the line. All I want to observe here is that this two-step model almost unavoidably suggests that we are moving *from* the world of the text (and its author) *to* today. This is the way people think of interpretation when they talk of applying ideas *from* the Bible *to* ourselves today. But that is the wrong way around.

Our job is not to take understanding out of the biblical text and drop it down into our world, as if it could then self-sufficiently take care of itself among all our twenty-first-century judgments and evaluations and commitments. Our twenty-first-century world is not that theologically robust. Rather, our job is to reverse the hermeneutical flow and to take our own attenuated theological vision and apprentice it to that of the text—to go and live in the world of the text, as a shorthand way of putting it.[29]

Critics of this idea sometimes suggest that this is an otherworldly or ivory-towered approach to biblical interpretation, all very well for a scholar but falling well short of the needs of the church on a week-by-week basis. I disagree. Crucially, immersion in the world of the text changes who we are. This is hermeneutics by way of character transformation, rather than trying to add character applications on to

---

29. For more on this key idea see Lash, "What Might Martyrdom Mean?," 75–92. I did not invent the phrase "reverse the hermeneutical flow" but learned it from various works of Larry Kreitzer, in the first instance from his two volumes in the early 1990s, *New Testament in Fiction and Film* and *Old Testament in Fiction and Film*, both of which are subtitled *On Reversing the Hermeneutical Flow*. Kreitzer uses the idea slightly differently.

the end of technical handling of the text. Again, although one could write (and I have written) about this at length, the merit of the idea in this particular case will be open for inspection as we employ it with regard to Psalm 23. So we will review the matter briefly in the final chapter of the book.

On a practical note, I might add that this is also a model that nourishes preaching ministry in the life of the church. It is not how I was taught to preach, but it is how I have pursued preaching ministry in my local church week by week, and I think it makes a practical difference to people's lives. It does so precisely by allowing the scriptural text to set an agenda and a vision for the daily life of those who gather for worship. Points of application will not do this. Capturing the imaginative vision of those who attend to the text has at least some chance. It takes time, but then any worthwhile cultivation of Christian character takes time. If readers of this book end up "at home" in the world of Psalm 23, then they will have been changed on their way there. To live in the world of the text involves and requires character transformation. So it will make all manner of difference in the life of the church.[30]

Approaching Psalm 23

The rest of this book will seek to offer an account of "Psalm 23 for the life of the church." For the sake of clarity, I divide up this single task into three artificially separated angles of approach. One might read them in any order, but there is a logic to their order of presentation here. I adopt the language of the worlds *behind*, *in*, and *in front of* the text.[31] I take these terms in their most straightforward and current usage to refer respectively to

30. And in principle, *mutatis mutandis*, in the life of the synagogue, with respect to Jewish character, although I am not qualified to comment on this in any detail and am aware of differences in the scope and nature of Jewish preaching.
31. The use of this language in biblical studies again derives from the work of Paul Ricoeur, though it proves complicated to track in his actual writings. For a user-friendly account, see Brueggemann, *Cadences of Home*, 59–61.

- the world that produced Psalm 23, including its author(s) and editor(s), and so forth;
- the world that is accessed by immersing oneself in the text, as a matter of attending to its words and phrases and meanings and connotations—what is most simply called "exegesis"; and
- the world "in front of" Psalm 23, which is the imaginative space opened up by taking Psalm 23 seriously.

All are important. None is self-sufficient. The understanding of each one will have implications for how the others are approached, and none can be understood in isolation.[32] But one must start somewhere.

Chapter 2 will explore "the world behind Psalm 23." Here we meet with David, the shepherd-king—in light of the psalm's title and its reference to David. If we knew who had written Psalm 23, when, and how, then that is what we would discuss in this chapter. But in the absence of much hard evidence, what we will mainly have to discuss are theories about those questions. Background information about Psalm 23 can take several forms, including historical reflections upon its author(s) and the world of shepherding at the time, and more literary-critical reflections upon how the text has landed as the twenty-third in an ancient collection of psalms. As long as one does not think that such considerations are the same as reading the text, this is all well and good. So here we will explore ancient shepherding, the status of David the poet—who was also a shepherd and king—and the compilation of the Psalter, without which we would not have had Psalm 23 preserved for us. I will reflect also on the significance of the lack of historically specific information in and about the psalm.

Chapter 3 explores "the world in Psalm 23." This is exegesis as traditionally understood. Word by word and phrase by phrase we will pick our way through the text. This can get detailed to the point of distraction at times, although in a couple of particularly complicated

---

32. That would take us back toward the problematic "exegesis + application" kind of split.

cases I signpost shortcuts for readers who are more interested in the conclusions than in why they are held. However, the basic goal of this chapter is to show readers how we get from the original Hebrew text to our generally understood English-language translations and interpretations, and what sort of interpretive flexibility there is along the way. Technical Hebrew discussion is cross-referenced to a brief appendix.

Chapter 4 then takes up "the world in front of Psalm 23." Here the focus is on ministry as we explore how Psalm 23 has been and could be used in the life of the church. This is the place, for example, to evaluate why and how the psalm is used in funeral ministry or how it could be of pastoral relevance to those facing "enemies" of whatever sort. Given that the psalm is often sung in hymnic versions or choruses, which tend to default to saying that one will be in God's presence "forever" or "forevermore," it is also appropriate to look at what sorts of hope it offers for not just this life but the life of the world to come.

I seek to draw together all these reflections in chapter 5, by way of honoring the theological vision of Psalm 23. My approach is via the challenging task of preaching the psalm, and I discuss there my own experience of preaching it in a range of contexts, as I have discovered some interesting ways in which it speaks. Of course, even a book as long as this on a text as short as this cannot foresee all that the psalm will yet say to thoughtful and faithful readers in times and contexts yet to come.[33] But I hope it will resource all such readers with clearer vision and with a firmer grasp of the text's interpretive, theological, and ministerial possibilities.

---

33. Or in other contexts around the world today. See the "global perspectives" gathered in Levison and Pope-Levison, *Return to Babel*, 55–72, which has readings from Latin America (Croatto, "Psalm 23:1–6"), Africa (Kinoti, "Psalm 23:1–6"), and Korea (Moon, "Psalm 23:1–6"). These are interesting, for example with Croatto's rendering of part of v. 3 as "paths of liberation," but are disappointingly brief and generally lack detail.

2

The World behind Psalm 23

Background

A long time ago in a setting far, far away . . .

Psalm 23 was written in Hebrew. It has also come down to us in a Greek translation as part of the so-called Septuagint (LXX), which dates from the third/second century BCE, with the Psalter probably translated in the early second century BCE.[1] It was then translated into Latin by Jerome in the Vulgate in the late fourth century CE—the version that dominated Western church life for many centuries.[2] Of much interest to scholars now but generally of rather less significance during those centuries, Hebrew Scripture was also adapted into early Aramaic paraphrases known as Targums and preserved in various degrees of alternative Hebrew forms among the Dead Sea Scrolls found at Qumran in the mid-twentieth century.

1. Briggs and Briggs, *Psalms*, 1:xxv.
2. Jerome actually translated the Psalter three times, of which the third was the version that attempted to get back to the Hebrew rather than work via the LXX. See Goins, "Jerome's Psalters," 185–98. Simple comparison between Vulgate versions is facilitated by consulting vulgate.org.

English translations of the Bible began with Wycliffe, whose fourteenth-century Bible translation worked from Jerome's Latin. Tyndale (d. 1536) translated from the Hebrew and Greek originals, and his work formed the basis for the justly famous 1611 King James Version (KJV). Coverdale, who assisted Tyndale, published his translation of the Psalms in 1535. It was Coverdale's version that became much read and loved as it was adopted into the Book of Common Prayer (BCP, first published in 1549) and subsequently prayed in churches as the standard English version until relatively modern times.[3]

I introduce all this information up front in this chapter because it forms the backdrop against which the details of our study will operate. To turn to Psalm 23 is to join a conversation, which has been going on since at least the time of the LXX, about what exactly the psalm says and how to understand it for those of us who are not ancient Hebrew-speaking Israelites. As I tried to emphasize in chapter 1, the traditions developed in the conversation we are joining are reliable. And on the whole, any decent English translation will be trustworthy, so we are not starting from scratch in our understanding here. But part of the project of this book is to show how we have arrived at the interpretations and understandings we have, and this involves digging around in all sorts of aspects of ancient and more recent history.

An interesting question in biblical studies is how much energy should be devoted to Hebrew alone in getting at "the original text" and how significant in turn are the variations and nuances of the early translations or versions. We will not ponder this interesting question in theory but will instead look at what does and does not occur in practice with Psalm 23.

This chapter will explore four "background" questions concerning the world "behind" Psalm 23: its author, the speaking voice we

3. A strikingly wide range of versions of Ps. 23—early and modern—may be found in the edited volume of Strange and Sandbach, *Psalm 23*.

encounter in it, the nature of shepherding as a key image lying behind the psalm, and the significance, if any, of our psalm being number twenty-three in a collection of 150 psalms. To some extent these four questions are independent, and readers may pick and choose which sections are of most interest to them. Indeed some readers may prefer to read the exegesis of the psalm in chapter 3 first and then turn to these background issues only when they realize that they want more information on them.

Author: Who Wrote Psalm 23?

Who wrote Psalm 23? The short answer is that we do not know. The traditional answer was David, the great shepherd-king and poet of Israel. The position we will develop in this book is that the psalm is "Davidic" in the sense about to be explored. While it might not be overly problematic to call the author David, the temptation to be resisted is to smuggle in a lot of background historical information from the time and life of David that is not actually found in the text of Psalm 23 itself and then use that information as the one true key to the meaning of the psalm. I will persist instead in the unfashionable belief that the meaning of Psalm 23 is found in the text of Psalm 23—a position I am willing to defend in principle but will instead focus on defending in practice.

To explore the issue of authorship we need to begin with the psalm's superscription, or title—printed in most contemporary English translations in small print before the psalm proper begins at verse 1. Most likely what you will find here at the beginning of Psalm 23 is "A Psalm of David," which may look like it rather settles the authorship question. So how can it be so complicated? Let me count the ways.

On Psalm Titles in General

Most psalms have superscriptions, and not all parts of them are appropriately called "titles," as a perusal of English translations of the beginning of various psalms (e.g., Psalm 60) will show. However, scholars generally call the superscriptions "titles," and in the case of the brief wording at the start of Psalm 23, it will be simplest to call it the psalm's "title."

Of the 150 Hebrew psalms in the Psalter, 116 are usually reckoned to have titles. You can arrive at this figure by counting the examples in an English translation. The matter is complicated by the use of the Hebrew *haləlû yāh* ("Praise the LORD," traditionally "Hallelujah") in a further sixteen examples (e.g., Pss. 111–113), which seems to function a little like a title, or at least a superscription, and is counted as a title in the Greek translation, the LXX. Following that line of thought, all the psalms in the LXX have a title except Psalms 1 and 2. Only six of the first eighty-nine psalms lack any kind of title in Hebrew (1, 2, 10, 33, 43, 71). Later in the Psalter it is more common for there to be no such introductory text (e.g., Pss. 93–97).[4]

In the 116 straightforward cases (with Hebrew titles), English translations almost always follow the convention of putting the relevant words in small print before verse 1, as they do here with Psalm 23. The incidental but awkward consequence is that Hebrew and English verse numbering may not match up. If the title is long enough (as it is in Ps. 22 for example), it is counted as a separate verse in Hebrew, and subsequent verse numbering is thus one verse different.[5] This issue does not arise in Psalm 23, since the short title wording is part of the opening verse in Hebrew. Thus while it is usually printed before verse 1 in English, both Hebrew and English end verse 1 at the same point. Conveniently, therefore, the verse numbering for Psalm 23 agrees in Hebrew and English.

The whole approach of printing the psalm titles in small print before verse 1 is deeply embedded in English translations, although it

---

4. The data on psalm titles can sustain book-length discussion and is most thoroughly analyzed in Willgren, *Formation of the 'Book' of Psalms*, 172–95, with a helpful tabulation of all the data on 404–11.

5. So Ps. 22 has thirty-two verses in Hebrew but thirty-one in English. In this book I always give verse references to the English verse number, unless clearly stated otherwise.

was not always so. The fourteenth-century Wycliffe Bible, translating from the Latin Vulgate (where Ps. 23 is actually numbered Ps. 22), has for verse 1: "The title of the two and twentithe salm. The salm, ether the song of Dauid. The Lord gouerneth me."[6] By the time of the KJV, in 1611, the relevant text is printed before verse 1, although in normal size. In the Book of Common Prayer, the titles are omitted, and what look like alternative brief titles are added in Latin, although they are actually the first words or phrase of Jerome's Vulgate text.[7]

Modern translations, availing themselves of elegant typographical options in modern printing, move to reducing the font size of the titles, often italicizing them, and in the notorious case of the New English Bible, a British project whose Old Testament translation appeared in 1970, the titles are omitted altogether.[8]

The small-print option—and much more so the extreme option of omission in the NEB—reflects the view that these titles are in some sense secondary to the psalm proper and were added later. This indeed is the NEB's justification for its editorial decision, written in a tone of some condescension: "The headings of the Psalms, consisting partly of musical instructions, of which the meanings have mostly been lost, and partly of historical notices, deduced (sometimes incorrectly) from the individual Psalms, have been omitted; they are almost certainly not original."[9]

6. Some editions will contemporize the spelling. "Ether" effectively means "or," according to the *Oxford English Dictionary* (see the entry for "either" at oed.com, accessed October 24, 2019). The Vulgate-inspired "govern" instead of "shepherd" will be discussed in chap. 3 below. The updated version would read "The title of the twenty-second psalm. The psalm, or the song of David. The Lord governs me."

7. The Anglican updating of the BCP in Britain, the twenty-first-century *Common Worship*, also omits the titles and omits Jerome's Latin too.

8. This was just one of many truly bizarre features of the NEB that was quietly dropped when it was updated as the Revised English Bible (REB, 1989). Although the NEB had a certain influence in the 1970s, especially in the UK, this has thankfully passed. The REB has had rather little influence anywhere, probably because it appeared in the same year as the NRSV.

9. From the NEB's "Introduction to the Old Testament" (pagination varies depending on edition), which was written by Sir Godfrey Rolles Driver (1892–1975), professor of Semitic philology at Oxford University.

There are some interesting evaluations at work in all this, and a certain lack of clarity about what the evidence is. I restrict myself to three points. First, we have no Hebrew manuscripts of the traditional book of Psalms that omit these titles. As noted, the opening words of Psalm 23 in Hebrew are (to anticipate our discussion of how to translate them) "A Psalm of David. The LORD is my shepherd . . ." Some Hebrew editions today, including the standard critical edition, print the opening words ("A Psalm of David") on their own line, but it is just as common to let the text run straight on.[10] The Hebrew text as received, in other words, includes the titles.

Secondly, there is indeed strong evidence that these titles were not "original," but it is evidence of an analytical sort rather than a textual sort. Without going into great detail: the titles are to some degree different in the LXX (though not in the case of Ps. 23), which suggests that they were seen in some way as separable from the poetic text that follows; they refer to points of musical detail or historical setting—as noted by the NEB—rather than seeming to be part of the poetry; and they function in the third person (referring, for example, to "David") even in cases where the psalm that follows is in the first person. On the third/first-person issue, Psalm 23 is a case in point, with its "A Psalm of *David* / The LORD is *my* shepherd . . ."

Thirdly, how does one evaluate this? There is no straightforward reason why being "original" should be the key issue. Some traditions give priority to the earliest recoverable form of a text or an idea, often linked to a view that the core ideas of a text should be traceable to a presiding creative genius, an "author" figure whose insight we seek to recover. On this view one goal is to downgrade the significance of later additions and possibly even remove them. Other traditions work with the idea that texts and ideas grow over time as communities develop their understanding, whether or not in complete agreement

10. The standard critical edition is *BHS*, the *Biblia Hebraica Stuttgartensia*. Other critical editions are in progress.

with an original author, which becomes to some extent a secondary issue. If it is indeed clear that the Psalms present us original poems with added editorial titles (to adopt perhaps the simplest view), this still tells us nothing about the relative significance of the titles until we have a framework for assessing how to handle later additions in general. Nor is this a problem unique to the Psalms, since editorial asides are not uncommon in the Old Testament.[11]

In the case of psalm titles, while we may deduce that the poem proper predates its title, we have no record of the texts being received into the Psalter without their titles. It thus seems most appropriate to treat the titles as part of the whole psalm: more specifically as early indications of how the poem proper was received, whether with regard to musical setting or proposed historical background (where relevant). A significant move in this direction was Brevard Childs's 1971 article that advocated for the historicizing elements of the psalm titles, which he saw operating as a kind of midrash: inner-biblical interpretation that mapped the relevant psalms into "canonical history."[12] In other words, within the canon one finds already the linking of text (the poem proper, in this case) with a historical context (found in the title) that serves to interpret the history (the "canonical history"), perhaps in some new and illuminating way. For Childs, what is significant here is that such interpretive illumination was not a postbiblical development that fell away from an original, simple historical reporting but was found within the biblical text already.

Childs makes a helpful point: the biblical text already stands in an interesting interpretive relationship with history, of the kind to be taken up in later, more creative styles of interpretation (such as midrash or, later, figurative reading). For our purposes, however, the simple point is that taking the psalm seriously as Scripture involves

---

11. They range from explaining vocabulary to puzzled readers (e.g., 1 Sam. 9:9, a kind of in-text footnote) to drawing a conclusion that does not relate directly to the world of the narrative (e.g., Gen. 2:24).

12. Childs, "Psalm Titles and Midrashic Exegesis," 137–50, quotation from 150.

letting the title play a role—not necessarily a straightforwardly historical one, but an integral one of contributing to how the text is received into the canon. Titles count. Interpretive work notwithstanding, correctly noting that titles are later and not original does not invite us to marginalize or ignore them.[13]

As a concluding comment here, it seems to me entirely fair for the BCP (and its update, *Common Worship*) to omit the titles, since their purpose is not to reproduce the book of Psalms but to present its 150 constituent psalms as prayers to be prayed in a worship service. But for a Bible translation—and indeed an interpretation of the Bible—to do the same is a different move, for the reasons rehearsed, and should be resisted.

On the Title of Psalm 23

I anticipate here the style of presentation and discussion of the text that will be adopted in chapter 3 when we offer an exegesis of Psalm 23. In brief: the text is presented in (transliterated) Hebrew, and then I offer my own straightforward translation, which is then discussed and interpreted in detail.

mizmôr ləḏāwid
A Psalm of David.

Although there are only two Hebrew words in this psalm title, they contain multiple interpretive possibilities. Each word occurs many times in other psalm titles, but on occasion the order is reversed, which does suggest that the two words function slightly independently. In other words, here are two things that can be said in the psalm title: one is that it is a *mizmôr*, and the other is that it is *ləḏāwid*—and

---

13. Having written this section, I pondered whether the situation is in fact analogous to the titles of books today—these are often the responsibility of the publisher, with input from the author varying. They are thus, in a sense, later and not original, but it would be odd to ignore their significance for reading and understanding the book.

one can say them in either order.[14] I am going to argue that the traditional interpretation, "a psalm of David" (KJV and most modern interpretations), remains the best option. But what exactly does it commit the reader to understanding?

Mizmôr is a noun formed from the verb *zāmar*, which means "to sing" (or corresponding musical equivalents). Comparably, a *zimrâ* is a song in Psalms 81:2; 98:5; and 118:14 (though NRSV and NJPS offer a minority report of "might" in this last instance: "the Lord is my strength and my song/might," with "might" relying on various judgments about Ugaritic parallels). The verb form *zāmar* ("to sing") occurs seventeen times in the Old Testament, fifteen of them in the Psalms, with the most striking example being its fourfold imperative repetition in Psalm 47:6: "Sing praises to God, sing praises; sing praises to our King, sing praises." Psalm 33:2 suggests it may have a wider musical reference than just singing when it says "with the harp (or lyre?[15]) of ten strings, *zammrû* to him." Perhaps therefore it is rightly understood as "to make music" more generally.[16] We can conclude then that a *mizmôr* is what you get from making music: a song or musical composition. The word occurs fifty-seven times, always in the title (v. 1) of a psalm, beginning at Psalm 3:1. A little over half the titles (twenty-two) of the forty-one psalms of Book 1 of the Psalter include the word as part of their titles. Its traditional translation as "psalm" in English comes via the LXX, which renders it as *psalmos*.[17]

A "psalm," then, is a song such as these over fifty exemplars found in this scriptural book. Whether, therefore, one should understand a

14. The reversed order (*ləḏāwid mizmôr*) occurs seven times in all (Pss. 24; 40; 68; 101; 109; 110; 139)—always in v. 1. I am unaware of a compelling account of the significance of this, other than to note the point made here, that the two words are in some sense independent.

15. Nicely left as "instrument" by the KJV!

16. So Goldingay, *Psalms*, 1:592. Vol. 1 covers Psalms 1–41 (2006).

17. *Psalmos* occurs sixty-two times in Pss. 1–150 in the LXX, since there are some other Hebrew words that are translated *psalmos* (e.g., the obscure *šiggāyôn* in Ps. 7, or *šîr* ["song"] in Ps. 46 [= LXX Ps. 45]), as well as one or two cases where *mizmôr* is not translated as *psalmos*. For discussion see Briggs and Briggs, *Psalms*, 1:xxi, lxviii–lxix, with its characteristic confidence about errors and confusions in the text.

mizmôr as fundamentally a song designed for a worship context, or whether the word had wider musical reference but is used here for worship contexts, is probably irrelevant to our appreciation of the word in the title. The book of Psalms within which Psalm 23 occurs is known in Hebrew as *təhillîm* (praises), which interestingly only picks up on one aspect of the book and arguably offers perspective on other aspects by leading one to see "praise" as the most significant lens. Thus Psalm 40:3, for instance, talks about a new song in the psalmist's mouth, described as "a song of praise" (*təhillâ*) to God. Perhaps the title "praises" suggests that the songs God gives to Israel are for praise first and foremost, although of course there are many other modes and moods in the Psalter too. Alternatively, maybe this helps to define "praise" more widely?

The note found at the end of Book 2 suggests that one can also see the psalms as "prayers": "The prayers [*təpillôt*] of David son of Jesse are ended" (72:20). Although this is no longer the end of the book of Psalms, nor even the end point of the Psalms "of David," it seems to have had the function at some time of concluding a collection, and in so doing calling the texts "prayers." The finished canonical book's Greek title (*Psalmoi*), as also its Latin title (*liber psalmorum*—book of psalms), probably remains as ambiguous as the Hebrew title: a book of praises that in fact constitutes more than just praise.[18]

In short: the word "psalm" in Psalm 23 points us to the text being a song, found in the holy book of such songs, and thus it is most naturally understood as a musical composition for worship or liturgical use. For now, I am skirting around a wide-ranging issue in Psalms scholarship: whether the Psalm texts reflect the unmediated outpouring of worship from a person who is praising God (a shepherd strolling through the field with a song in his heart, as it

---

18. The title *Psalter*, in contrast, appears to derive from the Greek for a musical (stringed) instrument—a *psalterion*, sometimes translated "psaltery" or "harp." The KJV uses "psaltery" twenty-seven times, and for an interesting case of how to handle the word, compare Ps. 150:3 ("praise him with the psaltery and harp" [KJV]) with modern versions.

might be in this instance), or whether they represent the poetically fine-tuned lyric of a worship song polished or even constructed for public use. It seems implausible to suggest that worshipers spontaneously hummed this song to themselves and then rushed to write it down before the moment passed. Much more likely the poetry is the work of reflection, conjuring up such an image of simple trust and so forth: not composed while out in the fields as such, although undoubtedly informed by such experiences, either at first or second hand. We will return later in this chapter to what implications this has, if any, for understanding who the first-person "I" is in the language of the Psalms.

The other word in the title, *lədāwid*, has occasioned even more discussion than *mizmôr*, since it pertains to authorship in some way. The Hebrew prefix *lə*– most commonly means "to." Like most short prepositions in many languages, there is some flexibility. One standard dictionary definition offers "to, for, in regard to" and clarifies that this is "to" in the sense of direction rather than actual motion.[19] Thus it is used, for example, in Genesis 3:6 when the tree is a delight *to* the eyes, and when the woman gives the fruit *to* her husband. So the psalm could be *to* David in this sense. We might say that it is David-facing. But what does this mean?

One traditional view is that the sense in which the psalm "belongs *to* David" is that he wrote it. I suggest that a complicating factor, not always considered by those who argue for or against David being the writer of any given psalm, is that we do not have a good grasp of what "authorship" was in the ancient world. Because we live today in a world where the majority of people capable of reading a text can also write one—as in physically producing a document using pen or paper or typing it electronically and printing it out or uploading it—we often have a misleading impression of what it meant to "write" something in ancient times. Given the low levels of literacy and the general division of labor between such people as prophets,

19. BDB, 510 (cf. 510–18 for full discussion).

priests, and scribes, we would do well to recognize a much wider range of possibilities.[20]

In an illuminating study of "Literacy in an Oral Environment," M. C. A. MacDonald draws some conclusions from a series of case studies from pre-Islamic Arabia that can apply to the world behind the Old Testament too.[21] Literacy in oral environments, MacDonald urges, is neither necessarily desirable nor a homogenous phenomenon. Rather like the emergence of "IT literacy" in our own recent experience, it will be welcomed by some, scorned by others, and achieved at different levels. A key feature is its link to memorization, for which a useful modern example might be that of a piano player working through a musical score. A detailed note-by-note "reading" will generally precede the use of the score (text) as an aide-mémoire that can be referred to in subsequent performance without being "read" in public in the manner in which we might normally understand reading today. This seems to me to capture helpfully the somewhat specialist nature of "texts" in daily life in the world of the Old Testament, as a sort of backup or record of significant oral performance(s). Indeed one can easily imagine Psalm 23 being a much prayed or sung "text," known by heart by many and actually read from a physical scroll by very few.

All this brings us back to the point made above, that the psalm is more likely a creative but finely honed performance than a spontaneous record of devotional affection. What would it mean in such a scenario to say that David "authored" this text? All sorts of possibilities arise quite naturally, none of which are likely to be provable: perhaps the text is presented in performance to King David, almost

20. Prophets could be priests (e.g., Jeremiah, Ezekiel), and presumably scribes (or sages) could be prophets as and when God spoke through them. But in general, the evidence—such as it is—suggests that scribes were not also prophets or priests, and the work and disciplines would have tended to make such a thing unlikely. A good review of these categories is Blenkinsopp, *Sage, Priest, Prophet*.

21. MacDonald, "Literacy in Oral Environments," 49–118. More generally on this issue see also Carr, *Writing on the Tablet of the Heart*, esp. 111–73, emphasizing the relative scarcity of written texts.

along the lines of being "sponsored" by him; perhaps it is dedicated to him; perhaps it is a prayer said for him; perhaps it is presented or dedicated or prayed in honor of him or the king who subsequently sits upon his throne. Then again, perhaps it is prepared as an addition to the repertoire of Davidic pieces: this song belongs to the "Davidic" collection.[22] Authorship seems less likely to have been an individual phenomenon than a matter of accrediting or "authorizing" a text (a "score") for public commemoration and performance ("reading"). One recent review of the issue concludes that "for practical purposes, all of the psalms are anonymous," and adopts an *–ic/–ite* suffix to capture the point: psalms are variously "Davidic," or "Asaphite," and so forth.[23]

Two further points are sometimes made here. First, Jesus and others in the New Testament refer to Psalm 110 on the understanding that they are hearing in it the voice of David (such as in Mark 12:36–37): David declares; David calls; all in the words of Psalm 110, which is indeed *lədāwid mizmôr* (of David; a psalm). However, Jesus and his contemporaries would have been operating with a sense of authorship much more comparable to that of the Old Testament than our modern independent and self-sufficient one. Presumably his and their point was simply that we encounter the "speaking voice" of David in hearing this psalm, much like we encounter the "speaking voice" of Moses in Deuteronomy, without this being a claim to a modern category of authorship. Such usage would fit with a psalm being "to David" somewhere among the range of senses discussed above, and many (or all?) of these senses would fit the point the psalms are making.

Secondly, people sometimes link the shepherd theme to David as shepherd. We will discuss this issue in detail later in this chapter.

---

22. Most commentaries rehearse these options, but often without accompanying reflection on what authorship might have meant in the first instance.

23. DeClaissé-Walford, Jacobson, and Tanner, *Book of Psalms*, 11. I shall refer to this commentary as "NICOT, *Psalms*" in notes. The specific commentary on Ps. 23 on pp. 238–46 was written by Rolf A. Jacobson.

The congruence of theme and biography is certainly worth noting and perhaps played its part in prompting the crafting and adoption of such a text in the Psalter. But it does not prove anything about authorship.

How best to capture all these points in a simple translation of *mizmôr lədāwid*? The old answer remains the best: "A Psalm of David." Commentaries occasionally seek alternatives, which can be a useful pointer to the issues discussed here.[24] But to say "David says" in our discussion of Psalm 23 is to stand in the tradition that sees these words as "Davidic," in some never-to-be-fully-known sense. As is often the case, there was wisdom in the tradition long before our own time.

I might close this discussion of the question of authorship with reference to a late 1990s introduction to the Psalms written by Bono, the lead singer of U2. As one might expect, his interest is more in the poetry than the historical details, but in reflecting on the status of King David vis-à-vis authorship and symbolic significance, Bono conjures up an interesting parallel between the collection of Psalms and the recordings of Elvis Presley. What difference does it make to know that Elvis did not write his own material? For any and all purposes of loving and responding to his music, basically none. And thus, says Bono, "To get back to David, it is not clear how many of these psalms David or his son Solomon really wrote." He concludes, "Who cares? I didn't buy Leiber and Stoller. . . . They were just his songwriters. . . . I bought Elvis."[25]

A song of Elvis and a psalm of David appeal to their named figures in slightly different ways, but the points of similarity helpfully capture what has been at stake in our discussion. The lesson here is particularly for those of us who spend more time analyzing creative work than celebrating it, even if analysis and celebration, in principle, may feed into each other in mutually reinforcing ways. When

24. Goldingay offers "Composition. David's." in *Psalms*, 1:344. NICOT, *Psalms*, as just noted, goes for "A Davidic Psalm."
25. Bono, introduction, xii.

all the analysis is done, finally comes the poet, who sees through to the heart of the matter.[26]

Voice: Who Is the Speaking Person/Persona in Psalm 23?

It may seem like a discussion that looks at the "persona" of the psalmist moves us away from a historical inquiry and toward a more literary exploration of how the text produces or projects an imagined character of its author. However, I am interested in this question largely as it gets filtered through historical categories (to be explained in a moment). In my view, it is surprising how little the category of "persona" has been used in Psalms studies, since it seems to be ideally suited to the task of exploring how the psalmist's voice appears in the psalm. Lately the terminology is beginning to appear, but it is worth first reflecting on the historical orientation of Psalms studies that has obscured it until recently. There will also be an interesting benefit to exploring the category of "persona" when we come to theological matters in later chapters, which illustrates in part the inseparability of our "behind"/"in"/"in front of" approaches. Nevertheless, those whose interest is solely in Psalm 23 may feel free to move ahead past this next general discussion to the section on Psalm 23, when I will turn to the specifics of how these categories might aid our reading of this particular text.

On the Speaking Voice/Persona in the Psalms in General

The study of the speaking voice in the Psalms has been a major historically framed question in Psalms studies throughout the modern era. It is perhaps most thoroughly explored in Steven Croft's published thesis *The Identity of the Individual in the Psalms*, which

---

26. It was Walt Whitman who wrote "finally shall come the poet . . . the true son of God" in the "Passage to India" section of his *Leaves of Grass*. The image was appropriated in striking fashion for Old Testament studies by Brueggemann, *Finally Comes the Poet*.

investigates who is being referred to by the use of "I" ("me") as the designation of the speaker in all its occurrences throughout the book. Croft examines three different conceptual categories: "either the individual suppliant is the king; or he is a private individual; or he is a minister of the cult."[27] He assigns each relevant psalm to one of these categories.

In some respects, the story of historically oriented attempts to identify the speaking subject in the Psalms constitutes the backbone of critical study of the Psalms in modern times, and Croft's book stands near the end of a long road, effectively mapping out the relevance in different cases of each of the three main options. Behind and in his work lie the core emphases of the giants of critical Psalms scholarship: Gunkel, with his form-critical classification that emphasizes the stylized nature of these religious poems as part of his pursuit of the forms of ancient Israelite religion; Mowinckel, with his emphasis on the cultic setting of each psalm, in particular liturgical contexts;[28] and the subsequent attempts by John Eaton and others to nuance their approach with regard to the importance of specific royal settings. This is hardly the place to try to review that great history of scholarship, not least since it ends up more or less all-encompassing as scholars debate genre classifications with a view to how they relate specific psalms to specific originating contexts and concerns.[29]

But regardless of how one identifies the speaking voice historically, it is clearly also appropriate to ask who the "I" ("me") is being presented as in the psalm, whether or not it is the historical identity of the author. One might in principle read Croft's study as supplying an answer to this question, but in practice his framework

27. Croft, *Identity of the Individual*, 13. The third category he parses further as "a cultic prophet, wisdom teacher, or psalm singer."

28. Croft says that his study broadly supports Mowinckel's emphasis "that almost all the Psalms were composed for use in the cult." *Identity of the Individual*, 13.

29. Most standard introductions to the Psalms will rehearse this scholarship in outline. A nicely judged example is Hunter, *Introduction to the Psalms*. Useful essays analyzing specific aspects of Psalms scholarship may be found in Johnston and Firth, *Interpreting the Psalms*. Especially helpful is Nasuti, *Defining the Sacred Songs*.

assumes that identifying the speaking individual is actually access of sorts to the author or performer of the psalm in worship, which remains a historical identification. It should be clear, however, that a psalm can be written in the voice of the king without being written by the king, or indeed without the king ever knowing about the psalm at all. This is one potential meaning of the *lədāwid* language explored above: the words of the psalm might be offered *in honor of* the king, but to be prayed by his subjects and others who will come afterward. Indeed, subsequent people who pray such "royal psalms," including all who do so today, make an analogical move to identifying with the king despite their own different location and identity. Interestingly, in the conclusion to his study, Croft points in this direction by suggesting that all of the voices he has canvassed may be understood as built upon one voice, "the voice of Israel responding to her God." This would indeed allow us to move toward a more literary and less historical approach, but Croft's study does not actually make such a move.[30] The wording of Croft's conclusion here echoes Gerhard von Rad's rubric for thinking theologically about the Psalms as speech that answers the God before whom Israel lives, a rubric which von Rad awkwardly included in his section on the theology of Israel's historical traditions in his magisterial *Old Testament Theology*.[31] Relating all these historical questions to theological concerns had become singularly complex by the mid-twentieth century.

The gains of the historical(-critical) approach are obvious: detailed attention to the text, analysis of ancient Near Eastern parallels and contrasts, careful consideration of matters of philology and historical plausibility regarding what the author may have been trying to

30. Croft, *Identity of the Individual*, 178. In other places, he resists proposals about liturgical use as originating context because he sees "an actual historical situation" as more relevant (e.g., 196n66 on Ps. 44).

31. Von Rad's treatment of the Psalms in his *Old Testament Theology* famously located them in a section of his discussion that was entitled "Israel Before Jahweh (Israel's Answer)." See von Rad, *Old Testament Theology*, 1:355–459, esp. 356–70.

say, and so on. All of this has made an inestimable contribution to our understanding of the Psalms in general and to many specific matters of interpretation. Nevertheless, I risk offering the opinion that the story of twentieth-century Psalms scholarship in outline is one of slowly covering over the spiritual vitality of the Psalms in the life of people of faith—Jewish and Christian—by way of historical conjecture, and then of having to work unduly hard to recover a dimension of the text that had become hidden in plain sight—namely, that these are prayers that serve to shape and nurture the faith of those who pray them.

From the perspective of such twentieth-century preoccupation with historical contextualization, I offer three observations on the long and winding road that links the speaking voice of the Psalms with broader spiritual and theological questions. The first relates to just what that link was in historical-critical categories, the second points to earlier theological modes of interpretation, and the third explores newer literary categories of interpretation. Again, the interrelatedness of all these angles of approach is clear: historical-theological-literary interpretation is all one activity, but it is to some extent a matter of where the emphasis falls.

First, the historical approach to the question—the pursuit of the original speaker.[32] The grand project of historical reconstruction of ancient Israelite religion did not set out to deny that there is spiritual vitality in the Psalms and that it is available for the reader today. However, the way Gunkel frames the inquiry shows him wrestling with tensions between formal religious expression in the cult and the occasional ability of the psalmist to break free and express matters of the heart. Most particularly, in his discussion of individual thanksgiving songs, Gunkel sees the psalmist learning from the prophets "to free themselves from the sacrificial worship in which their poetry had developed. *The soul steps free before God, liberated from the*

32. See here especially Bosma, "Discerning the Voices in the Psalms (I)," 183–212. In a second article, Bosma moves on to the question of how the Psalms' human words relate to revelation. "Discerning the Voices in the Psalms (II)," 127–70.

bonds of the cult.[33] Some characteristic value judgments are at work in Gunkel's time: notably that original (prophetic) genius was right in its vision of God, while formal elements such as priestly structure and liturgy represented a drift toward legalism—hence the desire to isolate such breakthrough moments as the thankful soul pouring out their praise. Von Rad is fairly unhappy with what he sees as this polarizing of cult and spirituality.[34] Instead, he insists that the proper focus of the interpreter should be the whole text as Israel's explicit witness to God and to life and faith before God (i.e., the text's "kerygma"). The "romantic" preference for a more subjective, indeed psychological, focus on the individual worshiper is to be resisted.[35] The burden of Carl Bosma's account of this matter is to show how one can respect von Rad's conviction here and still make sense of the voice of the worshiping individual in and through the text. The categories will sound familiar: the voice from the heart (or perhaps the soul, the *nepeš*) is filtered through the cult, owned variously by kings or priests or some authorized covenant representative, and is something of a normative sounding of Israel's faith.[36] The key point is that we hear *both* the praying individual *and also* a more formal, perhaps stylized, liturgical language.

Secondly, we turn to more traditional theological approaches to the question—understanding the speaking voice not in originating historical categories but in fundamental theological categories. As early as Athanasius we find the conviction that the Psalms speak both prophetically (of Christ) and also "psychologically"—that is, with respect to the soul both of the psalmist and of the reader who

33. Gunkel, *Introduction to Psalms*, 210, emphasis in the original. Gunkel (1862–1932) died without completing the book, but Begrich explains that the relevant chapter here was Gunkel's work (see Begrich's foreword to Gunkel's *Introduction to the Psalms*, vii).

34. Von Rad, *Old Testament Theology*, 1:368 critiques Gunkel on this point, including citing the italicized text in the Gunkel quote above.

35. My argument here follows Bosma, "Discerning the Voices in the Psalms (I)," 184–87. Bosma cites von Rad, *Old Testament Theology*, 1:105–6 on kerygma, in von Rad's "Methodological Presuppositions" section (105–28).

36. Bosma, "Discerning the Voices in the Psalms (I)," 193–212.

finds that these psalms serve as a mirror to their soul.[37] Such a dual conviction sustains Christian reading through centuries, culminating perhaps in Calvin's commentary on the Psalms, in the preface to which he writes of the book as "an anatomy of all the parts of the soul."[38] Classically such a view of the Psalms as speaking to the journey of the soul could be held alongside seeing the voice of the Psalms in other (christological) categories. What becomes clear with the benefit of hindsight is that the link between the original human author and the nature of the voice in the text has always been more complicated than simply working out what was first said and then applying it to later contexts, as indeed I argued in chapter 1. The goals of historical criticism and of theology in the service of the church deploy this complexity in different ways, but in a certain sense identifying the speaking voice in the psalm depends on the framework within which one reads the psalm, whether that be a (re-)construction of ancient Israelite worship or a construction of Christian (or, differently, Jewish) theology, or whatever overarching scheme is in view.[39] For now I wish only to note that the classic interest in the Psalms as the "mirror of the soul" can fit alongside the recognition that we may not be being granted access to the inner workings of the original psalmist's soul: it is what the text does with the portrait of the soul that matters.[40] We will return in chapter 4 to the other side of early Christian reading and its relating of the text to Christ.

Thirdly, what of newer literary categories of interpretation? These are about understanding the speaking voice of a psalm as whatever

37. See Athanasius, "Letter to Marcellinus on the Interpretation of the Psalms," cited extensively by Bosma, "Discerning the Voices in the Psalms (I)," 187–90.

38. Calvin, *Commentary on the Psalms*, 1:xxxvi, cited by Bosma, "Discerning the Voices in the Psalms (I)," 109; cited and discussed also in Selderhuis, *Calvin's Theology of the Psalms*, 23, who goes on to report Calvin's conviction that "all emotions of the human heart—joy, anger, temptation and sorrow—can be found there."

39. The exploration of this point with regard to modern critical accounts of genre is the particular achievement of Nasuti, *Defining the Sacred Songs*, esp. 52–55 but throughout.

40. This is essentially Bosma's main concern with his "first problem" of Psalms interpretation.

the text puts forward regardless of our ability to know its historical author. It may well be the somewhat self-involved nature of biblical studies that left Psalms study tied more to historical matters than poetics or aesthetics, especially in the modern era. Whatever the reason, the result seems to have been an overlooking of the more literary category of "persona" as relevant to the reading of these ancient poems. Fortunately, this is now changing. I learned the category of "persona" from its application to prophetic literature in the fine study of Jeremiah by Timothy Polk. He explores the constructive question of how to understand Jeremiah as a character in the book named after him, rather than as a historical figure.[41] It has taken rather longer to make its way into Psalms study, despite a passing reference in one 1985 article that does indeed show its potential.[42] The building blocks for the move to persona as a useful category have gradually come into view through reflection on how the readers/pray-ers of the Psalms relate to the "I" as they read each psalm today; in other words, this becomes a literary-hermeneutical question rather than a historical one. Both James Mays and Patrick Miller wrote illuminating articles exploring what they call this kind of "anthropological" approach to the Psalter, where the subject is "the self whose voice is heard in the prayers."[43] It seems to me that what Mays and Miller are achieving in these pieces is the long-overdue extraction of Psalms study from historicizing tendencies, and a recovery of the classic framework for letting the Psalms speak to the soul.

41. Polk, *Prophetic Persona*, a book developed out of his 1982 Yale PhD dissertation. Readers who know the book of Jeremiah will appreciate that Polk's approach skirts all sorts of intractable historical puzzles. His first chapter ("Biographical Interest," 7–24) offers a detailed account of the issues, though two of his long footnotes are also key: 177n28 and 184n12.

42. Parkander, "'Exalted Manna,'" 122–31. Parkander actually focuses on God as the subject matter of even the more difficult psalms but introduces her study with reference to the category of "persona" (122), which she may have imported from reflecting on George Herbert's poetry, since she uses it also in her discussion of Herbert's *The Temple* (129).

43. Mays, "Self in the Psalms," 51–67 (quote from 67); see also his "Question of Identity," 46–54; and Miller, "What Is a Human Being?" and "Sinful and Trusting Creature," in *Way of the Lord*, 226–36 and 237–49.

By this somewhat circuitous route, we have come back to a reading of a psalm that asks not after its author but its "persona." The persona of a poem functions rather like the narrator of a story: it is the identity of the "I" in each case. In their helpful introduction to the topic, Jacobson and Jacobson write that "the author of the psalm stages the poem in such a way that a particular voice is heard or experienced. . . . To ask who the psalmist is, and to think about the relationship that the reader may have with this 'person' who composed the poem, leads to asking the basic but important question of who the persona is in the psalm, and what that persona means to me."[44] Other introductions to the Psalms have likewise reconfigured the various aspects of Psalms study around the question of the speaking voice,[45] or the importance of performing the Psalms, where "the reader of psalms is compelled to take up the subject position of the speaker—'I' or 'we'—and is carried forward by the psalm's rhetorical movement."[46] To date, the most thorough examination of the area is the unpublished thesis of Nathan Dean Maxwell, which deploys a "persona-critical reading" of Book 4 of the Psalms.[47] Maxwell's exemplary survey of the issues ably demonstrates that "modern study of the Psalter has generally equated the 'psalmist' of the text with the historical poet, whoever that may have been."[48] He focuses instead on the *persona*: "the metaphor of the mask, derived originally from the ancient stage, which denotes the literary voice within a poem. The 'voice' of a poem is the character the poet creates, who speaks the words of the verse that the audience experiences."[49] In my view, this turn toward the literary enables Psalms scholarship to take the best

---

44. Jacobson and Jacobson, *Invitation to the Psalms*, 95–96. Their whole discussion on 89–117 explores examples rather than discussing the idea in theory. For a programmatic account, see also Brown, "Psalms and 'I,'" 26–44.

45. This is the governing rubric of Dawes, *Psalms*, surveying the voicing of praise, shalom, dissonance, penitence, hope, spirituality, and theology.

46. Brown, *Psalms*, 61.

47. Maxwell, "Psalmist in the Psalm."

48. Maxwell, "Psalmist in the Psalm," 132.

49. Maxwell, "Psalmist in the Psalm," 81. On 81–90, he helpfully locates the category with respect also to narrators and implied authors.

of the historical specificity of an author focus and to reconstrue it in terms of the text in front of us. It thus also chimes with the theological interests shown by von Rad and other earlier elements of the interpretive tradition.

On the Voice/Persona of Psalm 23

It is time to draw this discussion toward Psalm 23: Who is the speaking voice in our psalm? Is it an individual reflecting on the vagaries of spiritual life? A wanderer in the wilderness? A shepherd? More specifically, could one say that it is the king? Or a priest or other cult minister in a text intended for liturgical worship?

The foregoing analysis has shown that this is not a question about authorship. However, the historical categories that one might have proposed for authorship (e.g., it was written by the king or a priest) can still apply as ways of thinking about whose voice is found in the psalm. Here Susan Gillingham's review of modern critical scholarship on the psalm, mentioned in chapter 1, is very helpful. She identifies five ways that historical readings of Psalm 23 have been developed in the twentieth century.[50] To make the analysis manageable, she restricts herself to approaches that have focused on God as shepherd as the dominant motif in the psalm, while recognizing that it is not the only motif. She also notes that proponents of each reading see their proposal in exclusive terms, since the project in which they are involved is identifying an author and an originating context for the text. However, armed with our discussion of persona, we can see that she succeeds in uncovering five possible personae for the speaking voice in the psalm that proclaims, "The LORD is my shepherd."

First is the biographical-historical reading that locates the resonance of the shepherd imagery in the person of King David, the

---

50. Gillingham, *Image, the Depths, and the Surface*, 46–62. I will not repeat the details she gives of who has put these forward. The "twentieth century" rubric is incidental, but—with the exception of a couple of passing references to mid-nineteenth-century commentaries—all the readings she cites in this section happen to be from 1898–1999.

shepherd-king of Israel.[51] Secondly, we have the cult-historical reading that interprets God as shepherd for kings of the later Davidic dynasty. A third approach locates the voice in the exile, offering a communal-historical reading of God as shepherd for the exilic community. A fourth reading emphasizes individual piety and thus places the origin in the restoration of the postexilic community—a "personal-historical" reading. A final approach is a messianic-historical reading that sees the Maccabean high priests of the second century BCE as the plausible candidates for voicing the psalm's cultic hopes.

It is hard to avoid the conclusion that scholarly ingenuity can find more or less any context in the history of Israel and come up with a plausible scenario for the location of the psalm. Gillingham's own conclusion reveals her to be similarly unimpressed: "Historical readings are a subjective process, because they have to start with the theological motifs in a passage and from this intuit as best they can the religious and social context."[52]

To anticipate one of the details that will be discussed in our exegesis in chapter 3, a particular example of stumbling over potential historical reference is the final verse's mention of the "house of the LORD"—which for now we might simply assume is the Jerusalem temple. Obviously this temple comes after David, which on a surface reading makes it odd to have David (as author) imagining long-term dwelling in the temple; the only thing he knows of the temple is that he is not allowed to build it.[53] While it seems therefore fair to say that Psalm 23 must postdate the construction of the temple, beyond this it is hard to see what degree of specificity is really possible in terms of using this verse to situate the psalm historically. The fifth of

51. I follow Gillingham's labels for the five approaches.
52. Gillingham, *Image, the Depths, and the Surface*, 62.
53. See 2 Sam. 7:4–14 and the full discussion of this point with reference to Ps. 23:6 in chap. 3 below. One could explore various complexifying issues here: that David built some sort of temple structure perhaps (echoed in the superscription of Ps. 30?) or that 2 Sam. 12:20 indicates use of "house of the LORD" language in David's time (perhaps for the tent that housed the ark, but the text is brief). To anticipate the later discussion, my point is that specific historical reference is not a helpful focus.

Gillingham's five historical approaches actually finds here a reference to the second temple in the second century BCE: such dwelling is imagined, for example, by "a member of the Temple staff, one who dwelt in the temple precincts."[54]

Even commentaries that retain a commendable focus on the theological and spiritual potential of the text for believers can be prone to overly historicized readings at this point. Thus, in a series aimed at marrying "probing, reflective interpretation of the text to loyal biblical devotion and warm Christian affection," and indeed in a volume that generally does this very well, Craig Broyles writes of Psalm 23: "The *cup* and the *table* of Psalm 23 may not be merely metaphoric. They depict a meal, and being at *the* house *of the* Lord they probably allude to the thanksgiving offering, which was to be shared as a communal meal with Yahweh, the priests, and the worshipers' family (Lev. 7:15–16; Deut. 12:5–7; 1 Sam. 1:3–4, 9; cf. Pss. 22:26; 36:8; 63:2–5). . . . Psalm 23 was thus a pilgrim psalm anticipating the worship rituals at the Jerusalem temple."[55] To which the best response is "Maybe." Broyles does have good reasons for thinking that pilgrimage may be at issue (and it may),[56] but there is a degree of overconfidence in the move from "may" to "probably" to "was thus" as the commentary unfolds, in the long string of biblical verses that actually do not resolve matters one way or the other, and in the concluding confidence that we have located the originating context of the psalm.

In another example, from an unabashedly scholarly account, Kraus discusses this verse in connection with von Rad's worries

54. Gillingham, *Image, the Depths, and the Surface*, 61, citing the work of Treves, *Dates of the Psalms*, which I have not seen. Gillingham restricts herself to commenting that Treves takes the reference to the "house of the Lord" "literally."

55. Broyles, *Psalms*, 124. The statement on the purpose of the series is found in the editors' foreword, xii. Italics are bold in the original, a convention indicating citation of the NIV. That "house" is not in bold may be an error.

56. Relating to his understanding of v. 6, which we will discuss in chap. 3 below. I am myself sympathetic to the resonance of pilgrimage here, without finding it necessarily a reference to actual pilgrimage. See further the end of chap. 4 below.

about spiritualizing, which we discussed above. Kraus does not find spiritualization here but metaphorical appeal to specific sanctuary language. But he drifts toward conjuring up certainty out of thin air: "It can be shown in Ps. 23:6, for example, that the one praying had been persecuted by his foes and is now experiencing how Yahweh prepares 'in the presence of my enemies' a table for the one they had victimized (v. 5). These factors indicate that the wish to remain in the house of Yahweh as long as one lives relates to the experience of protection in the sanctuary."[57] Again, this is not impossible, but *how* it might be shown is omitted, and there seems to be no link between his correct account of what Psalm 23 does say and how these factors "indicate" his conclusion.[58]

One does not have to be a postmodernist or even the son of a postmodernist to find such tendencies frustrating. The standard interpretive misstep of mistaking persona for author has plagued Psalms scholarship throughout the modern era. To repeat the claim of chapter 1 on this point: historical conjecture is a worthwhile exercise because it might open up illuminating proposals that we could then explore to see whether they shed light on the text. But in this case historical conjecture seems to become a free pass to a certain lack of poetic sensibility: to imagine that a poet could long to dwell in the temple only if they were already in the temple seems odd.[59]

One other brief example must suffice to indicate why we will go no further down this path. At the other end of the psalm, in verse 1, does "The Lord is my shepherd" point us toward royal imagery? This suggestion may seem counterintuitive to twenty-first-century

---

57. Kraus, *Theology of the Psalms*, 160.

58. One's confidence is not boosted by the single appended note, "This interpretation differs from that offered in the *Commentary*"—by which Kraus indicates that this discussion in his *Theology of the Psalms* (German original in 1979) is not in agreement with his own previous commentary on the Psalms, written in 1960 (5th edition in 1988–89).

59. Variant readings of v. 6, such as Broyles offers, do point toward the psalmist at some point being in the temple, so this need not be a cut-and-dried issue, but my critique is of overconfident identification.

readers, but a disciplined historical imagination notes that "shepherd" was a key category for understanding the purpose and role of the king in the ancient Near East. Data for this claim can indeed be found. Specifically, the laws of Hammurabi see Marduk as shepherding his people, and in the Old Testament we find kings portrayed as shepherds, while Ezekiel 34 offers an extended image of Yhwh as shepherd.[60] In other words, King Yhwh is the God who shepherds, and in particular shepherds the psalmist in Psalm 23. So far so good.

There are then two ways in which one can attempt to make interpretive capital from these observations. One is helpful and may be found, for example, in Mays's reading of Psalm 23 in his Interpretation commentary: "To say 'The Lord is my shepherd' invokes all the richness of this [royal] theological and political background as well as the pastoral. The metaphor is not restricted to associations with what actual shepherds did; it is informed by what the Lord has done and what kings were supposed to do."[61] This is exactly right. The poetry "invokes" royal as well as pastoral reflection. We could call this a literary observation about the persona of the psalmist. One would not want to go further and call this a royal psalm, nor draw any conclusions about its place of origin or the identity of its author. But the second route that one might take is indeed to say that we have thus located a "royal psalm" and to insist that the interpretation of Psalm 23 should seek to relate its concerns to matters of kingship. If that were what Psalm 23 talked about in any substantive manner, then there would be no problem, but since it is not, at least in any obvious sense, we may leave the royal connotations on the level of appeal to

60. For details see NICOT, *Psalms*, 240–41. Although the NICOT commentary on Ps. 23 was written by Rolf A. Jacobson, he cites a key article by his NICOT coauthor: Tanner, "King Yahweh as the Good Shepherd," 267–84. On the pervasive metaphor of the shepherd-king across ancient empires, see Varhaug, "Decline of the Shepherd Metaphor," 16–23. In a manner relevant to my conclusions here, Nel argues that the range of the shepherd metaphor gradually reduces through Scripture to focus on the core pastoral imagery. Nel, "Yahweh Is a Shepherd," 79–103.

61. Mays, *Psalms*, 117. I insert "royal" into this quote to capture his preceding paragraph, in which he rehearses some of the data just noted.

Yhwh as provider, carer, and leader in a whole range of ways. Since that is what the psalm plainly says anyway, it is at least arguable that the whole historical diversion to kingship was not worth taking.[62]

Let us attempt a positive conclusion. The persona of Psalm 23— the speaking voice of its poetry—is not limited to being a king or a priest or a temple worshiper, although all of those could inhabit its persona. The psalm is conspicuously vague with regard to who is saying it, when, or where. And this is good news, since it is precisely this openness to being appropriated by many different speakers in many different situations that leaves the psalm open to persistent reappropriation down through the centuries by worshipers of Yhwh, the God of Israel. This is true whether such worshipers were ancient Israelites, today's Jews or Christians, or arguably even late modern people of no particular faith at all, as we will see in our later discussion of the psalm in funeral ministry. All that can be built up out of a "persona-critical" reading of the psalm will be what little the psalm itself tells us about a person living before Yhwh. Imaginative seriousness in interpretation may be sharpened by reflection on the historical categories we have considered, but it is not determined or governed by it. It thus turns out that one result of all our critical study here is to affirm that Psalm 23 can and does speak plainly today.

Focal Image: What Is the Significance of Shepherding in Interpreting Psalm 23?

Perhaps some readers will think that the whole preceding discussion has majored in saying that scholars are predisposed to construct clever theories and would be better off not doing so. That has not really been the point, as I have tried to allow for the possibility that theories

62. In principle, one might say that only the royal king-shepherd would have the boldness to affirm that Yhwh was "my" (personal) shepherd, and so the persona of the psalm must be royal. Again, this is possible. But we cannot show that only kings were bold, so it must remain at best a possibility.

can be useful for all sorts of reasons, not least for informing our imaginations. But what of the popular attempt to gain interpretive benefit from reading Psalm 23 with one eye on the insights afforded from thinking about shepherding? In my view, a similar argument will apply. I thus attempt a brief rehearsal of the pros and cons of appealing to knowledge of shepherding as a key to reading the text of Psalm 23. Interestingly it is not scholarly works that mainly do this but rather the kind of devotional works noted briefly in chapter 1.

Before turning to details, it is worth recognizing an assumption that probably influences all such popular works regarding this matter. The assumption is that the author of Psalm 23 was in fact David the shepherd, and therefore the psalm straightforwardly reflects the life experience of its shepherd-author. If this is granted, then one can see that a shepherd in the twentieth or twenty-first century might well say that shepherding experience unlocks what the text talks about, if due allowance is made for cultural differences between shepherding then and now.

Even granting the assumption about authorship just for the sake of argument, I still think this is mistaken. The psalm is not straightforwardly about shepherding. It starts with "the LORD is my shepherd," so it is immediately metaphorical. The voice speaking in the psalm (what I have called its "persona," though we are assuming for a moment that it is David the shepherd) is presented as that of a sheep, not the shepherd. The issue is how to interpret what a shepherd has written, not how to interpret the experience of shepherding, and while of course it may be helpful to understand shepherding in order to interpret what a shepherd has written, some traps lie in wait, as we will see. The issue is in fact the same as having a priest interpret a psalm written by a priest or a king interpret a psalm written by a king: this *may* help the interpretation, but whether it does or not would have to be examined in practice.

I have no interest in being unduly negative about devotional spiritual works, which have their place in principle, though that place would primarily be concerned with the biblical text and spiritual life rather than with shepherding.[63] For the sake of the discussion I consider one well-known example, then note the existence of many others, and finally look at a different sort of example that is a little more successful.

First must come the well-known book by Phillip Keller, *A Shepherd Looks at Psalm 23*, first written in 1970, although—to my complete surprise—it is listed as the number one bestseller in the "Hebrew Bible" category on a certain well-known internet bookseller's site on the day I write this, nearly fifty years later.[64] Keller (1920–97) tells us that he grew up in East Africa, where he learned the life of Middle Eastern herders, and that he later worked as a sheep rancher. He adds, "It is, therefore, out of the variety of these firsthand experiences with sheep that the following chapters have emerged."[65]

Now the reader of Keller's book will learn many uplifting and true things, and on another occasion it would be good to honor them. Sadly I must press on to comments specifically exploring the interpretive significance of shepherding, such as these:

> From early dawn until late at night this utterly selfless Shepherd is alert to the welfare of His flock. For the diligent sheepman rises early and goes out first thing every morning without fail to look over his flock. It is the initial, intimate contact of the day. With a practiced, searching, sympathetic eye he examines the sheep to see that they are fit and content and able to be on their feet. In an instant he can tell if they have been molested during the night—whether any are ill or if there are some which require special attention. . . . This is a sublime picture of the care given to those whose lives are under Christ's control.[66]

63. I have set out more fully my understanding of the nature of spiritual reading of the biblical text and the problems of appealing to extraneous background information in *Jesus for Life*, 91–103.

64. I looked it up on Amazon.com in late 2019 to be greeted by its "#1 bestseller" status. Different editions of this book have different paginations, so I have not cited specific pages but do give chapter references and the scriptural phrase to which the chapter attends. Keller wrote very short paragraphs—I have ignored some paragraph breaks.

65. Keller, *Psalm 23*, introduction.

66. Keller, *Psalm 23*, chap. 2, "I Shall Not Want."

In comments like this, Keller projects from his own experience as a shepherd to affirm what God is doing and why God is doing it. This does raise difficult questions about the nature of care imagined here. Does God have to check up on what has happened "in the night," for instance, as if God's charges may well have been attacked ("molested") since last they were observed? Likewise elsewhere Keller emphasizes how hard a shepherd has to work (in his chap. 4, "Beside Still Waters"), which may be true but is not what the Psalmist chooses to say about God.

But, secondly, the key point I wish to make is illustrated in quotes such as these:

> The greatest single safeguard which a shepherd has in handling his flock is to keep them on the move.[67]

> Both in Palestine and on our western sheep ranches, this division of the year is common practice. . . . During this time [the end of the year] the flock is entirely alone with the shepherd. They are in intimate contact with him and under his most personal attention day and night. That is why these last verses are couched in such intimate first-person language.[68]

> Just as with the sheep, there must be continuous and renewed application of oil to forestall the "flies" in my life; there must be a continuous anointing of God's gracious Spirit to counteract the ever-present aggravations of personality conflicts.[69]

I would characterize what Keller has done here as moving from the text to experiences he has had, and then talking about the lessons from those experiences as if he were still talking about the text. This is a common move in popular preaching and teaching, and what it achieves in rendering vivid lessons from life experience can obscure

67. Keller, *Psalm 23*, chap. 6, "He Leadeth Me in the Paths of Righteousness . . ."
68. Keller, *Psalm 23*, chap. 7, "Yea, Though I Walk . . ."
69. Keller, *Psalm 23*, chap. 10, "Thou Anointest My Head with Oil."

the fact that the text itself is eclipsed in the process. In these examples, Keller supplies details that are not clear in the text (or not present at all) and then addresses the abstracted ideas rather than the text. He has slipped into talking about shepherding instead of what the shepherd has written about.

Thus we are pressed to recognize the importance of being always on the move, which is an idea mysteriously absent from Psalm 23 itself. We learn about the shape of the sheep's year as a pattern for understanding the psalm, without noting that the psalm gives no such narrative shape to its poetry. We consider the need for the constant application of (medicinal) oil as an image of continuous Spirit-anointing, but in the process lose the psalm's image of a host of a meal offering a welcoming of (a single) anointing. In the slightly whimsical style of lengthy nineteenth-century book titles, I might suggest that this exhibit would be more accurately entitled *A Shepherd Looks at Psalm 23 . . . And Then Talks about Some Things It Reminds Him Of.*

If I belabor this point, it is because I think this issue is so common in popular handling of the biblical text, with the sad result that Scripture serves as little more than reassuring resonance for points that are actually being drawn from elsewhere.[70] But I also wish to pinpoint this problem because it can get shaded into a different issue, with which it should not rightly be confused.

So thirdly, and in my view less problematically, Keller reads metaphorically. One might say he "allegorizes," although I have no wish to enter into a detailed analysis of what counts as good or bad allegory. Perhaps allegory, for our purposes here, may simply be thought of as a kind of metaphorical reading. Admittedly, he does not himself present his reading as a metaphorical one, but I think that could be done (with some profit, I might suggest). Consider these examples:

70. A disquieting study of comparable phenomena in contemporary American spiritual life, although framed slightly differently, is offered by Strawn, *Old Testament Is Dying*, e.g., 1–18 and 131–55.

As with sheep, so with Christians, some basic principles and parallels apply which will help us . . . [e.g.] a sheep simply having too much wool. . . . Wool in Scripture depicts the old self-life in the Christian. It is the outward expression of an inner attitude.[71]

What David referred to as a table was actually the entire high summer [mountain] range.[72]

Actually what is referred to by "house" is the family or household or flock of the Good Shepherd.[73]

I would not have thought that wool was a sign of the old life, but once proposed, it is an image one might work with (perhaps!). I personally would desist from Keller's use of "actually," and instead restate some of these observations more as "the 'house' may point us to God's people," or "the table can be read as a mountain range where the sheep may rest." Such metaphorical reading can be worthwhile, and my concern here is that, recognizing the problem of textual eclipse in the previous examples, one might then dismiss the kind of metaphorical move Keller makes as further evidence of the same problem, but it is not. I have no particular stake in whether these three examples are all equally good, but I do think that this mode of reading in itself is not necessarily a problem. It is all a matter of whether a metaphor or an allegory takes us deeper into engagement with the text or—like the eclipsing examples above—simply changes the subject.

I have on my shelf other examples of devotional books on Psalm 23 that lack Keller's grasp of some aspects of the nomadic Middle Eastern context and that default to shepherding examples drawn from the beautiful hills of England or the plains of America: it is like this; it is like that; are we not—like sheep—so stubborn; green pastures speak to us of a nice walk in the countryside; and so forth.

71. Keller, *Psalm 23*, chap. 5, "He Restoreth My Soul."
72. Keller, *Psalm 23*, chap. 9, "Thou Preparest a Table . . ."
73. Keller, *Psalm 23*, chap. 12, "I Will Dwell in the House of the Lord for Ever."

I had intended to offer such further examples but was struck by the wisdom of a brief comment by Kenneth Bailey on this matter: that such authors "apply experience from sheep-herding in Africa, Asia and America to Psalm 23. Occasionally it fits and is useful."[74] And with that Bailey moves on, drawing instead on a few comments in manuals written by those with older or Middle Eastern experience. Bailey actually includes Keller's book in his comment, but for Bailey the key issue is always cultural fit. While that is certainly one important issue, the problem of talking about something other than what the text says is not at heart a matter of cultural awareness; it is a matter of attentive reading of a given text. And with respect to the Bible, attentive reading is a theological practice at root, filtered through literary attention to detail and only sometimes dependent on matters of cultural awareness.

This brings me to conclude this short section on shepherding by considering Bailey's own example. Kenneth Bailey (1930–2016) was an American who grew up partly in Egypt and spent many years teaching in Lebanon and later in Bethlehem. His writings persistently draw upon his experience of Middle Eastern culture and ways of reading or responding to stories, which leads him also to emphasize chiastic or "ring" structures in biblical texts, sometimes over even very long passages. His final book explored the imagery of *The Good Shepherd*, starting with a detailed reading of Psalm 23.[75] How does it fare according to the argument I have been developing?

Perhaps unsurprisingly, it fares rather better than any other example I have encountered. Here is part of his reflection on verse 1: "No sheep is ever taken out to pasture alone. The cost of the labor involved would be prohibitive. A flock is thereby always assumed. But in this famous psalm, the focus is on the individual."[76] This is exactly

---

74. Bailey, *Good Shepherd*, 16.

75. Bailey, *Good Shepherd*, 13, includes a discussion of his relevant cultural experience. His reading of Ps. 23 is in chap. 1 (31–65), and he does indeed find it to be a "ring composition" (33).

76. Bailey, *Good Shepherd*, 38.

the right way to handle background information: note its framing of the matters raised in the text by way of broader background detail, but then the move back to focus on what the text actually says. I will draw on some points of Bailey's reading in our exegesis in chapter 3. Here I would note that what he achieves in appealing to details of shepherding is fundamentally a vivifying of the imagination so that we can pay better attention to the text. Thus in connection with verse 2 he notes that green pastures are not a year-round phenomenon and hence represent something of a longed-for ideal; with reference to "for you are with me" in verse 4, he observes that sheep have no defenses of their own and thus can *only* rely on the shepherd for help.[77] At other times, he is more than happy to spiritualize or read metaphorically, and he knows that he is doing it.[78]

I have used the case study of shepherding as a way of drawing out the legitimacy and limits of appealing to background information in the reading of Psalm 23. The core issue is whether the information serves greater attention to the text and its subject matter, or whether that information eclipses the text. The eclipse is a common feature of critical study that displaces attention to such matters as king and cult, as we saw in the previous section. But it is also a too-common feature of popular reading. In my view this observation will apply to all reading of Scripture, not just Psalm 23. The lesson is worth learning well.[79]

Text: How Does Psalm 23 Fit into the Psalter?

One final "background" matter remains for brief consideration: the location of our psalm in the Psalter. We read it today as the twenty-third

---

77. Bailey, *Good Shepherd*, 40–41, 49.

78. Indeed the startling epigram at the front of the book is taken from the Babylonian Talmud: "Midrash is the hammer which awakens the slumbering sparks in the anvil of the Bible." Bailey, *Good Shepherd*, 11.

79. Those who have studied the history of biblical interpretation will recognize that I draw the key image of "eclipsing" the biblical text from the analysis offered by Frei, *Eclipse of Biblical Narrative*.

of 150 psalms. But how did it get there, and is that fact of any particular significance? The data we have for answering such questions is almost all literary in nature—that is, it consists of deductions from looking at the Psalter, rather than of independent historical evidence about how the Psalter was put together.[80]

First, a relatively minor technical point: the numbering of the Psalms is different in the Hebrew and Greek traditions. The 150 psalms of the Hebrew Bible Psalter are comparable to Psalms 1–150 in the LXX.[81] But for most of those 150 psalms, the numbering differs because the LXX combines Psalms 9–10 into one (and in due course splits Ps. 147 into two).[82] As a result, Psalm 23 is numbered Psalm 22 in the LXX (and the Vulgate). Some older translations (especially in the Orthodox and Catholic traditions) follow the LXX numbering because this numbering was the more traditional system used in the early church. To make sense of the relevant Bible references in older sources (such as we saw with Wycliffe at the beginning of this chapter), it is worth knowing that our psalm was Psalm 22 in earlier times, but in this book I always call our text Psalm 23, for simplicity.

More generally, one of the striking developments of Psalms study over the last forty years or so has been the turn toward giving attention to the "shape" and "shaping" of the Psalter. Since I intend to make only minimal use of this development, I will not attempt to do justice to all that has been explored here, fascinating though much of

80. It is not quite true to say that there is no historical evidence on this matter, but such as there is does not help us with Ps. 23. The main historical evidence concerns differing arrangements in Dead Sea Scrolls psalters, which prompts us to think that Books 1–3 of the Psalter were "a settled matter before the time of the Dead Sea Scrolls," whereas Books 4 and 5 were not and came later. See Holladay, *Psalms through Three Thousand Years*, 76–77, and 95–112, quote from 77.

81. This awkward phrasing allows for the fact that the LXX includes a Ps. 151. Ps. 151 is actually not irrelevant to our concerns in this chapter, since it is a brief rehearsal of some episodes from the life of David as a young man, saying that the Lord "took me from my father's sheep, and anointed me with his anointing oil" (v. 4). Unlike Ps. 23, Ps. 151 *is* in part about David, including as shepherd boy. It seems to be drawn largely from 1 Sam. 16–17.

82. There is a further complication around Pss. 114–116 that need not detain us. It all works out in the end.

it is.[83] One of the core questions such work explores is easy to state: Should one locate some part of a psalm's meaning and significance with reference to its place in the Psalter's collection? (Another core question goes the other way: How do individual psalms in their specific locations in the book contribute to thinking about the purpose and message of the Psalter?)

This is not a traditional interest of readers of the book, as indeed it is often not an interest of readers of other books of collected hymns or poems, who may reflect that they never (or rarely) ask whether there is any significance that such-and-such a poem is on page 23 of a book, is followed by another poem on a different topic on page 24, and so forth. Thus some scholars remain unimpressed by such concerns except in the broadest possible sense of receiving the individual psalms as part of the whole book.[84] One might, for example, say that it is helpful to recognize that Psalm 1 is an opening of sorts and Psalm 150 a fitting conclusion, but beyond this perhaps there is not much to say.

My own view is that there are two separate issues being unhelpfully conflated in this kind of work. One is whether any kind of editorial arrangement of psalms is deliberate, and thus whether one can talk of a purposeful shape to the whole Psalter. Although this is an interest in editors rather than authors, it is still effectively a "behind-the-text" question. The latest full study of this topic sees the case as, at best, not proven, and most likely not provable.[85] But a more relaxed question asks whether there may be mileage in *reading* the Psalter as a book, with attention to what sorts of links and thematic emphases might emerge in such a reading—to some extent regardless of whether they

---

83. The trigger for the interest appears to have been the reflections of Childs, *Introduction to the Old Testament*, 504–25, and in turn the thesis of his student Wilson, *Editing of the Hebrew Psalter*, usefully summarized in Wilson's "Structure of the Psalter," 229–46. See further deClaissé-Walford, *Shape and Shaping of the Book of Psalms*; deClaissé-Walford, *Introduction to the Psalms*.

84. The award for least-interested Psalms scholar in this regard goes to Goldingay, *Psalms*, 1:36–37, who cites rabbinic precedent on his side.

85. See Willgren, *Formation of the 'Book' of Psalms*.

were deliberately brought about by an editor at any point. On this kind of literary approach I suspect there are indeed some interesting things to say about the shape of the Psalter, although Psalm 23 is not particularly prominent in such readings.

Approaching a reading of the whole Psalter, one notes that the 150 psalms are arranged into five books, either in echo of the five books of Moses or for some largely obscured reason that may have been subsequently echoed in turn by editors of the books of Moses. There seems to be some degree of thematic emphasis in some of the books: Book 3 (Pss. 73–89) is often taken to reflect on the turmoil of life in exile, while Book 4 (Pss. 90–106) perhaps imagines a new sense of the LORD as king of the whole earth, for example.[86] But it is hard to discern any particular significance regarding Book 1 (Pss. 1–41) other than that these are more or less all psalms "of David."[87] On an older understanding, the use of YHWH as the divine name in these psalms, in contrast to the preference for *'ĕlōhîm* in Psalms 42–83 (the so-called Elohistic Psalter), suggested that Book 1 derived from the Southern Kingdom during the time of the divided monarchy.[88] But overall the interpretive insight from such observations is meager with regard to a psalm like Psalm 23.

As it happens, Psalm 23 falls within a particular series in Book 1 that *has* attracted attention: the sequence in Psalms 15–24, which is sometimes thought to make up a particular ring or "cluster" of

86. In addition to the survey of deClaissé-Walford, *Introduction to the Psalms*, 85–111 and 134–40, which focuses on these matters, see also the engaging narrative analysis of Parrish, *Story of the Psalms*.

87. See the discussion earlier in this chapter about the limited number of exceptions, most obviously Pss. 1 and 2. DeClaissé-Walford, *Introduction to the Psalms*, 59–72, draws few conclusions about Book 1 apart from the preponderance of laments found in it. Rather differently, McCann explores the beatitudes of Book 1 to focus on its portrait of "human happiness." McCann, "Shape of Book I," 340–48. Most likely these two writers are highlighting aspects of (different) subsets of Book 1 at best.

88. In addition to the discussions of such issues found in the resources just listed, a helpful brief survey is offered by Holladay, *Psalms through Three Thousand Years*, 67–81.

Psalms that reflects "a sophisticated level of editorial organization."[89] There are certainly some interesting features of this sequence that seem to invite comment. The series may be represented as follows:

Psalm 15—entrance liturgy

Psalm 16—song of trust

Psalm 17

Psalm 18

Psalm 19 = center

Psalms 20–21

Psalm 22

Psalm 23—song of trust

Psalm 24—entrance liturgy[90]

Psalms 15 and 24 are both "entrance liturgies," concerned with who may come into the presence of Yʜᴡʜ. The centerpiece of the arrangement is then Psalm 19, in which God the creator provides the *tôrâ* (the "law" as it is often translated) as the crown and climax of creation. In his reading of this series, Brown suggests that the structuring of the sequence of psalms around Psalm 19 relativizes the various mentions of temple or other refuge in the surrounding psalms and suggests that all such references therefore point in the fullness of time to God's *tôrâ* as the place where God dwells, and to which God's people long to be drawn.[91] On this reading, Psalms 16 and 23 then serve to orient the reader (or the pray-er, or the pilgrim perhaps) to seeing that

89. So Brown, *Psalms*, 97. This point goes back to some key studies of Auffret, Miller, and Hossfeld and Zenger: references may be found in the sympathetic summary of Gillingham, *Image, the Depths, and the Surface*, 68–70.

90. Brown, *Psalms*, 97, provides a slightly fuller chart and also in due course offers a (not particularly convincing) reason for seeing Pss. 20–21 as one element instead of two.

91. This is a simplified summary of the account of Brown, *Psalms*, 97–107. A spirited alternative reading, still locating significance in deliberate editorial arrangement, is Sumpter, "Coherence of Psalms 15–24," 186–209.

trust is ultimately in God's *tôrâ*. Brown suggests that 23:1, with its emphasis on "lacking nothing," is fulfilled in the provision of *tôrâ* in Psalm 19:8a as "complete" or "whole" (*tǝmîmâ*, often translated as "right" in English versions). Everything points to God's perfect provision of his *tôrâ* ("law," "instruction") at the center.

If such a reading is right, then this would indeed make a difference to some elements of a reading of Psalm 23, though perhaps not too many of them.[92] It seems to me that it is best to see this reading as overlaying another interesting level of resonance between Psalm 23 and its surrounding texts, rather than fundamentally changing how one reads Psalm 23. I also wonder whether there could be value in aspects of the reading, pertaining more to the bracketing and central psalms (15, 19, 24) without making every psalm in the sequence integral to the argument. But what this discussion does is remind us that how one frames a text in literary terms will always tend to make a difference to how its import is perceived. Once again, Gillingham offers a fine survey of several such options that have been pursued with respect to Psalm 23, and I can do no better than to summarize here the seven concentric frames within which she reviews literary readings of our psalm:

1. As a self-contained poetic prayer, affirming confidence within doubt
2. In the context of Psalms 22 and 24 (see below)
3. In the context of Psalms 15–24, affirming confidence in the midst of life's crises
4. In the context of Psalms 1–41, as sung for temple liturgy
5. In the context of the whole Psalter: "a daring expression of personal faith"

---

92. Another example sometimes given is the occurrence of the word for "my cup" (*kôsî*) in 16:5 and 23:5, as "the only times this term is used in the Psalter" (Gillingham, *Psalms through the Centuries*, 2:101), but this is only true of the term "cup" with "my" added, and "cup" (*kôs*) also occurs in various forms four other times.

6. Within the whole Hebrew Bible: looking toward the future hope of Israel

7. Within the Christian Bible: concerning the fulfillment of prophecy[93]

It is interesting perhaps that the difference between numbers 1 and 3 in this list is not strong, and the emphasis of number 5 would probably rightly be noted in any focused exegesis of the psalm itself anyway. But the overall point that (literary) context makes a difference to what sorts of themes and emphases matter most is well taken.

The second of Gillingham's seven reading frames addresses the experience of reading Psalms 22, 23, and 24 together and in order. The key perspective added, she suggests, is that we are helped "to see the psalm's expression of trust as part of a process, rather than an end in itself. . . . In this reading the faith of the psalmist of Psalm 23 could be seen as more resolute."[94] There are indeed sufficient notable links of vocabulary between Psalms 22 and 23 to make this kind of sequential reading worth pursuing. DeClaissé-Walford maps out what she calls "striking" verbal connections and concludes, "In Psalm 22 the psalmist feels surrounded, threatened, and bereft of the presence of God. In Psalm 23, the psalmist is still surrounded and threatened, but God is present, and for the psalmist, that fact makes all the difference."[95] Psalm 24 then offers a celebration of Yhwh's kingship and glory in response.[96]

93. Gillingham, *Image, the Depths and the Surface*, 62–77. I have in the main adopted her subheadings, though slightly simplified.

94. Gillingham, *Image, the Depths and the Surface*, 67.

95. DeClaissé-Walford, "Intertextual Reading," 139–52, here 149. Her own approach bases this reading on a historical claim about the intentional sequencing of these psalms, rooted in finding significance in their form-critical difference from most of the surrounding psalms in Book 1. I find this less persuasive.

96. The LXX title in Ps. 24:1 adds, "Of the first day of the week," prompting the early church to find reference to Christ's resurrection there (so Augustine, *Expositions of the Psalms* 1:246, for example), and opening the way to read Ps. 22 as a passion psalm, Ps. 24 as a resurrection psalm (later more commonly an ascension psalm), and Ps. 23 as a christological psalm pertaining to "Christ's benefits," to use Calvin's term. However, I have been able to find no trace of this in modern Psalms scholarship.

It certainly seems to me worth asking questions like this, in case they should turn out to be illuminating. Perhaps that is the case here. I suspect, though, that what such readings offer is a helpful angle on how to look at a (mini)sequence of poems, be it 15–24 or 22–24, and that this is simply a *different* reading that attends to some relatively well-grounded textual observations rather than a *better* reading. With regard to Psalm 23 itself, it is worth asking how our focal psalm might contribute to that wider perspective. But I am not sure that these different (literary) readings make an especially convincing or even a particularly marked contribution to the reading of the details of Psalm 23. Another way of putting this point is to say that a reader (or worshiper) who turns directly to Psalm 23 without regard to its surrounding psalms will not in so doing miss something essential, although they will of course, by definition, miss the experience of reading it in a larger context. Neither approach is inherently the right or wrong one.

To sum up, it might have been the case that the literary framing of Psalm 23 was significant, but it turns out to be a matter of limited (though not zero) interest. All things considered, in what follows I will therefore take the more traditional route of turning directly to Psalm 23, aware of its setting in a wider collection, but without considering immediately adjacent texts as especially relevant.

Conclusion

In this chapter we have reviewed four aspects of the world behind Psalm 23: its author, its voice, its focal image, and its arrival on our reading horizon as a particular text within the book of Psalms. This has led us to consider the psalm as effectively anonymous, but helpfully "Davidic," with due respect paid to the secondary but integral psalm title. It has led to an investigation of the link between the living spirituality of the psalmist and the ways in which that was factored through formal literary and liturgical contexts to be a public text, without losing spiritual emphasis. We also explored the concept of the psalm's "persona" in order to focus on the voice of the psalmist in the psalm. We asked about the significance of having a knowledge of (ancient) shepherding as a kind of test case for how to make wise use of background information in the reading of a biblical text; such knowledge informs our imaginations but does not properly invite us to move away from a focus on the text itself. And we considered proposals that have found canonical significance in reading Psalm 23 in its specific location—in Book 1 of the Psalter, in Psalms 15–24, and between Psalms 22 and 24—but we did not find these frames of reference essential to our reading of Psalm 23.

Readers may feel that the conclusions of this chapter have tended toward the negative. There is much we do not know, and no amount of scholarly ingenuity or spiritual reflection will conjure up additional information. But I have nevertheless wanted to maintain a tone of positive attention to the text, using any and every tool that may help us, whether it is careful historical inquiry or detailed literary consideration. In the end, the very lack of specific information about Psalm 23 is partly what has allowed it to roam freely in the imaginations of readers down through the centuries—that and its specific content, of course.

An unusual take on Psalm 23's fresh appeal in multiple new settings is offered by Hugh Pyper, who reads this "self-reproducing" characteristic of Psalm 23 as its "selfish gene": it replicates itself into endlessly renewable contexts and "survives" when many other texts perish, because it is so "ambiguous" and "malleable."[97] It may indeed be a text marked by a degree of ambiguity and a certain malleability— readers can to some extent adapt it to their own ends—but the text still certainly says some things and certainly does not say other things. In the end the nature of its actual claims can only be addressed by a proper exegesis. It is time to turn to the world *in* Psalm 23 and to a detailed and careful critical reading of the psalm's text.

97. Pyper, "Triumph of the Lamb," 384–92.

3

The World in Psalm 23

Exegesis

In chapter 1 we looked at some reasons why one cannot pursue a straightforward, objective account of the text without a range of judgments and commitments always being in play. In chapter 2 we saw how differing estimates of the historical background behind the text, and its significance, have an impact on readings of the psalm. However, none of this implies that close attention to the text is either impossible or inessential. On the contrary, it remains a cornerstone of faithful interpretation. This chapter is given over to such detailed consideration of the text of Psalm 23.

At times the path through this chapter is a little steep and gets waylaid on tricky details. I have been tempted by David Firth's passing note on Psalm 23 that "in some respects, this Psalm is so clear, that there is no real need to comment upon it."[1] Lucid as his own brief remarks are, for our purposes we need rather more detail. Fundamentally, what follows takes Psalm 23 phrase by phrase and word by word and dwells with the text in a sort of exegetically quiet and

1. Firth, *Hear, O Lord*, 36.

soul-restoring way in order to see *what the text says*. We will take a slow and detailed route and seek to explain how and why the psalm is read the way it is and has been. The reader will realize that what results is frequently open ended and influenced by a range of necessary interpretive judgments on textual, historical, literary, hermeneutical, and theological matters. But the reader will also see that the psalm does still say many things clearly. The open-endedness is not without limit.

This chapter is written to be comprehensible to those following along in English, although of course it refers to various ancient languages too. Christians have never had a theological commitment to saying that only the original Hebrew (OT) and Greek (NT) texts are "the Bible"—they have instead allowed that translations of the texts, such as into English, are the Bible too. Among the many implications of this theological commitment is the observation that English translations can be just as much inspired text as the Greek and Hebrew originals that they translate, despite the often-made claims to the contrary.[2] Nevertheless, the wisest readings of English Bibles will attend to questions of how our English translations relate to the relevant texts in the ancient languages that we introduced at the beginning of chapter 2. It is simpler to see how this works out in practice than to ponder it endlessly in theory. An appendix will offer some brief technical analysis of the Hebrew for those whose reading would be enlightened by such details.

The Hebrew text is preserved for us in a way that indicates lines and half-lines, which vary in length considerably in Psalm 23. To break the reading up into small sections, I have followed the helpful presentation of the text by Jan Fokkelman, who finds twenty sense units in the psalm (including the title).[3] While the rhythmic sense and poetic structure of the Hebrew is contested, I follow Fokkelman simply because it makes for ease of presentation.

2. The best discussion of inspiration as it relates to the specifics of the biblical text is Chapman, "Reclaiming Inspiration," 167–206.
3. Fokkelman, *Psalms in Form*, 34.

I begin the discussion of each verse with a transliteration of the Hebrew text so that readers can see what words we are discussing. I then offer what is effectively a word-for-word translation, insofar as that is possible and/or makes sense. This initial step is not intended as a fluent translation and serves purely to orient the reader to the discussion that follows. At the end of the chapter I gather up all the discussion of options and conclude with my own suggested translation.

Undoubtedly overstating his case, David Clines has called Psalm 23 "the best known but worst translated chapter of the Bible."[4] Perhaps it is the best known, but as regards the quality of our usual translations, I think any difficulty is due simply to the hazards of translating poetry and poetic imagery in general. Thus we will profit from working carefully through the details to see how we arrive at the psalm as it has been known and received, and in general loved, in English.

Verse 1

yhwh rōʿî lōʾ ʾeḥsār
Yʜᴡʜ is my shepherd. I will not lack.

The four Hebrew words in this verse fall into two pairs. The first is about God, the second about "me." The link between them is left implied, which means that there is some scope for interpretive options, and we will consider this after discussing the two pairs.

The first word of the first pair is the divine name, Yʜᴡʜ. As is well known, this is the name of Israel's God, traditionally translated as "the Lᴏʀᴅ" in English translations, and even more traditionally, this name is never pronounced by Jewish worshipers, who substitute the word *ʾădōnāy* ("Lord") in spoken Hebrew both in ancient times and today. Other substitutions were and are possible (e.g., *hāšēm*, "the

4. Clines, "Translating Psalm 23," 67–80, here 67. He seems overly worried by what sheep literally can or cannot do.

name") but need not occupy us here. This convention is marked in our Hebrew texts by effectively omitting the vowels of the name to make it unpronounceable.[5] The identity of Israel's God vis-à-vis wider conceptions of "g/God" in the ancient and modern worlds is a question of intense interest and no little complexity. The earliest settled tradition for rendering YHWH into another language was the LXX's decision to go with *kyrios* ("Lord"). As a more or less direct result, the tradition in English is to write "the LORD," with the small caps indicating that this is an occurrence of the word YHWH in the Hebrew original. A scholarly equivalent, after a period in the modern era of suggesting "Yahweh" as a reconstructed form, is to write YHWH in English-language contexts. This allows an informed reader to see the form Y-H-W-H and perhaps to vocalize it to themselves as "the Lord," which would nicely echo the convention in reading Hebrew texts. Further discussion of this general issue may be sidelined here, although in fact one further matter will be raised below by Psalm 23:1 itself.[6]

A *rōʿeh* is a shepherd.*[7] The word comes from *rāʿāh*, a verb meaning to shepherd, to pasture, or to graze. The *-i* suffix that creates the form *rōʿî* means "my," hence "my shepherd." Rendered into Greek, the construction turns "me" into the object of a verb "to shepherd," hence "The Lord (*kyrios*) shepherds me" (NETS). In neither case, however, is it entirely clear where the emphasis lies. As Muraoka puts it, in such cases as this "it is difficult to determine whether or not one of the constituents is meant to be prominent." He gives Psalm 23:1 as an example that leaves one wondering, Is the question behind this utterance "Who is my shepherd?" or "What is [YHWH] for me?"[8] Given the way that this bold assertion opens the psalm, perhaps both angles are in view.

5. In fact, the text includes the vowels of *'ădōnāy*, slightly adjusted, to remind the reader to say "adonay." The vowel-omission option is also sometimes tried today, when people write "G–d."

6. The important question for Christians of the identity of YHWH vis-à-vis Jesus will be taken up in chap. 4.

7. An * in the text in this chapter refers the reader to a note on the Hebrew in the appendix.

8. Muraoka, *Biblical Hebrew Reader*, 89.

It is not so rare for God to be described as a shepherd. In Psalm 80:1 the psalmist begins, "Give ear, O shepherd of Israel!" Psalm 95:7 (and comparably 100:3) implies that God is the shepherd in an acclamation that focuses on the people as "the people of his pasture, and the sheep of his hand." But to say that the Lord is *my* shepherd is uniquely personalized and individualized, which some may have been inclined to see as a pointer to the voice of David alone, the "man after God's own heart" (1 Sam. 13:14).[9] Even so, the point of the psalmist saying that the Lᴏʀᴅ is his shepherd is clearly to encourage others to adopt and appropriate the language too, so that all who follow in the greater "family of David" can also say, "the Lᴏʀᴅ is *my* shepherd."

The only truly comparable Old Testament use of *rōʿî* is in Isaiah 44:28, at the end of Yʜwʜ's remarkable speech of divine power that is conspicuously set against all the indications that exile has had the better of Israel. "I am Yʜwʜ" begins the declamation (44:24), followed by a string of affirmations about what Yʜwʜ alone can do and does, anything up to fourteen great claims (depending on how one counts them). This climaxes in the final verse of the chapter with the startling announcement that Yʜwʜ "says of Cyrus, 'He is my shepherd [*rōʿî*], and he shall carry out all my purpose,'" briefly illuminated in a final line as referring to the rebuilding of Jerusalem and the laying of the foundations of the temple (Isa. 44:28). Cyrus was the king of the Persian empire in the sixth century BCE, and the extraordinary prophetic claim here is that this incoming foreign ruler will serve Yʜwʜ's purposes and thus bring about the end of the long-endured Babylonian exile, which is by and large what happened. I doubt there is a historical link between the two verses; that is, the psalmist is probably not writing with the intent of calling to mind Isaiah 44, and neither is the prophet writing in conscious echo of Psalm 23. But the intertextual link may possibly impress a reader of the two texts, with Isaiah 44 taking all the uplifting confidence of

---

9. Ps. 23:1 fits entirely with David saying it, but as discussed in chap. 2, this does not equate to demonstrating that David said it.

Psalm 23 and pointing it in the direction of Cyrus in a counterintuitive indication that Babylon will not have the last word, and with Psalm 23 offering a distant echo of the extraordinary claim about Cyrus as God's appointed shepherd (about to be called God's "anointed" in the very next verse, 45:1). All that Cyrus did—on God's bidding—reflects for us the shepherdlike qualities of God. While there is truth in both claims, I suspect one should not make too much of any link.

It is often observed that in the ancient world royal figures could be described as "shepherds" and that this language therefore has royal connotations.[10] Thus it is not a totally new angle but rather a specific focusing that is introduced in this opening phrase when Jerome's Vulgate reads, *dominus regit me*, "the Lord rules (over) me" or "governs me" (or "The Lord is my ruler"). The Latin text of Psalm 23 overall does retain most of the psalm's direct shepherd connotations, but here in verse 1 Jerome makes a move that has considerable impact on the interpretive tradition and ends up shifting the focus to the Lord as ruler.[11] Jerome actually pulls away from this wording when he retranslates the Psalter from a more Hebraic base and offers instead *dominus pascit me*, "the Lord shepherds me." But it is the earlier translation that carries most weight in the subsequent tradition.[12] Rendering YHWH as "LORD" fits hand in glove with the notion of ruling or governing, but Jerome's translation obscures the image

10. See the discussion of background in chap. 2 above and the review of examples in Gillingham, *Image, the Depths and the Surface*, 47–48.

11. Or "governor." Interestingly this term crept into the Psalter in English via Coverdale's rendering of Ps. 8, adopted by the BCP: "O LORD our Governor, how excellent is thy Name" (8:1). Coverdale generally followed Jerome's lead, though not in 8:1.

12. See Goins, "Jerome's Psalters," esp. 189–92, for discussion of Jerome's first light revision of the Old Latin, then his "Gallican" Psalter (so-called because it became prominent in Gaul), based still on the LXX, and then his third attempt, known as his "Hebraic Psalter," which tried to balance fidelity to the Hebrew with the constraints of producing a Latin text of artistic merit. The Gallican version would in the end carry most weight in the tradition. Waltke and Houston point out that it was also the version used by Jerome himself in his own commentary (*Psalms as Christian Worship*, 417). They emphasize the impact of this specific decision in Ps. 23:1 on later readers (418–24).

of shepherding with its simple regal affirmation: the Lord (Yhwh) is in charge. Clearly a shepherd has "lordly" oversight of the sheep: a shepherd is hardly a model first-among-equals leader. But there are many other aspects of shepherding, as we have seen, and these have become obscured in the Latin translation of verse 1. Given its enduring significance as a translation in the church, this change of emphasis has considerable impact for subsequent readers.

This may also be the occasion to note an intriguing trend in modern (twentieth-century) translations and paraphrases of Psalm 23, which set out into the linguistic wilderness of trying to update the image of "shepherd" in the hope of refreshing one's understanding of 23:1. One can find versions that offer the Lord as shipmate, boss, pilot, pace-setter, probation officer, (space) controller, and teacher.[13] Engaging as such attempts may be, the drawback is when the range of connotations is shifted away from the range suggested by "shepherd." In each case a particular point of relevance is secured at the expense of letting the text cast the right linguistic shadow. In this sense, Jerome's "ruler" and modern paraphrases have the same problem. It is interesting to note that *The Message*, often thought to be a free paraphrase itself, goes with "God, my shepherd." Eugene Peterson, its author, generally knew when to let the text wander and when to keep it close to home, as we will see when we come to verse 4 in due course.

The targum of Psalm 23 (i.e., its early Aramaic paraphrase) strikes out in an altogether different direction: in place of "The Lord is my shepherd," it has "It is the Lord who fed his people in the desert" (and concludes, "They lacked nothing").[14] The "me" has become Israel. Jonathan Magonet reviews how this becomes a "strong tendency to read the Psalm as a collective statement about the wilderness

13. All these are recorded in Strange and Sandbach, *Psalm 23*, 132–42. The majority are intended not as actual translations but as popular paraphrases.
14. See Stec, *Targum of Psalms*, 61. The Psalms targum is in general somewhat discursive; see the introduction by its translator David M. Stec, 1–24, esp. 2–4. It was perhaps written sometime between the fourth and the sixth centuries AD (2).

period," followed—though not universally—by various rabbis who wrote the succeeding *midrashim* down through the centuries.[15] This line of thought is carried on through the targum, which refers to the restoration of the soul "with manna" in verse 3 and begins verse 4, "Even when I go into exile . . ." For our purposes it suffices just to note that this occurred, since it shows that a simple text can give rise to wide-ranging traditions of interpretation. In Jewish tradition, to oversimplify, this is seen as a productive move toward letting the text speak afresh, rather than a worrying failure to restrict oneself to a purported original meaning.

The second half of verse 1 states simply: *lō' 'eḥsār. Lō'* is a word that negates what follows, which is a first-person verb "to lack/be lacking."* The word is also used with the negation, for example, to describe what happens with the gathering of the manna in Exodus 16:18: "Those who gathered much had nothing over, and those who gathered little had *no shortage*." The verbal link with Psalm 23 is brought out in Exodus 16 in the KJV and ESV, both of which say that the one who gathered little "had no lack."

The interpretive question most clearly posed by the word is how to understand its "tense," which is complicated because Hebrew verbs do not have tense (past/present/future) in the same way that English verbs do. The simplest way to understand how Hebrew verbs are distinguished is to see them as either ongoing or related to a specific point in time.[16] Most commentators opt for emphasizing both the ongoing nature of the verb and the fact that there is no obvious delay; that is, although the ongoing nature of "not lacking" will indeed last into the future, it is already in place. Thus Briggs and Briggs assert, "The imperf[ect] is not future, but a present of habitual experience,"

15. Magonet, *Rabbi Reads the Psalms*, 52. Rashi is an exception, reading it as about David. (*Midrash* was a form of annotated interpretive commentary practiced by the rabbis. As a Hebrew word, its plural is *midrashim*.)

16. This is traditionally called a distinction between "perfect" (complete[d]) and "imperfect" (ongoing), which are labels that bother grammarians who recognize that such categories do not fit Hebrew well. But the labels are very commonly used.

and translate it, "I have no want."[17] Goldingay likewise offers, "I do not lack."[18] English translations mainly follow the KJV's "I shall not want," though NJPS captures the nuance with "I lack nothing." In theory "I shall not want" may be open to the possibility of being present as well as future, but the use of "shall" in the KJV is governed by an older English (British) paradigm in which "I shall" was simply an (irregular) straightforward future comparable to "he will," and would thus in modern English (especially American English) be the same today as the future-tense "I will not want." It is probably the poetic impact of the KJV in Psalm 23 that has prompted widespread retention of the "shall" in English translations. The BCP offers a nice way of holding it open: "therefore can I lack nothing," which is taken up in various hymnody down through the years, such as the second verse of "In Heavenly Love Abiding," with its "My shepherd is beside me and nothing can I lack."[19] This use of "can" helpfully avoids being overly specific about now or the future, although the shorter options ("lack nothing"/"do not lack") have merit.

It is also worth asking in what sense one lacks nothing or will not lack. Clearly not in every conceivable sense.[20] The Psalms themselves bear ample witness to the fact that life is full of trouble and reason for concern, as indeed Psalm 23 will show in due course. The point must be that in some sense—to be determined by further reflection as the psalm progresses—the person who prays Psalm 23:1 has confidence that God is a God who meets needs and who is not caught unawares by one's difficulties. Perhaps more specifically, verse 1 points to letting YHWH decide what it is that I need, in the very process of ensuring that whatever it is, I will not lack it. That my accounting

---

17. Briggs and Briggs, *Psalms*, 1:207–8.
18. Goldingay, *Psalms*, 1:344.
19. Written by Anna Letitia Waring in 1850.
20. As so often, when one switches to this more substantive kind of question, many commentaries fall nervously quiet, and it is the theologians who have more to say. For a reading of "lacking" here that relates it to whether or not we receive the revelation of the glory of God, see Barth, *Church Dogmatics* II/1, 645.

of what I need will differ from Yhwh's seems probable, but Psalm 23 is partly in the business of training my sense of need to be better attuned to what God provides. Arguably one could even say that at root, "not lacking" is a way of phrasing the claim that all one needs is God, because then one has a shepherd who watches over everything. Only a failure to grasp poetry as the open-ended celebration of thankfulness for provision would find Psalm 23:1 to be a statement of overconfidence or willful lack of realism.

This understanding of "not lacking" draws implicitly on the link between the two halves of the verse.[21] That link is interestingly highlighted in the BCP version noted above: "*Therefore* can I lack nothing." In other words, it is the specific point that Yhwh is my shepherd that permits the affirmation that I (can) lack nothing. It is as if 23:1 is describing the theological grammar of Yhwh being my shepherd: I am provided for—and being provided for means fundamentally that Yhwh is my shepherd. Do I still have concerns—even physical or emotional or social needs? Very likely yes, just as the sheep of the shepherd are not guaranteed permanent good health or food. But they will experience such needs in a context of care, and that—the psalm urges—makes all the difference.[22]

Verse 2

bin'ôt deše' yarbîṣēnî

In pastures of green he makes me lie down

21. Other ways of pondering the link (or lack of link) between the two parts of the verse are possible. A good discussion is Magonet, *Rabbi Reads the Psalms*, 50.

22. As I was finishing the first draft of this book, I received from my friend and former OT professor, Deryck Sheriffs, a picture of a tombstone in Wuppertal, South Africa, written in Afrikaans, that reproduces the beginning of Ps. 23 as "Die Here is my herder, Ek kom niks kort nie"—"The Lord is my shepherd, I don't come up short." Deryck explains, "To 'come short' or 'get caught short' is a delightful South African expression for being caught out, found wanting, going to fail, to run out of options, be in trouble" Personal correspondence, Nov. 22, 2019. To me it seems to strike just the right note.

ʿal-mê mənuḥôt yənahălēnî
By waters of rest he leads me

Despite the confident assertions of various commentators, the structure of the poetry of Psalm 23—how its lines fit together into strophes (or "poetic verses")—is hard to discern. I suspect not much hangs on this. The structure is hard to discern because the individual images flow in relatively simple procession, and (allowing for one or two clear shifts of focus) the reader is invited to experience them one at a time. I thus take these two affirmations of verse 2 together, although some prefer to pair the second with the beginning of verse 3.

Both affirmations of verse 2 follow the same structure: naming a pastoral location and then saying what God does to/for me in that location. We should see these as two pictures that begin to offer examples of what it means to be cared for by the shepherd of verse 1.

English translations of verse 2a seem almost uniformly influenced by the KJV: "He maketh me to lie down in green pastures" (updated to "He makes me lie"). The first word, *binʾôt*, has a *b–* prefix that generally means "in" and is followed by a plural form of the word *nāwâ*, which is the feminine form of the word for "pasture."* The Hebrew word order, literally "in pastures of green," is simply a result of the way that the grammar works, but its function is identical to an English adjective ("green"). Thus, despite the familiar hymn—which I will discuss in a moment—there would be no need to reorder the phrase as "pastures green," except oddly that now in English it sounds more appropriately poetic, largely as a result of this very hymn. In fact, the word "pastures" can be a more general dwelling place,[23] but it is qualified here immediately by the word *dešeʾ*, a word for "green vegetation" or "green grass." The greenness emphasizes the newness of the growth: this is grass with life in it. The word is not common in the Old Testament but does occur twice in Genesis 1 as part of

---

23. Though it is coincidental that the famous hymn version of Ps. 23 ends with a reference to "my dwelling place," the underlying vocabulary is different.

the description of God creating plant life on the third day: "Let the earth sprout *dešeʾ* . . ." (Gen. 1:11, cf. v. 12), which is immediately parsed in terms of herbs/plants, trees, seeds, fruit—and hence many translations render *dešeʾ* as "vegetation" in Genesis 1 (e.g., ESV).

Verse 2 thus locates us "in green pastures," where there is life and evident provision. What happens there? A single verb comprises all the elements of what happens, in typical Hebraic practice, by putting subject, object, and action all into one word: *yarbîṣēnî*.* The verb *rābaṣ* means "to stretch/lie down," and it occurs here in a "causative" form—that is, someone causes someone else to stretch or lie down. The subject is undisclosed, other than being masculine singular, hence it is "he," the shepherd of verse 1. The suffix on the word (*–ēnî*) indicates that this is happening "to me." Put all that together and we have "he causes me to lie down," which will sound familiar from all the English translations that say, "He makes me lie down." I do wonder whether the word "makes" brings with it today connotations of insistence that are unhelpful. The image is rather that the shepherd has brought me to a place where I lie down; this is provision, and only in a distant second-sense compulsion. Eugene Peterson offers, "You have bedded me down in lush meadows" (MSG), which captures several nuances well.

Those who find the backstory of shepherding practice fundamental to following the psalm will sometimes suggest that this is a midday image, as the shepherd breaks the daily walk with a period of rest in a place of abundant provision before going on with the "leading" at the end of the verse. Perhaps so. Such a reading is an example of what we discussed in chapter 2: attentiveness to shepherding rather than to what the text chooses to foreground. One need not make too much of it as key to Psalm 23.[24]

Having commented on the word order here, and indeed in the sentence to come, I should note an oddity about the classic hymn that,

24. Even less likely to be a key is Dahood's confident assertion that "verses 2–3 are a description of the Elysian Fields," where the psalmist is led "into Paradise." Dahood, *Psalms 1–50*, 145, 146. Dahood's general approach is discussed later in connection with v. 4.

as sung, appears to retain the Hebrew word order of putting the verb after the mention of "green pastures": "In pastures green he leadeth me."[25] Attention to its punctuation reveals that the well-known first verse of the hymn does in fact follow the breaks of the psalm text:

> The Lord's my shepherd, I'll not want.
> He makes me down to lie
> In pastures green. He leadeth me
> The quiet waters by.

Note that verse 2a of the psalm text occupies line 2 and the first part of line 3 here. Then verse 2b occupies the rest of line 3 and line 4, as follows:

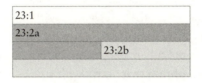

However, I am inclined to think that most people who sing the hymn do not realize this, although perhaps this is simply to generalize my own experience. For years I have sung the third line of this verse—"In pastures green He leadeth me"—assuming that this is one statement that is duly completed by line 4 (". . . the quiet waters by"), on the understanding that the waters flow through the green pastures. At least I now realize that that is the understanding I have had while singing, perhaps somewhat unawares. The tune and the rhythm of the sung hymn all point to line 3 being one thought unit: the meter of the tune pauses naturally after "down to lie" at the end

25. Strange and Sandbach, *Psalm 23*, attribute this hymn originally to Francis Rous (1579–1659) and William Barton (1603–78), and it is the revision of this version in the 1650 Scottish Psalter that survives in hymn books today, sung to the tune of Crimond. Some printed versions put "he leadeth me" at the beginning of line 4 of the hymn's first verse, which makes it compare oddly with all the other verses but emphasizes the point being made here.

of line 2 and not after "in pastures green," and there is a sense to be found in the hymn sung this way. The end result is that I (and, let us assume, at least some others) have inadvertently imagined that there is a nicely poetic word order at hand that seems to mimic the Hebrew word order but does so by mixing and matching different bits of the text. There is of course nothing wrong with understanding the hymn either way. But in matching it up to Psalm 23, something oddly creative has happened. Thus, when I propose translating verse 2a as "in pastures green he makes/lets me lie down," it is the poetic style of the hymn that makes it seem more natural than it might have been.

Making continued use of this word order oddity, we come to verse 2b: ʿal-mê mənuḥôt yənahălēnî, "by waters of rest he leads me." Once again the KJV has carried the day for most English translations with its "He leadeth me beside the still waters" (although the NIV changes "still" to "quiet"). ʿAl is a preposition that tends to mean "on" or "upon," but the context here makes "by" a more natural translation. Mê mənuḥôt* is a phrase that starts with a plural form of the word for "waters" and clarifies it by linking it to a second word showing the purpose of the waters: they are for rest (nûaḥ). What are "waters for rest"? In the world of Psalm 23, in these particular dry lands of the ancient Near East, we are less likely to be talking about rivers that are unusually pastoral in their gentle running, since rivers in general—at least ones that could be located by green pastures, say, and not the Nile or the Euphrates—would generally have been low volume and quiet. The image is probably one of the waters that adjoin the fields, where the resting sheep can take water. The word mənuḥâ more generally means "resting place" when, as indeed almost always, it is not attached to water; a good example is its double use in Psalm 132 (vv. 8, 14) to describe the resting place of the ark of the covenant after it is carried in procession. So this is a resting place that happens to be a water feature, as it were, nicely captured by the NJPS paraphrase: "water in places of repose." Goldingay helpfully explains, "The sheep may drink and lie down by the pool, again knowing they can get up and have another drink."[26] The NIV's "quiet waters," adopted also by Alter,[27] may therefore strike just the right note, even if it is sad to lose a potential structural parallel between "pastures green" and "waters [of] quiet."

The delayed verb in this case is *yǝnahǎlēnî*,* a word that again combines the subject ("he"—the unspecified third-person masculine subject), the object ("me"—denoted again by the suffix), and the action of the verb, which in this case is *nāhal*, "to lead," or "guide," or "bring to a place of rest." Putting this together gives us "he leads me." *Nāhal* is not a common word (it occurs only ten times in the Old Testament). Psalm 31:3 is a clear parallel that we will consider in connection with verse 3 below. Isaiah 40:11 imagines another context where Yhwh leads his people like a shepherd leads a flock (as also does Isa. 49:10). There is not much quiet rest in Isaiah's great declaration of being led through the wilderness on the return from exile, as indeed there is little that is restful about the exodus-celebrating "Song of the Sea," which uses the same verb to sing praise to God: "You guided them by your strength to your holy abode" (Exod. 15:13).

In contrast, the shepherd of Psalm 23 brings me to a place of life-giving rest: I lie down by green pastures, and I am led to water that will be there for me not just momentarily, but—in its own quiet way—as and when I need it. If *dese'* does carry any sense of vegetation, then this is food and water that nourishes life in the care of Yhwh my shepherd. The "leading" is low on emphasizing movement through the wilderness. It is once more about provision, a good resource in peaceful times.

Verse 3

> *napšî yǝšôbēb*
> My life he restores

26. Goldingay, *Psalms*, 1:350.
27. See Alter, *Hebrew Bible*, 3:70.

yanḥēnî bəmaʿgəlê-ṣedeq
He leads me in right(eous) paths

ləmaʿan šəmô
For the sake of his name

This verse continues and perhaps completes the scene of verse 2, as the psalmist continues to rejoice in provision, restoration, and guidance—although again, actual movement seems low on the list of emphases one might discern here. These three short lines are often taken as lines 4, 5, and 6 of the psalm thus far, making up a second couplet and then comprising a third. In outline,

Verse 1: the LORD is my shepherd / I do not lack
Verse 2a: green pastures / lie down

Verse 2b: still waters / leads
Verse 3a: soul / restores

Verse 3b: leads / right paths
Verse 3c: sake / name

It is clear from this simplified presentation that structures and parallels are not strong, with the clearest parallels being the ones noted already between 2a and 2b. I am not persuaded that there is much to be gained from speculating on specific structural divisions of the psalm, other than to observe that these three verses do go very well together and that verse 4 will take us on to a consideration of walking and movement (though of course it could still be considered from the perspective of the rest that is celebrated in vv. 1–3). Here I will simply take the three sections of this verse one at a time.

The verse begins with *napšî yəšôbēb*, a noun followed by a verb. The noun is *napšî*, "my soul." The *–î* suffix once again indicates that it belongs to "me." The word in question here is *nepeš*, classically translated as "soul" but capable of a wide range of ways of connoting the whole person: from "breath," to life, body, self, being, and, of course, soul. The key point is that Hebrew conceptions of the person tended to be aspects of thinking about the whole person: I am characterized by my body, and then again I am characterized by my spirit, and then again it is my emotions, or my desire, that most mark me out as the subject of whatever is being discussed.[28] So *nepeš* is a very flexible word as it gets translated into English, since the modern world tends toward imagining the human self as comprising of parts (body, mind, spirit) in a way that does not match ancient conceptions. This can lead some to ponder whether it is really right to say that humans have "souls" in biblical terms, but this is a confusion created by the fact that Hebrew (and Greek) is different from modern English and that we are not trying to label self-evident parts of a whole so much as wondering what the best way is of describing the whole in different dimensions or aspects.[29]

It is certainly true that the result of consistently translating *nepeš* as "soul" is that many readers imagine that the Bible is interested primarily in the immaterial aspects of the self, while the physical is less significant before God. Such misunderstanding is to be resisted. So what are the options? In some ways "my being" is a helpfully focused translation, but in English it introduces a note of abstractness that sits uneasily with the nature of the poetry in which we find the word. There is a good case for making "person" or "life" (depending on the context) our default translation; "life" is Alter's preference, for example. Here in Psalm 23:3 it is my whole life that is restored. Language being what it is, the poetic weight of the KJV and

---

28. Among various options in the literature, we have "my vitality" (Waltke and Houston, *Psalms as Christian Worship*, 439) and a helpful discussion by deClaissé-Walford, "On Translating the Poetry of the Psalms," 190–203: despite semantic range and nuance of meaning, *nepeš* is more or less consistent in the Psalms and means "the all of who one is" (p. 196).

29. I do not intend this as a technical discussion. The best discussion I know of these matters is Di Vito, "Old Testament Anthropology," 217–38. More broadly I have benefited from Green, *Body, Soul, and Human Life*.

subsequent centuries makes it easy to say "he restores my soul" when we try to articulate this point. Equally, minds beholden to a certain literalism with modern categories might misunderstand the restoring of "my life" to refer to recovery from some near-death experience, which cannot be ruled out as one example of what verse 3 could be imagining, but it would be overly limiting as the actual translation.

What happens to "my life" here? The verb *yəšôbēb** resumes the unidentified "he" as subject[30] and comes from *šûb*, to "turn back" or "return." In the form in which it occurs here it has a slightly stronger ("intensive") sense and thus naturally means "recover," or indeed, as traditionally, "restore." We thus arrive at "He restores my life (/soul)." Would "refresh" be a suitable verb to capture the point here, or even "renew" (NJPS)? This is probably a summation of sorts of the preceding two lines: I am cared for and provided for, and the life-giving food and water and rest do indeed give me life. This applies to anyone, whether they are already feeling good in life or whether they are struggling. As yet the struggling remains distant in this psalm, but it will come in due time.

Jerome's influential Latin translation (the Vulgate) renders this first phrase *animam meam convertit*: "he has converted my soul." This may have contributed to a sense of the restoration at stake here being a spiritual one (hence "my soul"). Jerome changed the verb to *refecit* in his later translation ("remade"), which does indeed recover more of the Hebrew sense, but as we have noted, it is the earlier version from the LXX (the Gallican version) that carried weight.

The verse continues *yanḥēnî bəmaʿgəlê–ṣedeq*, which breaks the pattern of delaying the verb to the end. Instead we begin with *yanḥēnî*, "he leads me" (with the now-familiar unidentified "he" as subject and with "me" as the object, indicated by the suffix). *Nāḥâ* is another verb that means "to lead" or "guide." It is not the same as the *nāhal* of the previous verse, though they clearly operate in the same broad

---

30. And since the word *nepeš* is feminine, this is one more reason—along with sense and considerations of word order—why we know that the subject of the verb must be "he."

semantic range and are found together in the verse we noted in connection with verse 2 above: "In your steadfast love you led [nāḥâ] the
people who you redeemed; you guided [nāhal] them" (Exod.15:13).
As with the version of Exodus 15:13 just quoted, the distinction is
sometimes made in translation between "led" and "guided" when
the two verbs occur in close proximity, but this is really a choice of
style and could be defended either way. The NIV alone demarcates
them in Psalm 23, with "he leads me" in verse 2 and "he guides me"
in verse 3. Most translations go for "leads" in both places.

The place where he leads me here in verse 3 is bəma'gəlê-ṣedeq,
a phrase that is open to two contrasting understandings in English.
The first word means "in paths of," with the word ma'gāl meaning
"path," often used in a metaphorical sense of a way of living (e.g.,
Prov. 2:9, 15, 18, and elsewhere).[31] The second word, ṣedeq, is a noun
meaning "rightness" or "righteousness," or what we might call a kind
of "uprightness." There is a longstanding confusion lurking here that
has created difficulties for English speakers trying to understand the
Hebrew link between doing something right and being righteous.[32]
Ṣedeq means to be right in a range of ways connoting propriety,
including on occasion the moral-ethical dimension of rightness that
we tend to translate as "righteousness." Following the KJV, most
translations suggest "paths of righteousness" (which is suggested
more distantly also by Alter's "pathways of justice"), but the NRSV
and NJPS restrict themselves to "right paths," with the NRSV placing
the more familiar option in a footnote. Which is the better option?

In terms of the poetry, the point is that both are permissible. For
sheep, probably little troubled by ethical dilemmas, the key question
is whether this is the right path, and the shepherd takes them the
right way. For the psalmist and any following after him, the right path
through life, such as is canvassed in Proverbs 2, for example, clearly

---

31. A useful discussion of this sense of a "walk" through life in the Psalms, including Ps. 23, is McCann, "'Way of the Righteous,'" 135–49.

32. A similar issue arises in Greek with the terminology for being righteous and
being justified, where the link is clear in Greek but obscured in English.

has moral connotations. The Old Testament does not know a way of life of theoretical righteousness that is not marked by practically doing the right thing. Obviously this is not to say that there was a perfect correlation between the righteous life and the right deed. David's own biography would be testimony to that. But failure to do what was right was not counted as part of a righteous life in some broader sense. Rather, failure to do what was right was confessed and forgiven in order to facilitate resuming the practice of what was right.[33]

It is this upright path through life that Psalm 23:3 imagines. I do not walk the path mapped out elsewhere (in Proverbs for example) alone. The LORD, my shepherd, leads me along it. The ambiguity of right/righteous is useful, even if it is confusing as to how to capture it in a translation. Holding on to that ambiguity requires only a certain degree of moral imagination. Eugene Peterson offers one way of imagining such a purposeful life: "You send me in the right direction" (MSG).[34] This may suggest that it is excessive literalness with respect to "paths" that actually trips up interpreters: it leaves the reader still situated with the sheep following the shepherd but offers a setting in which moral issues seem to be hidden from view. Going "in the right direction" is nicely ambiguous here and points toward the underlying idea that God leads me in the right way through life. It is not the poem's purpose to stop and ponder any particular doctrine of righteousness at this point.[35]

The final two words (*ləmaʿan šəmô*) are traditionally translated "for his name's sake," again with modern translations tending to

---

33. For an excellent discussion of "the righteous" in the Psalms, including the role of confession, the significance of imitating God in acting rightly, and how to understand the (many) occasions when the link between right living and right "result" seems absent, see Wenham, *Psalms as Torah*, 149–66.

34. Peterson puts all of vv. 2–3 into second-person "you" address, which is a shift that only comes in v. 4 in the psalm itself.

35. A thorough—but to my mind inconclusive—study is offered by Abernethy, "'Right Paths' and/or 'Paths of Righteousness'?," 299–318. He also thinks part of the stumbling block is failure to read more imaginatively than what sheep want. Abernethy's review of data from the Psalter points in multiple directions, but he favors "righteousness" as a translation.

follow the KJV. While the first word (*ləma'an*) often means "because of" or "on account of," the phrase as a whole seems to mean "to maintain reputation or character."[36] This is to take *šēm* ("name;" the suffix *-ô* tells us that it is *his* name) in the sense of "reputation"— a sense that persists in English in a phrase like "his good (or bad) name."[37] This is the nuance sought in the NJPS rendering: "as befits His name." Although the standard translation is fine in its way, Clines may be right that it could be clarified as to how this relates to what has gone before. Accordingly, he adds "all" to the beginning of the line, helpfully suggesting that it is the recital of all that we have seen so far in verses 2–3 that adds up to the reputation of YHWH my shepherd. Hence Clines's translation: "all to uphold his repute."[38] Allowing for "name" still to carry that wider sense of reputation, this invites us to translate as "all for the sake of his name"; that is, all this care and provision in verses 2–3 point to what makes YHWH my shepherd and assures me of the "not lacking" of verse 1. Another advantage of adding "all" in translation is that it rounds off this section of the poem so far and prepares us for the new thought and emphasis of verse 4.

Verse 4

> *gam kî-'ēlēk bəgê' ṣalmāwet*
> Even though I walk in the valley of shadow-death
> *lō'-'îrā' rā'*
> I will not fear evil
> *kî-'attâ 'immādî*
> For you are with me

36. BDB, 775.

37. Clines's discussion of this phrase ends helpfully, as we shall see, but he seems unduly mystified by the "lazily literal" translations of the standard English translation, suggesting—rather oddly—that it is neither good English idiom nor particularly intelligible. Clines, "Translating Psalm 23," 74.

38. Clines, "Translating Psalm 23," 80.

šibṭəkā ûmišʿantekā
Your rod and your staff
hēmmâ yənaḥămunî
They comfort me

With verse 4 we come to a slight change of focus—a new reflection. As noted above, while this could be part of the reflection on life written from the perspective of pausing in the soul-restoring pasturelands of verses 2–3, there is more a sense of moving on to consider anew threats of various sorts. It is a long verse that seems to constitute its own relatively self-contained section of the psalm, though as with all our structural observations, this should not be overpressed, since this verse fits perfectly well with the shepherd/sheep imagery preceding it and with the language of provision and comfort following it.

After noting several times that the psalm thus far has been static, we see that verse 4 begins with movement: *ʾēlēk* means "I walk." The sentence begins with *gam*, famously "yea" in the KJV, and generally a connective used to mean "also" or "moreover."[39] Here the opening phrase *gam kî*– is best understood in a concessive sense as "even if." The context of my walking, shortly to be overcome in the next part of the verse, is *bəgêʾ ṣalmāwet*.

The first word (*bəgêʾ*) is simply "valley of," with a *bə*– prefix that would typically mean "in," or as we would more naturally say of progress in such a location, "through." "Valley" (*gayʾ*) occurs only here in the Psalms, but is easy to imagine as one of the many ravine-like paths found in Israel. Elsewhere we find Isaiah's great vision of restoration announcing that every valley (*gayʾ*) will be lifted up (and every mountain and hill made low)—a vision of leveling the land to make straight and straightforward progress on the great and glorious return from exile. Short of this world-transforming vision coming to pass, valleys remain difficult obstacles, offering paths characterized more by difficulty than righteousness.

39. Thus the very three options ("also, moreover, yea") offered by BDB, 168.

It is the final word in this opening part of the verse that has attracted attention: *ṣalmāwet*. The issue raised by this Hebrew word is that it looks like a compound of two simple nouns: *ṣēl* ("shadow" or "shade") and *māwet* ("death"). It is tempting then to offer an etymological derivation of a meaning like "shadow of death," and of course this will be familiar to English readers since it is the KJV option, retained in the ESV. What is unusual is that Hebrew does not normally have compound words like this. The standard way Hebrew says "X of Y" (e.g., "the son of David") is to string the nouns together in a chain but to keep them as separate words.[40] That is precisely what is already happening in this phrase where X = "valley" and Y = *ṣalmāwet*. But is it happening inside the word *ṣalmāwet* itself? On an initial straightforward reading, probably not.[41] It seems awkward that *ṣalmāwet* is what would have been written in Psalm 23:4 had "shadow of death" been intended. This does not necessarily rule it out as a good translation, but the route to arriving at it will be a little complicated.

When I went on a walk through a long dark valley path in Israel (through the *Wadi Qelt*, east of Jerusalem and heading toward Jericho), I was part of a large group that always made two provisions for such journeys: those wanting the invigorating walk would plunge into the step-by-step adventure, while those less inclined to physical exertion would take the bus around to meet us at the other end. I hereby advertise that the discussion to come is a little like that walk, and that some may prefer to take the bus to the conclusion, rejoining us down below. I will try to keep the discussion clear in

40. Readers who know Hebrew will know that this is achieved by putting any noun preceding the last in the chain in the construct state.

41. In theory, one could at this point study whether Hebrew really does not work with composite/compound nouns. Dahood says that "composite nouns in Hebrew are more frequent than grammars allow," but his evidence is (1) that there are examples at Ras Shamra (i.e., not in the Hebrew Bible itself) and (2) that there are some comparable cases in the Psalms that he lists, but they do not really equate to being composite nouns in the way that *ṣalmāwet* would have to be. See Dahood, *Psalms 1–50*, 147. Clines thinks it "more likely" that the word is a compound, though he ends up avoiding "death" in his translation ("Translating Psalm 23," 76, 80).

English to those who do not know ancient languages. But there are some steep moments.

———————————— ⌄ ————————————

For a straightforward example of "shadow of" in a Hebrew psalm, consider Psalm 17:8, "Guard me as the apple of the eye;[42] hide me in the shadow of your wings." "Shadow of your wings" here is two words in Hebrew, showing the "X of Y" approach as one would expect: "shadow of" (ṣēl) and "wings" (kənāpeykā). That is perhaps what one would have anticipated in Psalm 23:4: ṣēl māwet ("shadow of / death"). Because it is not what we have, scholars ponder their options here.

The standard scholarly solution is to propose an alternative form of ṣalmāwet, which is "repointed" to ṣalmût. The "pointing" of a Hebrew word refers to the system of vowel "points" and other marks that are added in and around the Hebrew letters. Only the consonantal text was passed down from the authors, editors, compilers, and earliest preservers of the Hebrew text. The vowels were added by the Masoretes, a group of Jewish scribes and grammarians working many centuries later (sometime between the sixth and tenth centuries CE). This "Masoretic Text" (hence the abbreviation MT) is the basis for all modern translations of the Old Testament. Different scholars have different preferences when it comes to how often one should take a stab at changing the Masoretic vocalization in order to come up with a more comprehensible text. Fashions have changed on this. The 1966–70 three-volume Anchor Bible commentary on the Psalms operated with a particularly noteworthy deployment of such emendation, resulting in large numbers of "fresh readings" that either commended the idea or showed its limitations, depending on one's view.[43]

42. The Hebrew here nicely illustrates the "X of Y" (construct) chain by actually saying "the little one of / the daughter of / the eye," though untangling that idiom is not our concern. Several translations and commentaries adjust to "your eye" in parallel with "your wings" at the end of the verse.

43. See Dahood, *Psalms*. Dahood's specific approach has not been followed by many people at all. For an example, his translation of Ps. 16:4 (admittedly a difficult

Its particular approach to Psalm 23:4 will come up below. The consonants of *ṣalmāwet* are *ṣ–l–m–w–t*[44]—*hence the possibility of reading it as ṣalmût.*

There are then two (slightly different) options. One is to propose that *ṣalmût* means "'gloom, darkness' with *–ût* a suffix for abstract nouns."[45] At this point evidence has to be gathered from other (ancient) languages, but there is a fair bit of it. So we are left with a possible Hebrew word meaning "darkness," for which we do not have an actual straightforward Hebrew example, but nevertheless there may be reason to suppose that this is what it said.[46] It was captured by Briggs and Briggs in 1906 with the translation "a gloomy ravine," where *ṣalmût* is "gloomy."[47]

A second option sees the "death" part of this word as actually a superlative qualifier—the most/best/greatest—with the result that *ṣalmût* means "darkest." Goldingay offers examples of how that might even work in English ("dead right," or "dead tired") that successfully point in a comparable direction.[48] He then translates as "darkest canyon," which is also the line taken by the NRSV, which gives "darkest valley," and NJPS, "valley of deepest darkness." Dahood's approach follows this line even to the extent of losing a separate reference to a valley: "in the midst of total darkness."[49]

It is worth noting that the gravitational pull of the KJV's "valley of the shadow of death" in Psalm 23:4 has helped to keep the phrase in both the ESV and the NIV. But it is also worth noting that

---

verse) gives, "May their travail-pains be multiplied, prolong their lust," reading it based on Ugaritic parallels as a curse on now-forsaken Canaanite gods (xxxii, 86, 88). I can find no trace of this in post-1970 translations.

44. Beginners need to know that "w" can also be written/pronounced "v" depending on what system of pronunciation is used. In modern Israeli Hebrew it is "v," but both approaches exist in biblical studies. It can also be adjusted by vowel points to be "u" or "o," so there are often several options.

45. Muraoka, *Biblical Hebrew Reader*, 126.

46. Clines thinks this is the option gaining ground, via parallels in Akkadian, Arabic, and Ethiopic. "Translating Psalm 23," 75–76.

47. Briggs and Briggs, *Psalms*, 1:207, explained on 211–12.

48. Goldingay, *Psalms*, 1:351.

49. Dahood, *Psalms*, 1:145, see 1:147.

ṣalmāwet (or various grammatical forms of it) occurs eighteen times in the Hebrew text of the Old Testament and that very few modern translations keep the phrase "shadow of death" in the other seventeen cases. Many of them (ten) are in Job, where poetic nuance in translation is probably even more complex than the Psalms. For a simple comparison, look at Job 24:17, where the word appears twice, and the KJV's "shadow of death" has been replaced by "deep darkness" in the ESV and NRSV. Probably the other best-known verse to use *ṣalmāwet* is Isaiah 9:2: "The people who walked in darkness have seen a great light; those who lived in a land of *ṣalmāwet*—on them light has shined." Here the ESV and NRSV go for "deep darkness" and have recently been joined by the NIV after it initially retained the KJV's "shadow of death." The NJPS, meanwhile, is content with simply "darkness" in both Job and Isaiah.

So far so good. We have a reasonable case for translating Psalm 23:4 as "the valley of deep darkness," repointing the Hebrew but not changing its consonantal text. But in fact the discussion to this point has been operating within the (standard) assumption that the goal of the reading is to get back to the (supposed) Hebrew original. Thus when Briggs and Briggs in 1906 opined that the Masoretic pointing of *ṣalmāwet* was "a rabbinical conceit," they intended this as dismissive.[50] Strip it away and get at the real thing: a "gloomy ravine" no less. However, it is questionable that we can do better than a construction of meaning of one sort or another—as we saw, the suggestion that the text should be *ṣalmût* is simply a different construction—and so to recognize that a way of reading has been constructed is not in itself an argument against it. Instead it is the first step: ways of reading must be clarified accurately so that one may then go on and evaluate, rather than saying that because we have labeled the reading, we can discard it. In the case of Psalm 23:4, no option is unproblematically straightforward, and so we might pause to consider whether early constructions are in fact aids rather than obstacles that need removing to get back to an original.

---

50. Briggs and Briggs, *Psalms*, 1:211.

This recognition of the potential value of the tradition—especially the early tradition—in facilitating a reading of the text can often be passed over too quickly, since it operates in a blind spot of a certain kind of historical pursuit of original meanings. Moreover, since that historical pursuit is characteristic of the kinds of critical exegesis that predominate in commentaries on the Hebrew text, it can be a blind spot embedded deep in the approaches of many modern readers.

Goldingay locates help even in the Masoretic pointing (the MT): the word is, he says, "suggestive," and the resonance of "death" in the "MT's pointing heightens its effect."[51] The targum also makes a move to understanding "shadow of death" as the function of the Hebrew. Having already strikingly adjusted "I walk" to "I go into exile," reading the psalm—as we may recall—in terms of Israel entering the trials of exile, the targum then goes on to say *bəmêšar ṭûlā' dəmôtā'*, which can translate word for word into "in (or 'by') the plain of / the shadow of / death."[52] The Aramaic here is definite, which may be an incidental grammatical feature but allows the possibility that it is reading the Hebrew phrase as a proper name: a particular valley, which is "the Shadow of Death." This is equivocal as to whether we should see a reference to death as such, but will turn out to be helpful as we trace ongoing attempts to understand the term. In any case, the targum seems to presuppose that the Hebrew is effectively the same as *ṣēl māwet*, "shadow of / death."

Simpler and earlier, the LXX translates the phrase in question as *en mesō skias thanatou*, "in the midst of death's shadow" (NETS). "Death" here has arrived as a word in the text (*thanatos*) and—as it were—now casts its shadow over all translators to come for many centuries.

---

51. Goldingay, *Psalms*, 1:351.
52. This is not Stec's translation (*Targum of Psalms*), where he has "in the valley of the shadow of death," (61) which is also possible, and is perhaps partly to echo the English translation of the MT, which is one translation feature of his edition of the targums. It is, however, the translation offered by Edward M. Cook ("Psalms Targum"). I am grateful to David Janzen for offering helpful reflections on this targumic verse, though he is not responsible for my use of them.

Jerome's Vulgate is particularly interesting since it first offers (in the Gallican version) *in medio umbrae mortis*, "in the midst of the shadow of death," and later revises in the Hebraic version to *in valle mortis*, "in the valley of death." The first captures the LXX, and the two would easily translate to the same wording in English. Coverdale, however, puts the two together to arrive at "through the valley of the shadow of death" (dropping "in the midst of"). This is then adopted into the KJV and also the BCP and thereby dwells forevermore in the English-language consciousness.[53] Poetic rendering of *valle* as "vale" also allows for the hymnic versions, such as "death's dark vale."

In light of this early understanding that 23:4 is in fact about the overwhelming threat of death, it becomes less plausible to suggest that the interpreter's first move in the face of Hebraic ambiguity should be to reconstruct the text to remove such a reference. More likely, it seems to me, the earliest evidence (Targum, LXX, Vulgate) indicates that the Hebrew pointing is already being understood as an awkward but possible attempt to say "shadow of death," and the fact that one would have expected it to be written differently becomes therefore less significant. Interestingly, Alter pushes back against philological concerns with the Hebrew here by saying "the traditional vocalization reflects something like an orthographic pun or a folk etymology . . . , so there is justification in retaining the death component." Largely for reasons of poetic simplification, he offers "the vale of death's shadow."[54]

The simplest interpretive option is to say that the dark shadows of 23:4 include the shadow of death as the most significant example of a dark shadow, if not as a direct reference to the shadow of actual death. Is it perhaps this sense of the lurking presence of death's threat in the text that compels more interpreters to an option such as "darkest valley" (NRSV) or "deepest darkness" (NJPS) than the linguistic evidence alone really supports? Before drawing any further

53. On Coverdale being strongly influenced by Jerome, see Goins, "Jerome's Psalters," 193.

54. Alter, *Hebrew Bible*, 3:71.

conclusions, it is time to rejoin the main party who have bypassed this particular wilderness trek.

⌃

The conclusion of our examination of the various scholarly reflections upon *ṣalmāwet* is that its original meaning may be hard to pin down precisely, but the traditional understanding of the word as referring to "the shadow of death" has a long pedigree and is either a good understanding or possibly just one meaningful, specific example of what the slightly adjusted word for "(deep) darkness" (*ṣalmût*) was suggesting. I wonder again whether a certain poetic imagination can catch the resonance of the wording in ways that allow death to be part of the picture without thinking that the verse is about death in a factual or straightforward way.

In this connection it is worth pausing over Eugene Peterson's striking move here: "Even when the way goes through Death Valley . . ." (MSG). Peterson often uses a sort of personification of qualities in *The Message* translation, which brings imagery into vivid relief.[55] Here he all but relocates the reader to the Mojave Desert, although this is left as an echo in the context of a poem clearly labeled a "David Psalm" and following a shepherd. Lo and behold, though, we have come to a modern telling that calls back to the ancient targums, treating the "valley of the shadow of death" as a proper name, but here clearly one that is used with symbolic reference. Only the most flat-footed reader, who will doubtless already find the path of poetry a rather forbidding one, will be led astray by this kind of reimagining of the language.

Finally, can the shadow in question be death itself? Rather oddly, Clines denies this possibility: "I should insist that the verse does not mean 'even if I should die,' for how would the rod and staff comfort me if I were dying?"[56] The natural assumption made by

55. For good examples see Ps. 1:1 or Mic. 1:10–15 (MSG).
56. Clines, "Translating Psalm 23," 76.

Clines is that the shadow is the shadow cast by death. The shadow, in other words, is experienced by the living. This could be true even in those contexts where the psalm may be appealed to in cases of death: at a funeral, for example. The shadow cast by death at a funeral is cast over those who remain, who mourn, and who see what death has done. The psalmist, on such a view, would be more like a mourner than the deceased, in the sense that the psalmist is experiencing the threat of death in a way comparable to that of the mourner.[57]

However, having labored to reinstate "shadow of death" as the translation for verse 4a, I now also wish to reckon seriously with the presence of actual death as one potential referent of the text. The "natural assumption" noted above is in fact a modern one, that "death" is simply physical, clinical death. In his remarkable work on resurrection in Jewish Scripture, Jon Levenson shows that this is not how death was understood in ancient poetry. Death was something more like a force that cast its influence (indeed, its "shadow") even within what we would now call the land of the living.[58] Levenson argues that Israelite poetry can see a person who is gravely ill or under assault as "dead," and he contrasts two views, where (A) is our modern one, and (B) is closer to the Psalms:

(A) Life ⇨ illness ‖ death

(B) Life ‖ ⇨ illness ⇨ death

In other words, we (under model A) see the business of illness transacted on the left of the key dividing line, with death separated off to the right, whereas the Psalms (under model B) think of illness as representing the encroachment of death into the ("lived") experience

57. The use of Ps. 23 in funeral liturgy, formal and informal, will be considered in chap. 4 below.

58. New Testament readers will recognize that Paul operates with a similar conceptual map, such as in Rom. 5–6. Most good New Testament ideas were in the Old Testament first.

of the sufferer.⁵⁹ Hence it becomes easier to see what a psalmist is talking about in a poem such as Psalm 116, where verses 3–4 say, "The snares of death encompassed me. . . . Then I called on the name of the LORD: 'O LORD, I pray, save my life!'" Then verse 8 celebrates, "You have delivered my soul from death." The psalmist experiences emergence from trouble/illness as "delivery from death."

Imagine then that we were able somehow to address the ancient psalmist in his own context and ask something like, "When you were talking about going through the valley of the shadow of death, was it actual death that you were confronting?" In light of Levenson's analysis, the word "actual" would conceal a misunderstanding, since I think the psalmist would be able to say "of course" but in the process be referring to death's encroachment upon life. As we will have opportunity to consider further in chapter 4 below, the modern (and postmodern) Western world could benefit from recovering something of this ancient understanding of death.

We have dwelt at length on this opening line of the verse, so let us recap. Verse 4 opens a new section that sees the previously static psalmist ("me") consider those occasions where I am journeying into dark places. Despite all the options and possibilities for understanding how to describe those places, there is a good case for saying that they are places darkened by the shadow of death—actual death and also its implications while still alive. How am I to make progress through this life at such times? This is what the verse goes on to address.

First, "I (will) fear no evil." The NRSV and NJPS omit "will." The issues recall those with "shall" in our translations of verse 1. There we had *lō' 'eḥsār* (negating the first-person verb "to lack"), and here we have *lō'-'îrā'*, negating the first-person verb "to fear" (*yārē'*).* However, "I will" has probably persisted in English translations because it (traditionally) captured a sense of intention—not just that the future will lack fear but that I intend or desire not to fear. As with

59. Levenson, *Resurrection and the Restoration of Israel*, 38–39, diagram on 38.

verse 1, this is relevant whether thinking of "now" or the future, and one could see this either way—reading verse 4 from the perspective either of the "rest" of verses 2–3 or as a new moment. The NRSV's "I fear no evil" allows more easily for the valley-experience to be now: this is happening to me and I do not fear.[60]

What is not feared is *ra'*, "bad" or "evil." This is a common word with a wide range of uses in the Old Testament, and for our purposes may be left as vague as Psalm 23 leaves it: things that are not good. (The sense that *ra'* means "not good" may be considered by way of the tree in the garden of Eden, which is called the tree of the knowledge of "good and evil [*ra'*]" [Gen. 2:9, 17], which clearly intends to mark out two conflicting but broad labels for how things may be.) The question this might raise for today's reader is to what extent there is a moral/ethical sense of evil in this verse, which is an issue that will come into focus when we arrive at "enemies" in verse 5. It is hard to say based on the word alone, because *ra'* can be used both for moral evil and more generally for things that are not right. Thus the wickedness (*ra'*) of humankind is great in Genesis 6:5—indeed, every inclination of the thoughts of the human heart was *ra'* in the same verse. But later in Genesis the seven "thin" (or "ugly") cows that symbolized famine were also *ra'* (repeatedly in Gen. 41), but not in any particular moral sense.

Thus the traditional translation of Psalm 23:4 may have traded on differing nuances of "evil" in older times that may be seen by some as misplaced today. The well-known hymn's underdefined "yet will I fear no ill" arguably has it just right. The word is normally understood here to refer abstractly to what is "distressful" or "harmful" in not being good, rather than to people who are *ra'*.[61] Thus the NJPS translates as "harm" ("I fear no harm"), while Goldingay translates as "disaster."[62] The unavoidable difficulty is in knowing

---

60. Goldingay notes also options of whether this conditional could or could not happen, on which Hebrew grammars divide, but adds that the context ensures it is a "real conditional." *Psalms*, 1:344.

61. Muraoka, *Biblical Hebrew Reader*, 126.

62. Goldingay, *Psalms*, 1:350.

how to connote the right level of relating the *ra'* to God's world: if "evil" overmoralizes the term for today, then "disaster" might lend itself to overextracting the term from God's involvement (as in the postbiblical conception of a "natural disaster"). Given that verse 4b does not itself specify any of this—indeed, hardly anything at all other than to say that I do not fear it—there is still a good case for leaving it as "evil" on the tradition-oriented grounds that this draws least attention to the word.

On what basis can the pilgrim through Death Valley confidently claim not to fear evil? The answer is given immediately: *kî–'attâ 'immādî* ("for you are with me"). Readers may be relieved to discover that there is basically no question as to what the Hebrew means here! But if the words are straightforward (*kî* = "for," *'attâ* = the second-person singular pronoun "you," and *'immādî** = "with" and a suffix that shows that it means "with me"), then this familiar language may mask a couple of issues. First, why does the psalm switch suddenly from third person ("the LORD/he") to second person ("you")? And a more probing question: What does it mean to affirm that God is "with me"?

The switch to "you" language seems like a strong indication that verse 4 begins a new section of the psalm. But it turns out to be at best only one option to sustain this way of demarcating sections, since the "you" language drops out at the end of verse 5, which is clearly and most simply linked to verse 6, where "the LORD" reappears, albeit only in reference to "the house of the LORD." Verse 6 also suggests a good way of understanding this issue, so I defer discussion of it to that point. For now it suffices to say that the intensity of the "I-You" encounter in verse 4 reflects the consideration of the bad/evil in the shadow of death in a way not provoked by the calmer waters of verses 1–3.[63]

---

63. It is a disappointing reflection on Old Testament studies that the switch from third to second person is almost always treated, when it is treated at all, as a trigger to investigate the psalm's structure, rather than to reflect theologically on what an "I-You" mode of dialogical address might be suggesting. For one example that notes

"You are with me" is a strong and striking claim. The nature of divine presence is frequently taken for granted in adopting language such as this: God is with us, God was with me, God be with you. People use language like this without always stopping to ask what it means. In the famous case of *Immanuel*, the meaning of this name in Hebrew is straightforwardly "God with us," and when applied to Jesus via Isaiah 7:14 and Matthew 1:23, it results in the Christian claim that in the person of Jesus one has "God with us." That makes for a coherent claim about divine presence (a christological claim), regardless of how a reader of the Psalms might evaluate it. But it does not get us very far with Psalm 23:4.

This is not the place for a theoretical discussion of divine presence, even just as it relates to the Psalms, although Samuel Terrien has suggested that "the motif of Yahweh's presence seems to constitute, alone, the generative and organic power of such a theology [of the Psalms]."[64] Terrien rehearses how divine presence could be understood through "cultic presence" (e.g., the sacrifices of the priests), or reflection on the inaccessibility of God, or moments of spiritual or mystical ecstasy, among other ways.[65] There is no other psalmic statement quite comparable to 23:4 in terms of a general claim that God is "with me," although the defeat of enemies prompts psalmists to celebrate God's presence (e.g., Ps. 32:7; 41:11), and hearing God's counsel—through torah meditation perhaps—also prompts celebration of being "with you [God]," as in Psalm 73:23–24. Indeed the targum to 23:4 offers, "Your word is my help," though the conceptuality is different.[66] Forgo-

<hr>

Buber's I-Thou conceptuality but presses on to questions of structure instead, see Marlowe, "David's I-Thou Discourse," 105–15. By contrast, Wiseman's "Thou with Me," 280–93, is a Buber-free zone. I have not been able to discover Buber directly addressing Ps. 23.

64. Terrien, *Psalms*, 46. Terrien is alert to the difficulties of pulling the 150 disparate psalms into a single statement of straightforward theological assertion. See his wide-ranging discussion of "Theology of the Psalms," 44–62. A key work on the area in general is his *Elusive Presence*.

65. Terrien, *Psalms*, 46–48.

66. In Stec's version, "your Memra is my support." On the Targumic use of "Memra" (word), see Stec's introduction: "*Memra* is used almost exclusively where

ing further analysis of what we mean by the language of "God with me," I note only that Psalm 23:4 is as underdefined with regard to this as it was a line earlier with regard to *ra'* ("evil"). If there is any specific sense in which God is "with me" in this verse, it is to be deduced from what follows. But I suspect that there is little such specificity. God is with me. This is fortification against trouble in the valley ahead. Perhaps the assurance comes from the celebration of divine provision rehearsed in verses 1–3. Perhaps it comes from the conviction that a shepherd does not lead me into the valley without accompanying me. Most straightforwardly, and above all, it is a reflection that the LORD who is my shepherd is my reason for confidence in the face of whatever *ra'* may befall me.

The shepherd imagery makes its last high-profile appearance in the psalm in the next phrase, *šibṭəkā ûmišʿantekā*, "your rod and your staff." The –*kā* endings denote the second-person masculine singular pronoun "your," which follows on from the switch to "you" language noted above. With the *û–* prefix meaning "and," this phrase means "your *šēbeṭ* and your *mišʿenet*," which would be straightforward if we knew what these two terms meant. Despite various attempts to distinguish between them, the safest thing to say here is that these are two stick-like implements such as a shepherd might have. The word for the first (the "rod," *šēbeṭ*) is a relatively frequent word, and I cannot resist citing a standard dictionary entry that picks its slightly bemused way through the data, noting among other things that it is evidently a common article for smiting and for beating, serves as an (inferior) weapon, and is used for shepherding sheep.[67] It seems, in effect, to be the tool of choice with which a shepherd can variously point, "encourage," and otherwise direct the sheep,[68] as well

---

God and humans relate to one another, as a device for keeping a proper distance between them" (12).

67. BDB, 986–87. The terms noted are mixed in verbatim amidst various data.

68. Though Muraoka says that the rod as weapon would not be directed at the sheep, which I imagine might be more a statement of principled intent than of fact for any given shepherd. *Biblical Hebrew Reader*, 126.

as attack protruding obstacles, and indeed be at hand as an inferior weapon—although Bailey urges more emphatically that the rod "is the shepherd's primary offensive weapon for protecting the flock from enemies, be they wild animals or human thieves."[69]

The second term (*miš'enet*) is much rarer (only occurring eleven times in the Old Testament) and seems to mean just "staff." On Bailey's account, the staff is a symbol of care for the sheep rather than a weapon against threats.[70] Even insofar as some want to say that a staff is a symbol of authority, it seems to me a stretch to say that this is necessarily royal imagery or that we have here a royal psalm on the basis of the connotation of an authority figure. It is sometimes noted that the "rod" [*šēbet*] is also used in royal contexts, such as Psalm 2:9, where a rod of iron will be used to break the nations, and it is true that ancient cultures could naturally have seen a crook as a royal symbol. But as argued in the discussion of shepherding imagery in general in chapter 2, the issue is only partly about potential ancient resonances, and more significantly it is about what the text of Psalm 23 goes on to make of the language. Not even the standard linking of this text with (King) David really connects the psalm with kingship, since his shepherding days are at best only loosely associated with his reign in Scripture in general.[71] Authority in the face of enemies (about to be referenced)? Yes. But royal authority? One would not think so unless already determined to find it.[72] To conclude our discussion of the rod and the staff, one might summarize the difference between the terms

---

69. Bailey, *Good Shepherd*, 50. The caveats of chap. 2 on discussions of shepherding are less relevant here in a discussion precisely of the nature of a shepherd's implements.

70. Bailey, *Good Shepherd*, 52–53.

71. The final three verses (vv. 70–72) of the lengthy historical recital of Ps. 78 are the nearest link but draw that link in terms of David's work in sheepfolds and with nursing ewes (NRSV). They feel a long way conceptually from the valley of the shadow of death.

72. So Craigie, *Psalms 1–50*, 204. Commentaries that emphasize the royal and kingly dimensions of the psalm include Mays, *Psalms*, 117, and Eaton, *Psalms*, 124, though not on this particular verse, but the theme is deeply rooted in much of Eaton's work on the Psalms.

here as that between the directive guidance available through the rod and the focus of the staff as the shepherd's symbol of authority and presence. The reason behind the mention of the two items is revealed in the next phrase.

First, the rod and the staff are emphasized as "they," *hēmmâ*. The poet would not have needed to say this, as is clear also in English, since "your rod and staff comfort me" makes perfectly good sense, although one must allow for poetic rhythm as a simple possibility for "recapping." In any case, introducing "they" provides a retrospective emphasis on the fact that the two items were just deemed worthy of naming as subjects prior to being attached to a verb. Secondly, the verb that closes the verse (*yənaḥămunî*) explains what the rod and the staff do. As we have seen throughout, the verb incorporates several elements: it is "imperfect" (incomplete, ongoing; the *yə–* prefix); it includes "me" as its object (the *–nî* ending); and the verb itself is *niḥam*,* "to comfort" (famously used in a double imperative "comfort, comfort my people" in Isa. 40:1). For an analogous example of the emphasis on personal "comforting," consider Ruth 2:13, where Ruth says to Boaz, "May I continue to find favor in your sight, my lord, for you have comforted me [*niḥamtānî*]." Boaz provides practical care for the newly arrived Ruth, allowing her to glean in the fields, protecting her from unwanted attention, and ensuring that water is available as she needs it (Ruth 2:8–9). Reading on in the book of Ruth, it becomes clear—if it was not already—that this practical provision flows out of his developing love for her. As with Ruth, so with the psalmist in the valley, at stake is the presence of heart-lifting and life-affirming comfort. That comfort will be practical in terms of what the rod and the staff achieve and symbolize, and it also reflects the love that Yhwh/my shepherd (the "you" of the verse) has for me.

I may be in the presence of death, but I am comforted. God is with me. One might suggest that the rod and the staff are the visible symbols of God's invisible presence, in turn suggestive of the shepherd in the valley as the visible symbol of God's presence. Evil, undefined and out of focus as it is to this point, need not be feared. The thankfulness easily discerned in verses 2–3 by quiet waters and good care now carries over into darker times. Death and its shadows do not take it away. Retrospectively, we also see now how the "lacking nothing" of verse 1 begins to be nuanced: I have what I need for facing the troubles that will inevitably come, as surely as verse 3 runs straight on to verse 4.

Verse 5

> *taʿărōk ləpānay šulḥān*
> You set before me a table
>
> *neged ṣōrərāy*
> In front of my enemies
>
> *diššantā baššemen rōʾšî*
> You anoint with oil my head
>
> *kōsî rəwāyâ*
> My cup overflows.

The "you" of verse 4, who was obviously the shepherd, is now often understood as becoming the "you" who is a host: it is a common observation of commentaries that the shepherd imagery of verses 1–4 here gives way to host imagery as we move toward a meal. In one sense, of course, there is truth in this. Thus far we have rested, been restored, and have walked in the company of the shepherd, and now a "table" is set, suggesting that we take time from our journeying to eat. Yet the idea that this is a major contrast seems misplaced. The table suggests a meal, but not necessarily a dining room. Most likely, in the loosely structured psalm as we have it, this image is another way station on the journey that we have been undertaking since the beginning, without at any point overemphasizing the journey or any particular sense of progress.[73] A particular reason for saying this will become apparent in a moment.

73. Cf. Craigie, *Psalms 1–50*, 207: "Although the shepherd imagery no longer dominates in the last two verses, it is still present in the transition."

The verse begins with *taʿărōk*, a second-person verb from *ʿārak*, "to arrange/set in order." Muraoka suggests that the word is often used when several things need to be set in a certain way.[74] This might suggest the traditional sense of "prepare" here, as in getting various aspects (of a meal) ready; although, more likely the particular sense of "prepare" comes from what follows. The NJPS's "spread" perhaps captures this notion of preparation of several things. The "setting" is done *ləpānay*, a standard Hebrew idiom meaning "before" (as in "in front of") with a suffix *−ay*, indicating that it is before "me." What "you" set in order before "me" in this instance is a *šulḥān*, "table."

The table in question could be any table, but the word is interesting, though arguably not as interesting as Rolf Jacobson's tour de force suggests when he writes, "The basic interpretive challenge is to discern what type of banquet table the poem imagines," before going on to rehearse tables of hospitality, thanksgiving, and ritual response to salvation, among others.[75] The word *šulḥān* can refer to a table in a broad number of contexts; for instance, it is used in the books of Kings to refer to the table at which King Solomon and his guests eat (1 Kings 2:7; 4:27; 10:5), a small table in a private room (2 Kings 4:10), and also the golden "table" for the bread of the presence in the temple (1 Kings 7:48).[76] It is also used many times for the table in the tent of meeting in the tabernacle (Exod. 25; 37; 40), where we read in particular, "You shall bring in the table [*šulḥān*] and arrange [*ʿārak*] its setting [*ʿērek*]" (40:4), using the same verb as in Psalm 23. One can see therefore why interpreters might see more than just a dinner setting here in Psalm 23:5, discerning perhaps some priestly or even temple echoes in the language. However, as with the question of royal imagery considered above and as argued in chapter 2, I suspect one mainly finds such echoes largely when eager to look for them.

74. Muraoka, *Biblical Hebrew Reader*, 127.
75. NICOT, *Psalms*, 244. Not all of the cases Jacobson considers include a word for "table," though that would not in itself rule out interpretive relevance.
76. A comparable range of uses could be seen elsewhere, but I am interested in the mixture of dining table, sacred table, and personal table that this usage evinces.

Among the many interpretive options put forward here is Terrien's thought-provoking point, which seems to me to make the best sense. While there are indeed Canaanite parallels for *šulḥān* that equally well mean "table" from long before the psalm would have been written, "it is forgotten that . . . its Arabic equivalent, even in modern times, continues to mean, not a piece of wooden furniture, but an animal skin or a woven rug thrown on the ground to keep food away from sand."[77] Although this specific nuance has not often been noted, it fits best in this context: someone ("you," whether the shepherd or not) pulls out a cloth and places it on the ground in order to set out the constituents of the meal implied here.[78] It is in this broader context that we arrive at the now-standard and (once more) KJV-influenced English translation: "You prepare a table before me." The table-as-(picnic?)-cloth leaves the image more straightforwardly embedded in the context that we have had in view thus far. Wooden (or other) dining furniture is not in view. Sustenance is the issue.

The next phrase, *neged ṣōrərāy*, is somewhat unexpected and worth careful consideration. The first word, *neged*, means "in front of." It has more of a simple locational sense than the verse's earlier *ləpānay*, "before (me)," which connotes something that is in front of me because it is for me, in some sense. But something can be "in front of" (*neged*) someone because that is simply a way of describing where the thing is. In this case, it is the table (*šulḥān*) that is both before me and also in front of the *ṣōrəray*. Is there possibly a confrontational aspect to this location (which is about to be described as "before my enemies")? This seems to be one aspect of the NJPS translation: "You spread a table for me in full view of my enemies." While "in

77. Terrien, *Psalms*, 241. In a footnote, Terrien adds, "The use of this Arabic cognate was heard by the author while a guest of Bedouin in (then) Transjordia (1934)," (*Psalms*, 241n3). A rare earlier suggestion along these lines is Briggs and Briggs, *Psalms*, 1:212, "mat or piece of leather spread on ground"—incorporated into BDB, 1020, presumably by the same Charles Briggs who coauthored the commentary.

78. Terrien, *Psalms*, 241, almost seems to suggest that there is no meal: the "setting in order" he imagines consists of "arranging" a meadow for the flock to rest safely by removing thorns, scorpions, and other "enemies."

full view" could be just a location, it seems to play up the relation of the setting to the enemies, which I will in due course suggest is not quite the right emphasis, for various reasons.

The word *ṣōrəray** is the participle of the verb *ṣārar*, which means "to be hostile" in a range of senses.[79] The participial form ("being hostile") can thus be used as a noun ("the one being hostile") as is standard in Hebrew, and from this comes the sense of the word as a noun meaning "enemy" or "foe," or "enemies" in this case, as the word is plural. The particular form of the word incorporates a suffix that indicates that these enemies are "mine." A good translation is therefore "my enemies," as any reader familiar with the psalm will have anticipated.

This should rightly raise a question: Who are my enemies, and what are they doing here in the psalm at this point? I will take these two questions in order, beginning with a brief rehearsal of the long-pondered question about the identity of one's "enemies" in the Psalms.[80]

The first thing to say, sufficiently simple that it is all too easy to pass over, is that the Psalms in general do not define "enemies." Apart from the recognition that the conceptual map of the world is divided into the righteous and the wicked—from Psalm 1's two ways to live at the very outset, and consistently all through the collection—there is not much that can be said by way of specific identification. Scholars labored from Gunkel onward to find points of historical identification, but in truth these are almost impossible to find in the text.[81] Our best option is to list the kinds of categories of enemies that could conceivably have been in view. To do this requires attention to the

79. BDB offers, "to bind, to tie up, to be restricted" (864).
80. The data on "antagonists" in the Psalms is helpfully set out by Croft, *Identity of the Individual*, 20–48, though he does not discuss Ps. 23 in his review.
81. A useful review of mainstream twentieth-century discussions is Hobbs and Jackson, "Enemy in the Psalms," 22–29. They support to some extent the view (much critiqued subsequently) of Birkeland, *Evildoers in the Book of Psalms*, that the evildoers are "gentiles" or "foreigners." I have not independently consulted Birkeland's book.

vocabulary used and plausible reconstruction of what sorts of threats life would have held. Thus a standard account would be that of Kraus in his *Theology of the Psalms*; his chapter on "The Enemy Powers" distinguishes national threats from individual enemies and in the latter category looks at vocabulary for enemy, foe (his translation of the term in 23:5), evildoer, wicked, pursuer, and so forth, including metaphorical language that describes them as (or like) armies, hunters, or wild beasts.[82] Too clear a separation of individual and national categories for enemies may be the result of overzealous (form-critical) classification by the scholars involved. Hence some want to include the alien and the aggressor as other key categories.[83] As David Firth has noted, grand schemes of classification do not convince, and one has to take each psalm and its specific references to enemies case by case in order to see what is being attributed to them.[84]

Of course, with regard to Psalm 23:5, this leaves us back where we started, not knowing the identity of the "enemies" in question.[85] In this the reference is not alone, as we saw with the discussion in chapter 2 of the general significance of the absence of background historical information for the psalm's ongoing applicability and relevance. But on this issue, it is important that we accord the right weight to the psalm's mention of (undefined) enemies, because grasping what the psalm assumes here is key for letting its own claims come across clearly.

This brings us to our second question: What are the enemies doing here in the psalm at this point? They seem to appear out of nowhere. Verse 4 spoke in passing of evil, which the psalmist did not fear, and of death and its shadows as the present example of evil that was

82. Kraus, *Theology of the Psalms*, 129–34. For comparable categories in symbolic and iconographic terms, see Keel, *Symbolism of the Biblical World*, 78–100.

83. Hobbs and Jackson, "Enemy in the Psalms," 24–25.

84. See the brief review of the limitations of the question in Firth, *Surrendering Retribution in the Psalms*, 9–10.

85. Insofar as commentaries consider this issue, they generally agree that they are left undefined or are literal (but still undefined) enemies. So, e.g., Craigie, *Psalms 1–50*, 208, and Goldingay, *Psalms*, 1:352, respectively.

being encountered. Nothing in verses 1–3 anticipates this turn, and nothing in verse 4 specifically prepares the reader for this mention of enemies, unless one simply equates them with—or focuses them somehow on—death. But the assumption must be that the average reader/hearer of the psalm is not to be overly surprised at this point, since they will share the view that enemies are indeed at hand. The moment of the turn to enemies may include an element of unexpectedness, but that enemies come into view is not surprising.

These observations prepare us to answer what seems to be the obvious question raised here, although since few commentaries address it, I might hesitate before saying it is as obvious as it seems to me. It concerns the oddity of this scenario on too serene an accounting of verses 1–4 (the valley of the shadow of death notwithstanding). If one overemphasizes the peacefulness of the picture so far, then one is left asking, Why would the shepherd, the LORD ("you"), prepare a table in such a location—before my enemies? A moment of reconsideration seems required here. The gracious provision that has characterized the psalm throughout, on good days and on bad, suddenly arrives at the preparation of a meal in the presence of enemies. Why would it do that? Why would God do that? Surely the answer lies in the assumption that there is no other option. There are always enemies, and while one need not (and does not) talk about them all the time, it can always be appropriate to remember that enemies are everywhere. In one sense this point would hold even if we do take the enemies as fundamentally exemplified by death. One need not talk about death all the time, but it could always be appropriate to remember that death is potentially at hand. And thus in a certain sense God's preparing a meal in the presence of the threat of death is because the threat is ever present. I am inclined to think that reading the enemies as "death" is more specific than it needs to be, but the reading still makes sense.

We move to the second half of the verse, which I take to continue the scene as we are sitting and eating in the company of the shepherd. First we hear that "you" anoint my head with oil. Then there

is a comment about a cup, which (once again) is left adjacent to its
surrounding text without any explicit link, so we are invited to draw
the link ourselves.

"You anoint" is *diššantā*.* This is not the standard word for
"anoint" and actually occurs rather rarely in this form. The word
has a sense of "being or growing fat," although here it is in a causative
form—that is, to "cause to become fat" (or "fatten"). But even in
this relatively unusual form it is hard to find other instances where
"anoint" would work as a translation. The nearest may be Proverbs
15:30, "The light of the eyes rejoices the heart, and good news *re-
freshes* the body."[86] But even this is a little way from "anointing,"
and the first thing to say here is that this is not in any technical or
cultic sense an "anointing," such as is found frequently through the
Old Testament when a priest or a king is anointed in a specific ritual.
Rather "its associations are sensual rather than sacramental."[87] This
is anointing in the lower-key social sense of welcoming a dry and
dusty guest to the table, and it symbolizes hospitality above all.[88]

There are two reasons why "anoint" persists as a translation. One
is that this is what the LXX says: straightforwardly "you anointed
[*lipainō*] my head with oil" (NETS).[89] This is still not the standard,
more formal word for "anoint" (which is *chriō*, from which comes
the English use of "chrism" for liturgical uses of anointing). It is used
in Psalm 141:5 (LXX Ps. 140:5) where it is followed by the NRSV,
though most translations there try to work with the Hebrew, which
does not say "anoint."

Secondly, whatever the verb means, it is done with oil on the head:
baššemen rō'šî is simply "with oil" (adding a *ba*– prefix, "in/with/

86. Note the wonderful KJV rendering of this: "A good report maketh the bones
fat," intriguingly echoed by NJPS: "Good news puts fat on the bones."
87. Alter, *Hebrew Bible*, 3:71.
88. Bailey, *Good Shepherd*, 58, citing Luke 7:36–50 as a relevant example (see
especially 7:46).
89. The Vulgate, however, has *impinguasti*, from *impinguo*, more normally "to
fatten" or "to fill" (a usage that persists in Italian, where again it is not the normal
word for religious anointing [*ungere*]).

by," to a common word for oil, *šemen*) and "my head" (the word for head, *rō'š*, with an *–î* suffix meaning "my"). So clearly translators are left with an inviting solution here: an act of some kind of "fattening"—perhaps a generous pouring—that is performed with oil on the head, and which in the LXX is understood, nontechnically, as "anointing." The simple solution is to translate as "anoint." Only Eugene Peterson resists the standard wording, using instead "You revive my drooping head" (MSG), an interesting option that combines the sense of "refreshing" that we noted above with an understanding that the "oil" is primarily symbolic of being cared for.

A similar openness attends the question of whether the verse goes on to talk about a literal cup and its filling or its symbolic resonance as an image of generous provision. Of course it makes sense to suppose that a meal would include a cup, but the language that follows is hardly matter of fact. The "cup" (*kôs*), which belongs to "me" (the *–î* suffix), is most naturally the kind of cup used in contexts where wine is drunk, such as in Genesis 40, where it is used five times as the word for the cup of Pharaoh in the cupbearer's dream.[90] Even when the word is used in darker, more metaphorical contexts, such as the "cup of his wrath" (e.g., Isa. 51:17), the cup in question is still such a cup. NJPS suggests that the issue is not the cup but the drink it holds: "My drink is abundant." The word that characterizes the cup in Psalm 23:5 is *rəwāyâ*, a cup of "saturation"—the word, at least in its slightly more common verb form, seems to connote a fullness of satisfaction, or "intoxication," as Terrien suggests.[91] Although commentators like to point out that "overflows" is not quite what the word means, it is the standard contemporary rendering of the KJV's "runneth over."

90. It is not the only word for "cup"—e.g., the cup hidden in Benjamin's sack in Gen. 44 is a different word—but in general, a cup seems to have been mentioned only in contexts where a noteworthy drinking utensil is imagined. The targum to Ps. 23:5 uses a Greek loan word from *chalix*, from which comes the English "chalice." Stec, *Targum of Psalms*, 61n8.
91. Terrien, *Psalms*, 241.

The LXX actually adjusts the sense to something more like "your cup intoxicates me like the best,"[92] rendered in NETS as "your cup was supremely intoxicating." Jerome follows this at first, though later drops "like the best" to stay closer to the Hebrew and says, "Your cup inebriates me." In each case, these versions refocus the sense of overflowing fullness from the cup to the psalmist.[93] Although that is not the same as the Hebrew, it captures something of the wider-ranging symbolic sense of what is happening in verse 5 than a more literal focus on a full/overflowing cup might. The Greek and Latin also adjust the reference to whose cup it is, as eagle-eyed readers may have spotted above: it is no longer "my cup" that is a source of joy, but "your cup." In context, this must refer to the cup of the host/shepherd/LORD; God's cup overwhelms me with life. Briggs and Briggs observe, with customary scholarly tight lip, "The Fathers generally find here a mystic reference to the cup of the Eucharist."[94] Well indeed, an overflowing cup that brings joy at a feast in the presence of my enemies sounds eucharistic, and it would not be the only occasion when a theological conclusion is drawn from the LXX that is not quite so obvious from the Hebrew. Rather intriguingly, the two recent commentaries I have consulted that attempt to read the Psalms "in Christ" both fail to note this help from the LXX and labor at trying to draw the link from the Hebrew alone.[95]

All in all it would be a pity to imagine this moment in the psalm as introducing any kind of formal (religious) action, as if the meal has been set and the weary traveler, on the point of enjoying life-giving

92. The best wine, perhaps? What has happened here is that the "goodness" of v. 6 has been transposed into the end of v. 5 and made to serve a different purpose. In LXX v. 6 it is only mercy that follows me, not goodness and mercy.

93. And thus Goldingay, persuaded by this, translates, "My cup amply satisfies." *Psalms*, 1:345.

94. Briggs and Briggs, *Psalms*, 1:210.

95. In one case Kriegshauser, *Praying the Psalms in Christ*, bases his whole project on the MT and reads Ps. 23 christologically but without reference to the Eucharist; odder is Reardon, *Christ in the Psalms*, whose Orthodox reading is specifically based on the LXX, but who reverts here to saying "my cup brims over" in connection with the Eucharist (44).

sustenance, has to pause and go through a liturgical act. More help-fully, it seems to me, this description of "anointing/fattening" and "satisfaction" can be seen as parallel and poetic descriptions of the life-giving sustenance itself. Is it the provision of the meal (and drink) itself that—in Peterson's phrase—revives my drooping head (MSG)? One need not say that there is a parallelism here that makes the two things identical (i.e., the meal and the generous provision of oil and cup), but at least one could imagine that in this sitting down to receive from the generous host, the meal and the general sense of refresh-ment are all inseparable parts of one experience. I propose a small step toward binding together these three acts in the verse (the setting of the table, the "anointing," and the intoxication) by translating the last two of them as participles ("pouring" and "overflowing"), pointing to the possibility that they are what happens in and through the meal at the table. Thus: "You set before me . . . / pouring oil . . . / my cup overflowing."

In a study of the imagery that crowds in as the psalm draws to a close, Sylva notes that there is a sustained note of celebration and joy in this verse, not least in the bringing together of oil with the "cup" that follows, which he takes to point in the direction of wine. Whatever the details (since Ps. 23 does not quite mention wine), it seems plausible to say that this meal in the wilderness, surrounded by enemies, is a moment of joy.[96] God does not just ensure the sur-vival of the enemy-beset traveler, but brings "intoxicating," joyful celebration too. I might have suggested "blessing" as a way of trying to capture this multisensory idea of being refreshed, except that that, too, conjures up images of a formal or liturgical act.[97]

In short, and contra all the various historical reconstructions that see verse 5 as referring (semi-)technically to priestly or temple prac-tice, I suggest that this is no new setting or formal echo of a separate

---

96. Sylva, "Changing of Images in Ps 23.5, 6," 111–16.
97. Peterson manages to get around this problem by putting the word at the end of the verse with "my cup brims with blessing" (MSG), which is the nontechnical sense of blessing I want to suggest.

act from the providing of a meal (and cup). Rather, more simply, we have stopped to eat, drink, and be refreshed at a makeshift way station (a "table") in the wilderness. This is joyful language that celebrates divine provision in the presence of enemies. It is almost, indeed, a more sense-oriented recapitulation of the "restoring of my soul/life" from verse 3. Confronting the shadows of death and enemies of various sorts, I can still lack nothing, as my shepherd/ LORD provides overwhelmingly for me; and more than lacking nothing, my body/mind/spirit (my *nepeš*) is strengthened and refortified for whatever comes next.

▓ Verse 6

> *'ak ṭōb wāḥesed yirdəpûnî*
> Surely goodness and mercy will pursue me
>
> *kol-yəmê ḥayāy*
> All the days of my life
>
> *wəšabtî bəbêt-yhwh*
> And I will return to/dwell in (?) the house of YHWH
>
> *lə'ōrek yāmîm*
> For length of days.

The final verse of the psalm draws together a responsive reflection to the generous provision so far. We will need to discuss the implications of the psalmist imagining themselves "in the house of YHWH" when we come to this phrase below, but as the verse begins, I think it makes sense to imagine that this is the restored and re-energized wayfarer of verse 5 giving thankful praise to the God who has nurtured them thus far. In that sense, we are still in the presence of enemies, still out in the fields or the shadows of the valley that were in view earlier, still indeed in the same imaginative scenario that began back in verse 1 and has persisted throughout.

The verse begins with a short connective word that is traditionally translated "surely" (*'ak*) here and elsewhere.[98] Clines makes an interesting point that the goodness and mercy that are about to be mentioned have the appearance of coming rather suddenly from nowhere, as abstractions in a text of (what he strangely labels as) "concrete particulars."[99] He suggests that one should understand goodness and mercy as in a certain sense reprising all that has been spoken of so far. He therefore inserts a connecting "such" at the beginning, while deferring "surely" to later in the line: "Such goodness and constancy shall surely be my companions" (anticipating a couple of other points to be discussed below). I wonder if he overplays the switch from particular to abstract, since, as we have seen, there is scope for reading details as symbolic of wider understanding in what has gone before—but the point is a good one. In my view there is a hint of gathering up the earlier lines of the poem in "surely," in any case.

The pair of words that together comprise the opening subject of the sentence are *ṭōb* and *ḥesed* (the *wā*– prefix is the "and"), arguably two of the most well-known Hebrew nouns. We start with their traditional sense of "goodness" and "mercy" and offer some nuances, especially in the latter case.

With *ṭōb*, the key nuance to add to "goodness" is a certain aesthetic sense. Things that are *ṭōb* are "pleasant, agreeable, good."[100] The range of "good" in English is probably comparable (a good friend; a good pizza; a good day out; a good sports performance)—the word doubtless has ethical connotations but serves many other purposes too. The switch in translation to an abstract noun, "goodness," is trickier, since in English this tends to be more ethical: a person possesses goodness but a pizza does not, really; and the aesthetic sense has more or less disappeared. Peterson responds to these issues by translating as "your beauty" (MSG), which picks up strongly on the

98. NICOT, *Psalms*, offers "indeed" (240). NJPS has "only." Oddly, Coverdale in the BCP gives "but."

99. Clines, "Translating Psalm 23," 80.

100. BDB, 373.

aesthetic point but introduces a "your" that might give pause for thought. Surely(!) the goodness and mercy of which verse 6 speaks are indeed YHWH's, but the text does not actually say it.

The second term, *ḥesed*, is more elusive. This is a notoriously difficult word to render into English, and attempts have included "love" (NIV; which is not wrong, except that "love" is a more emotionally oriented word in modern English), "steadfast love" (NJPS; and it is also the usual translation of *ḥesed* in the ESV and NRSV, though not in fact here, where they both say "mercy" under the influence of the KJV), "covenant love," "loyalty," and—more traditionally—"mercy."[101] So awkward is the task of translating the term, in fact, that the joint authors of the NICOT Psalms commentary give it up as a bad job: "One peculiarity of this commentary is that we have opted not to translate the Hebrew term *ḥesed*, but simply to transliterate *ḥesed* and treat it as a loanword from Hebrew to English—similar to 'shalom.' . . . The *relational nature of the term* cannot be overemphasized. It describes the duties, benefits, and commitments that one party bears to another party as a result of the relationship between them."[102] Readers of this fine commentary are required effectively to learn the Hebrew term and to do so by seeing how it is used, which is often, given that according to the NICOT commentators, 130 of its 255 OT occurrences are in the Psalter. It is one of the qualities of God in which God is said to be "abounding" in the famous verse in Exodus 34:6: "The LORD, the LORD, a God merciful and gracious, slow to anger, and abounding in *ḥesed* and faithfulness." It is, perhaps, "love-with-covenantal-commitment," but that is not going to work as a translation, obviously.

For "goodness and mercy," then, think "good-with-a-sense-of-the-beautiful and love-with-a-sense-of-covenant-commitment." These

---

101. The Hebrew term has regularly been the subject of entire monographs. A readable orientation to such studies is Sakenfeld, *Faithfulness in Action*, who suggests that "loyalty" is the least worst option.

102. NICOT, *Psalms*, 7–8. Different conventions lead to *chesed* or *ḥesed* as equally justifiable transliterations. The word begins with a "ch" sound such as one finds in Bach, or a Scottish loch.

are God's good and generous blessings for a world in the shadow of death and for pilgrims in the presence of enemies. When they are used together, which is not very common, the effect is of a very strong statement of God's provision. Indeed, this is the only place in the Old Testament where the two terms are put together as the joint subject of a sentence.[103]

The verb that is attributed to them is the one word in the whole psalm that in my opinion has been persistently poorly translated in English. The word in question is *yirdəpûnî*,* which has an ongoing (imperfect) sense (marked by its *yi–* prefix) and a suffix (*–nî*) that means it is applied in turn to me, and it is in the third-person plural (the *û*; i.e., it has goodness and mercy as its subject). At the heart of it is the verb *rādap*, which typically means "to pursue." It tends to mean "pursue" in a somewhat negative sense, but it all depends on who is doing the pursuing and why. For example, when Joshua and his men attack the people of Ai in Joshua 8, various forms of the word are used five times (vv. 16 [twice], 17, 20, 24) as pursuit leads on to killing. That is entirely negative. But in this, as in so much else, context is king. It can just mean "go after" (as when Gehazi goes running after Naaman to catch up with him to talk in 2 Kings 5:21), and in some cases it is entirely positive, as in Psalm 34:14, "Depart from evil, and do good; seek peace, and pursue [*rādpēhû*] it."[104]

The conclusion should be clear. Goodness and mercy (*ṭōb* and *ḥesed*) will not just "follow" me, but they will "pursue" me. It is almost

---

103. The words occur together in a range of ways, such as when God's *ḥesed* is described by the adjectival use of *ṭōb* (Ps. 69:16, for example). In Mic. 6:8 one of the things that is good (*ṭōb*) is to love *ḥesed* (mercy, kindness . . .). It is simplest to say that there is no comparable use of "*ṭōb* and *ḥesed*," and Briggs and Briggs, *Psalms*, 1:212 describe the phrase as a "*hapax legomenon*," i.e., only used once. Two potential cases of their conjunction (though dependent on textual emendation, and lacking a connective *w–*) are discussed in Barré, "Formulaic Pair," 100–105, discussing Pss. 69:16 and 109:21.

104. All this rather mitigates against Clines's suggestion that "'pursue' would be unintelligible here." "Translating Psalm 23," 80. Oddly, Muraoka, *Biblical Hebrew Reader*, 126, says—correctly—that the "verb often means 'to hunt down, chase with a hostile, malicious intent,'" but without assisting the reader to see the importance of the context.

as if the verse attributes both agency and initiative to these divine characteristics here, whereas "follow" might suggest a sort of tagging along with me. Instead, (God's) goodness and mercy are dogged and determined in their pursuit. If this sounds odd, I suspect it is simply a matter of the persistence of the traditional translation, which I have often wanted to defend or rehabilitate in some way. But here, for reasons that we will explore more in later chapters, I think there is real merit in sticking with the clear meaning of "pursue." The LXX leans this way already (using *katadiōkō*, "to search for diligently," translated by NETS as "pursue" no less).[105] The God who has been faithful thus far in the psalm will surely continue to provide for me, in the form of his *ṭōb* and *ḥesed* following in close pursuit wherever I may yet go.

The duration of this provision is simply stated: "all the days of my life" (*kol–yəmê ḥayāy*). There is little confusion over the meaning of the Hebrew here: it is a chain of words linked together in typical Hebraic fashion. Thus *kol–* means "all of," *yəmê* is a plural meaning "days of," and *ḥayāy** is "my life." It may be that uncertainty over how to translate the imminent phrase (as traditionally in the hymn versions) "forever"/"forevermore" makes translators cautious here. Most translations stick with the slightly awkward English "all the days of my life," rendered more normal by Eugene Peterson as "every day of my life" (MSG). In any case, the goodness and mercy have ahead of them a lifelong project of staying close to me—which is good news for the psalmist (and bad news, one supposes, for the enemies).

Two questions loom large as we come to the end of the psalm and read its closing lines. First, what is the nature and significance of the reference to the house of Yʜᴡʜ? And secondly, what does the final two-word phrase mean? Both raise questions of understanding, or perhaps of reference. Before we arrive at these issues, however, the verb (traditionally "I shall dwell") is slightly complicated. Here, as with the discussion of the "shadow of death" in verse 4 above, I have chosen to offer a bypass for the bus tour and to conduct what

---

105. Jerome stuck with "follow" (*subsequitur*).

turns out to be a somewhat thorny discussion about the verb in an excursus below. In my opinion, this is a matter where the average reader can safely skip ahead to the conclusions. But for those who like to know how everything is done, the joys of a different proposed reading once again await.

The oddity before us in verse 6 concerns the verb *wəšabtî,** which is indeed an unexpected form. As vocalized, the verb is *šūb*, "to return." It is in a form that makes it function like an imperfect (ongoing) verb and is in the first person; hence it would most naturally mean "and I will return." Or in such a context perhaps the *wə–* prefix that is often "and" might just as well mean "then": "then I will return." (On the issues of present or future nuance with "will"/"shall" in the first person, see the discussion of v. 1 above.)

Defenders of this reading offer a range of ways of understanding it, including making the perfectly fair point that this is what the Hebrew text says. A thoughtful study of hospitality and its practices by Arterbury and Bellinger suggests that "returning" fits the context of a guest at a table very well, since "guests return to their host's house whenever they are in the region again."[106] This is perhaps the strongest defense of the reading, although it seems to rely in turn on seeing the "house" of Yhwh that is about to be mentioned as any place of hospitality, which is an aspect of the reading they do not fully explore. They also note Broyles's reading of the word as "return" in his commentary, which relates the returning to the annual pilgrimages to Jerusalem. This does see the "house" as the temple—on which see below—although of course the pilgrimages have to be supplied as a potential context.[107] There are thus two rather contrasting approaches

106. Arterbury and Bellinger, "'Returning to the Hospitality of the Lord,'" 387–95, here 394.
107. Broyles, *Psalms*, 126. Cf. the discussion of Broyles above in chap. 2 where I noted that his reading depended on a particular way of taking v. 6, which is the one here discussed.

here to seeing the word as "return."[108] Note that on Broyles's view, it makes most sense to see the psalmist as already in the temple, in order to express the wish to return there.

Turning to the LXX, we have *katoikein me*, which is "my residing/dwelling"—the infinitive form of "dwell" is functioning like a verbal noun would (and does) in English. This seems to be "translationese" Greek, an awkward phrasing that serves only to echo how the Hebrew is being understood. The Vulgate is initially similar and awkward: *ut inhabitem*, "that I may dwell." This is later modified and smoothed to *habitabo* when Jerome switches to the Hebrew, although this does not really affect the meaning. It becomes clear that the LXX (followed by the Vulgate) is presuming that the word in question is in fact *wəšibtî*.* Here the *wə–* prefix is a simple connective, "and," and the verb that follows is not *šûb* but *yāšab*, which does indeed mean "to dwell." It is in a form that functions just as its Greek translation did: an infinitive serving as a verbal noun. It also has a suffix, *–tî*, that identifies it as mine: hence, "my dwelling." Remembering that the pre-Masoretic text has consonants only, this difference is the difference between two ways of understanding the three consonants *w–š–b*. As the pointed Hebrew stands, it is a connective prefix (*w*) with a two-letter word *š–b*, and as understood by the LXX, it is a connective (*w*) followed by a three-letter word *y–š–b*, where the initial ("weak") *y* has disappeared, as often happens. Here it effectively gets replaced by the new prefix (which is a good example of why sometimes there are genuinely a couple of different options for what form a Hebrew word might be). Both options offer a reading that preserves the consonants of the Hebrew text, with one of them imagining (perfectly legitimately) that another letter has dropped out.

In this case, we may note that the LXX reading ("my dwelling") has been favored by English translations, partly because the evidence

---

108. An interesting and entirely different argument in favor of this reading is offered by Cooper, "Structure, Midrash and Meaning," 112, based on midrashic echoes of the Jacob narrative and comparing the wording of Gen. 28:21 with Ps. 23:6.

of the LXX itself is that this was an early understanding of the text. If you have been following closely, you will realize that on this reading we need to supply a form of the verb "to be" in English in order to make the sentence read smoothly. However, although such a move is common in Hebrew (and Greek, as well as in many languages), this is not actually a straightforward case where the verb "to be" can naturally slip into the text. In effect, on this alternative reading, we are imagining the verse something like this (simplified for illustration):

(6a) goodness and mercy [subject] will follow [verb] me [object]

(6b) and my dwelling [subject] in the house of the LORD [indirect object]

One *can* insert "is/will be" in (6b) here, but the sentence is simply awkward, not naturally inviting a first-person verb in its second half since "I" has not been its subject thus far.[109] As for what tense one would supply, it is not specified, and one could legitimately say "and my dwelling is/will be in the house of the LORD." Poetically, "will" can allow the possibility that I may already be so dwelling, and equally that I will continue to do so. If we now fix the awkwardness of "my dwelling shall be" and retain the KJV-influenced, archaic "shall," we finally arrive at the standard translation: "And I shall dwell in the house of the LORD."

You will see that there is no "right answer" to the question of which understanding is better. Some scholars propose that we follow the Hebrew with "I will return to the house of the LORD," while the majority are happy with the convention of English translations, which represents a repointing of the Hebrew. Those who defend this latter course often appeal to the parallels with Psalm 27:4—"One thing I

---

109. Supplying omitted forms of the verb "to be" makes most sense when there is a simple subject-predicate clause presented without a verb in Hebrew, e.g., "David king" becomes "David is king."

asked of the LORD, that will I seek after / *to live in the house of the* LORD *all the days of my life*" (NRSV with parallels italicized; though ESV and NIV both follow KJV and have "dwell in the house of the LORD"). Although the order of the two phrases in the italicized part of this verse is reversed, the wording is all but exactly the same as Psalm 23:6, and in 27:4 "dwell/live" is indeed *šibtî*. However, in the case of 27:4 the reversed order of the clauses removes the need for a connective *w–* prefix, which results in making 27:4 definitely a form of *yāšab*, "to dwell"—that is, it rules out the possibility that it might be *šûb*, "return." This could be a strong argument in favor of reading the same sense back into Psalm 23:6, although it overlooks the fact that supplying the verb "to be" is not at all difficult in 27:4, as compared to its awkwardness in 23:6. In 27:4, where the whole phrase is the object of the first-person verb "asked," one can elegantly insert the verb "to be" without difficulty: "My dwelling [is] in the house of the LORD." Now there is undoubtedly a pull from one verse to the other, since these are the only two uses of the phrase "the house of the LORD" in Books 1–3 of the Psalter, and the extended phrase ("all the days of my life") does occur both times. But the argument is just that: an argument, not conclusive proof.

Minimally, adding further weight to reading it as *wəšibtî* ("and my dwelling") is that the location of this returning/dwelling is about to be specified as *bəbêt–yhwh*, where the *bə–* prefix is arguably best translated as "in," and it is more elegant grammatically to "dwell in" than to "return in." However, we have met this inseparable preposition *bə–* four times already in the psalm and so far have been content to translate it as "*in* pastures green," "*in* right paths," "*through* the valley," and "*with* oil," so while it would be unusual to translate it "*to* the temple," it would not be impossible.[110]

---

110. The real issue of course is what counts as elegant and permissible in Hebrew, but the gist of this paragraph makes the point appropriately. The lengthy entry for *šûb* in *DCH* 8:273–98 includes the relevant sense of "return" as the eleventh of thirty-five possible nuances of the verb in the Qal. Lo and behold, it finds an example of its use with the *b–* preposition in Hosea 12:6 ("return to your God") where *b–* means "to"

What have we shown? The Hebrew text ("return") makes sense, though is slightly awkward with regard to returning "in" the temple, but it was already not being followed by the LXX. It probably (though not necessarily) assumes that the psalmist is in the temple. The alternative suggestion ("dwell") makes sense in comparison with Psalm 27:4, though the case is not conclusive and the result is awkward in 23:6. But the strongest argument for it is that it is the reading adopted by the LXX.[111] Readers may find their judgment between the options influenced by how probable they think it is that the psalmist is located in the temple, longing to "return" (whether on an annual pilgrimage or not). If one chooses that option, then it turns out that our whole poem has been framed in retrospect by a worshiper now a long way from quiet waters or the valley of the shadow of death. This is not impossible. My personal opinion is that it is less likely. I wonder whether it does not inadvertently effect a switch in the final verse from the *persona* of the psalm (the voice that speaks throughout) to the author, and takes a claim that the author may have been in the temple and merges it with the speaking voice claiming to be there. But, like all options, this is not provable either.

Goldingay exercises a commentator's privilege to include both, explaining briefly how both could be right, and translating "I will return to [MT]/dwell in [LXX]."[112] He suggests that in practice it makes little difference.[113] In both cases future occupancy of the house of the LORD is confidently envisaged. As a final observation here, it is worth noting that willingness to work with both textual variants when they cohere in terms of meaning has a long pedigree, and that

---

(282), which shows that Ps. 23:6 *might* mean "return *to* the house of the LORD," as indeed is noted, as positive support for this reading, by Cooper, "Structure, Midrash and Meaning," 112. Is one comparable example enough? I have sympathy with readers who may feel that we are now past the point of discharging the obligation to pay attention to the details.

111. Followed by the Vulgate and also found in the targum.

112. Goldingay, *Psalms*, 1:345, 353.

113. Goldingay, *Psalms*, 1:353, following a short article making this point by Knauf. Knauf, "Psalm xxiii 6," 556.

in such instances too much energy focused on which is "the right reading" seems misplaced—this excursus notwithstanding![114]

————————— ⌃ —————————

For those who skipped the "small print," let me summarize: the verb as written in Hebrew (with its Masoretic vowels added in) is "then I will return" (wəšabtî*). For two (or maybe three) reasons, most English translations and commentators presume that the vowels are not quite right, and the word should have been written "and my dwelling [shall be]" (wəšibtî*). The first reason is that the LXX reads it this way, suggesting this was an early understanding. The second reason is by way of comparison with almost identical wording in Psalm 27:4, where in fact it has to mean "dwell" (since the small difference between 23:6 and 27:4 is enough to remove the ambiguity in 27:4), although there is an awkwardness to this parallel with 23:6 that makes it a bit less conclusive. A possible third reason is that the returning or dwelling is "in" the house of the LORD, as we will note in a moment. How much difference this choice of translation makes may depend a little on how we handle the rest of the sentence.

The place where I will dwell (or to which, conceivably, I will return) is "the house of the LORD" (bəbêt-yhwh). The name of the LORD returns for its only use subsequent to verse 1, but the LORD has never been out of focus throughout. We have met the bə– prefix in every verse of the psalm except the first, and we have thus already seen some of the wide range of English translations it can sustain depending on context: "in" (pastures green); "through" (the valley); "with" (oil). So while it would most naturally mean "in" here—"in the house of"—it could perhaps mean "to" (the house of).

But what is "the house of the LORD"? Perhaps the phrase could be taken in an abstract sense to refer to any place where God is

114. An interesting discussion of textual variants working alongside theological concerns about the text speaking in either way is Johnson, "Living, Active, Elusive," 83–102, which notes that Augustine could let variant readings stand if they did not affect the exegesis (97).

worshiped, but the most obvious specific reference for this phrase in the Old Testament is the great temple built by Solomon (1 Kings 6–8). Admittedly, given that David is told not to build this temple but to leave the project for his son (2 Sam. 7:4–14), this would be a strange reference in a psalm "written by David." Even if the psalm is instead honoring or pertaining to David in some way (as we discussed in chapter 2), reference to the temple would be odd since it might remind hearers of David's disqualification from building it. But what really makes the more specific reference plausible is imagining that the psalm was written to be sung in the temple by later worshipers, who are thus invited to slip here from the imagined world of the psalm to the reflection on their present experience praising the LORD, who is their shepherd and provider.

Would this then tell us anything about the date of the origin of the psalm? Apart from saying that it is from the time of Solomon or later, not really. The point about worshipers singing in the temple is not the same as arguing that the persona of the psalmist is located in the temple. This was also discussed in chapter 2. However, with reference to the detailed discussion above, we may note that a psalmist longing to "return" to the temple has doubtless been in it at some point.

Are there other alternatives for what the phrase *bəbêt-yhwh* could mean here? While there was a separate word for temple in the Old Testament (*hêkal*, which could also mean "palace"), the specificity introduced by saying that this is the house *of the* LORD can really only allow reference to a particular place. There are some uses of the phrase "house of the LORD" in books set before the temple account in 1 Kings 6–8, and in such cases it seems to refer to a specified place such as the tabernacle or a shrine.[115] It is just conceivable then that the

---

115. References to "the house of the LORD" in the text preceding the account in 1 Kings are Exod. 23:19; 34:26; Deut. 23:18; Josh. 6:24; Judg. 19:18 (omitted by NRSV following LXX); 1 Sam. 1:7, 24; 3:15; and 2 Sam. 12:20. It is of course possible that some of these project the phrase back in light of later usage. This list does not include references to "house" where the context might indicate that the house of the LORD is in view.

reference to the house of the LORD in Psalm 23:6 could have been to some pre-temple location, perhaps pertaining to a nomadic celebration at some shrine or recalling some long-gone tabernacle. I judge this unlikely because it would be such a leap out of the presenting Davidic context. It does seem simplest to assume that the place is the temple. Finally, since the point in verse 6 is not really one of historical reference, perhaps it does not matter much that we have only a best guess rather than proof that one particular reading is right.

The key point to make here is that the psalm arrives at an assurance that transcends the immediate imagery of the poem. The assurance works on two levels quite naturally. The psalm assures the traveler, who has been the poem's subject throughout: the wayfarer conceptualized as the sheep, breaking their journey by quiet waters, traveling through dark valleys, nourished by rest and food, and invited to ponder longer days of praise than the days of toil and difficulty already experienced. It also assures the implied audience of the psalm, those who are using this psalm to worship YHWH in and after the days of the poem's composition, including readers today.

It seems odd that most commentators who reflect on this phrase seem to assume that the speaker must be in the temple physically.[116] It would make equal sense to say that the worshipers associate themselves with the ongoing worship of the temple, wherever they may be themselves. After all, anyone singing or praying or liturgically appropriating this psalm has already managed the mental shift necessary to describe themselves as the sheep of the shepherd, and no one imagines this over-literally. They have also said "for you are with me" in verse 4, which, as we saw, is a use of language that covers over a range of literal understandings. All it requires here at the end of the poem is to maintain that kind of flexible approach to saying "I will dwell in" the temple. Jewish and Christian praise down through the centuries has

---

116. E.g., Brueggemann and Bellinger, *Psalms*, 124–25, and many others. The case of Broyles basing this view on reading "return" as the verb in v. 6 has been noted above and makes more sense. Here I am addressing those who stick with "dwell" but still see it as evidence of the poet being in the temple.

found it possible to affirm such words as "I will dwell in the house of the LORD" from wherever on the earth they are offering praise. Once again, over-historicizing the reading really does not help.[117]

How long will I dwell in the LORD's house? The answer in Hebrew seems simple: *lə'ōrek yāmîm*, which means "for length of days." The *lə*– prefix is the same as the one we met in connection with the psalm's title ("to/for/by/about David"), and it introduces a phrase that points ahead into the future. How far it points into the future is less obvious, as is generally the case with Hebrew expressions indicating time to come. As a rule of thumb, Hebrew phrases that look far ahead generally mean "for sufficiently long that we do not need to worry how long precisely." This is the sense sought by translation options such as "days without end"[118] or "for long days."[119] While such a reading is usually noted in a footnote, no major English translation has followed it.[120] Most, in fact, follow the KJV's lead again and translate this phrase as "forever," although the NRSV gives "my whole life long."

We may be helped toward seeing the strengths and weaknesses of "forever" as a translation by comparing the three other cases in the Psalms where such a phrase appears. The most interesting example

117. It may be noted that in the first three books of the Psalter (Pss. 1–89), there are only two uses of the phrase "house of the LORD"—here in 23:6 and in the parallel verse in 27:4, which we looked at in connection with the dwelling/returning wording in this same verse. Might this connect these two verses as rare pre-temple references intended more loosely? I do not think this is likely. Again, more loosely worded references occur (e.g., to "house" Ps. 36:8, to "courts" in Ps. 84:10; and Book 2 may intend the same in its Elohistic phrase "house of God" in 42:4; 52:8). This might suggest that the Psalter is generally avoiding the kind of slippage between then and now that I am suggesting here. However, subsequent psalms continue to refer only infrequently to the "house of the LORD" (one reference in Book 4, in Ps. 92:13; and six references in Book 5—116:19; 118:26; 122:1, 9; 134:1; 135:2), so it seems simplest to say that the focus of worship in the temple was not the temple itself, at least not very often. I would then be reluctant to draw historical conclusions from this, even if it may be a worthwhile line of reflection for those who write liturgy, hymns, or praise songs.

118. Craigie, *Psalms 1–50*, 204.

119. Goldingay, *Psalms*, 1:352.

120. In this case we are not helped by either the LXX or the Vulgate, which both simply translate the Hebrew expression word for word, resulting, e.g., in "for length of days" (NETS).

is Psalm 21:4, where the psalmist says regarding the king, "He asked you for life; you gave it to him— / length of days forever and ever." The phrase at the end here (*ʿôlām wāʿed*) clearly pulls in the direction of "forever and ever," with the result that it seems odd to all translations to use the same word or phrase for the "length of days" part of the verse. Perhaps this psalm suggests that good long days may endure forever, which would lean toward Psalm 23 imagining the long days rather than forever; although equally one could say that Psalm 21 is simply piling up time-pointers to emphasize that we are looking at time without limit. Elsewhere the phrase means "long life" (Ps. 91:16, where it belongs to the psalmist in practical terms, and thus "forever" does not fit) and a more undefined sense of "forevermore" (Ps. 93:5, where it describes the holiness of the temple [the LORD's house, in fact]; here the NIV has "for endless days," NJPS has "for all times," and Peterson imagines "to the very end of time" [MSG]).

My own conclusion here is that none of these phrases were intended in any specific sense to point to a technical conception of precise duration. The usage in Psalm 91:16 arguably shows that the focus in such a phrase points most naturally to this life, and this makes very good sense in Psalm 23:6. This would suggest avoiding the translation "forever," and perhaps this is the thinking behind NJPS's "for many long years." However, this seems to me overly worried by later issues regarding time and eternity with which Hebrew poetry is not especially concerned. Likewise, English uses of "forever" that operate with a vague sense of "for a very long time/long enough" are reasonably common and hardly considered misleading.

It is true that the most straightforward way of saying "forever" (*ləʿōlām*) is not used here, so it is worth asking why the specific wording ("length of days") might have appealed to the psalmist. In a thoughtful analysis of the possibilities here, Janzen makes the intriguing suggestion that Psalm 23 ends on a note of "the experience of the act of praise and its attendant joy, a praise and joy on occasion issuing in a suspension of all sense of time," where the sense of "presence before the everlasting God" seems itself to be everlasting.[121] In other words, "length of days" imagines the days of praise stretching out to seem longer than normal. I suspect Janzen is right, though this is a nuance hard to capture in translation.

Does this sense of time-distorting praise spill over into saying that the comforted pilgrim has the promise of dwelling in God's presence forevermore—in the next life? For the reasons just rehearsed, it seems unlikely that the psalm's author was primarily seeking to make that point. But in the light of Janzen's argument and our own wider considerations, a positive answer to this question—affirming the sense of "forever"—seems best. Indeed, once the reader (whether ancient or modern) has asked the question about whether the promise of divine presence endures beyond death—a question that will most naturally arise in precisely those cases where the psalm is used in connection with funerals or bereavement—it seems to me that the answer must be yes. To capture that openness in translation, I suspect that "my whole life long" (NRSV) or "for the rest of my life" (MSG) are both serviceable, since they can trade on the same openness about how long my life is in terms of both what the Hebrew psalmist might have said and also what today's hopeful pilgrims might say with regard to life before and after death. But overall it seems simpler, and just as helpful, to let the ambiguity be based around the word "forever." Once again the KJV leads us in the right path.

The poetic tenor of verse 6 overflows the boundaries of clear meaning and precise reference. In a final outpouring of trust and confidence in the shepherd LORD who has led me through the journey of the psalm as a whole, I imagine goodness and mercy chasing after me forevermore, and I realize that God's presence is not just for the momentary trouble with my enemies. I dwell in it for equally

---

121. Janzen, "Revisiting 'Forever,'" 204. Janzen's essay correctly notes that the work of Levenson, *Resurrection and the Restoration of Israel*, which we discussed in connection with v. 4, dispenses with many older objections to the translation "forever" that were based on thinking that Jewish Scripture had little or no interest in an afterlife.

long. The enemies have not gone away—not least in the sense that God's presence in verse 6 continues the celebration of the meal of verse 5—but the enemies have faded from view. The view is taken up entirely with God. Psalm 23 would not want to leave us with any other final impression.

Translation

Readers who have persevered through this analysis will by now be fully aware of just how much poetic ambiguity and openness of resonance accompanies many phrases and words in this psalm. It would thus be unwise to suggest that any translation can be a final word. Rather, a good translation offers maximum light by which to read the text or maximum clarity by which to hear the text. In particular it allows us to experience the pressure of the text of Scripture upon today's reader (or addressee), and I have wanted to balance the right and proper openness in our exegesis with a real commitment to letting the psalm's text impress itself upon us appropriately. Justifications for the translation offered here have been rehearsed above, but readers will have noted that more than once we were left with a "possibly" or a "perhaps." With these caveats in mind, I translate as follows.

Psalm 23

A Psalm of David.

> [1]The LORD is my shepherd, therefore I cannot lack.
>
> [2]In pastures green he lets me lie down;
> by quiet waters he leads me;
> [3]He restores my life.
> He leads me in the right direction
> —all for his name's sake.

⁴Even though I walk through the valley of the shadow of
 death,
I fear no evil,
for you are with me;
Your rod and your staff,
they comfort me.

⁵You set before me a table
in the presence of my enemies:
pouring oil generously over my head,
my cup overflowing.

⁶Surely goodness and mercy will pursue me
all the days of my life,
and I will dwell in the house of the LORD
forever.

4

The World in Front of Psalm 23

Ministry

How does Psalm 23 speak to Christian ministry in the twenty-first century? Our exegesis in chapter 3 has already revealed some of the many ways the psalm may speak to our present horizons. In this chapter, I explore four areas of the life and mission of the church in which Psalm 23 can and does make a significant contribution. Taking them in the order in which they occur in the text, we first consider the psalm's witness to rest and protection in a busy world, then how it offers encouragement in the face of death, then how it speaks to our engagement with enemies, and finally the ways in which Psalm 23 gives voice to hope. While all these issues would apply in their own way also to Jewish readers and those serving in Jewish communities and congregations, our concerns in this book are with the text in the life of the Christian church.[1] I therefore preface the discussion

1. I would be uneasy presuming to address Jewish readers on matters of Jewish wisdom and practice. The next note points to one popular Jewish reading of Ps. 23 that shows how it can be done, though it is largely addressed to all readers. For

by attending to the ways in which Psalm 23 is taken up in the New Testament and in Christian theology.

Jesus and Psalm 23: A Christian Theological Account

In an interview to promote his self-consciously post–9/11 book, *The Lord Is My Shepherd: Healing Wisdom of the Twenty-Third Psalm*, Rabbi Harold Kushner was asked, "Does the 23rd Psalm mean something different to Jews and Christians?" He replied, "Absolutely. . . . Christians claim ownership of the psalm as much as Jews do. They love it just as much and maybe even know it better."[2] Perhaps so. It might be that Psalm 23 is read more often in Christian worship than in Jewish worship, partly as a result of its prominence in church funeral services (which we discuss below), although Kushner does note its use in Jewish funeral services and makes it clear that the psalm is widely known and loved in Jewish circles too.[3]

But is Kushner right? Does Psalm 23 mean something different to Jews and to Christians? The answer to this question lies somewhere in the range of yes and no, depending on what exactly is being asked. In what could become a very abstract discussion, I offer one paragraph of theoretical reflection on this issue and then restrict myself to outlining a Christian account of Psalm 23 and its relationship to Jesus Christ.

Christian reading of the church's Old Testament Scripture has been confused in the modern era for a range of reasons, but in large

Jewish scholarship looking at Ps. 23, see for example Cooper, "Structure, Midrash and Meaning," 107–14, which explores rabbinic insights in reading some details of Ps. 23 as "a poetic/midrashic reflection on the life of Jacob" (110)—and especially Gen. 48:15. More generally, note also Cooper's "Some Aspects of Traditional Jewish Psalms," 253–68, which sadly does not consider Ps. 23. A good introduction to relevant scholarly issues in reception is Sawyer, "Psalms in Judaism and Christianity," 134–43.

2. Kushner, *Lord Is My Shepherd*. See https://www.beliefnet.com/faiths/2003/09/what-the-psalmist-meant.aspx (accessed November 13, 2019).

3. Ps. 23 is traditionally said at the beginning of the third Sabbath meal (*Se'uda Shelishit*) every Sabbath, so I am not quite persuaded that it is necessarily better known by Christians. I am indebted here to *Koren Siddur*, 684–87.

part because of the shift to looking at original meaning and context as uniquely determinative for interpreting a Bible text. This is not to say that the church was always right in older times, that there is nothing helpful in modern interpretation, or even that original meaning is not worth exploring as fully as we can. The exegesis offered in chapter 3 models many elements of that approach. But as I have said all along, it is artificial to separate the worlds behind, in, and in front of the text, and the reader brings to the interpretive task certain perspectives, contexts, and interpretive interests that shape the reading—sometimes in small ways and sometimes profoundly. So as a whole, Christian reading weaves in and out of specific Christian commitments alongside attention to literary (textual and philological) study that offers insights that are indeed the same for Jews and Christians. Is Psalm 23 therefore different for Jews and Christians? Yes and no. And how much more is it different (and also the same) for interested bystanders who profess no faith, or a different faith? This does not mean that interpreters should seek diverse perspectives just for the sake of it, as if it were inherently good to have lots of readings. Rather it means that interpreters should assess the virtues of being generous and hospitable to multiple readings and perspectives depending on the various agendas at work—both their own and other people's. For Christian readers there are two obvious resources of wisdom that it would be strange to ignore in reading Psalm 23. One is the Jewish wisdom and insight on a text that emerged out of ancient Israel from a tradition that would give rise to varieties of Jewish faith. The other is the Christian wisdom and insight on a text that has been received and honored in the history of the church and in the varieties of Christian faith. Other traditions will need to make their own decisions about what sort of engagement with other voices is constructive. Here I speak from and to a Christian conviction that it is good for Christian readers of the Old Testament to learn and read widely, beyond Christian writers, while also not losing sight of how a text like Psalm 23 speaks to Christian convictions. It is the Jewish scholar Jon Levenson who notably issues a plea for Christians to own their Old Testament readings as Christian projects in the interest of better serving Jewish-Christian dialogue than is possible if the respective faith convictions are bracketed out.[4] So in what follows, I attempt to do just that.

There are three interesting questions one might explore with regard to specifically Christian interpretation of Psalm 23. (1) In what sense, if any, is it about Jesus? (More broadly, perhaps, How is YHWH in Psalm 23 related to the God known in trinitarian terms by Christians as Father, Son, and Holy Spirit?) (2) More generally, how does reading Psalm 23 in the light of the New Testament and Christian theology make a difference? A third question might allow us to build up toward that second question, although it may result in a different set of inquiries: (3) How did the early church (and indeed any "premodern" church) read Psalm 23 in the days before historical-critical concern with original meaning became so determinative? Other interesting questions and variations immediately suggest themselves (e.g., What might a charismatic Spirit-oriented reading of Psalm 23 look like?), but these three will keep us busy enough. In fact the second question, on the difference it makes to read Psalm 23 in the light of Christian understanding, will also effectively be the topic of the remainder of this chapter. This first section of the chapter will therefore mainly restrict itself to questions 1 and 3, which in abbreviated form ask, "Is it about Jesus?" and "How was it traditionally read by Christians?"

Is Psalm 23 about Jesus? Well again, this is a "yes-and-no" question, depending on what specific issue is being raised. Today's Christian approaches to this question tend to fall into three different categories, which overlap a little. Some take the original meaning as key and answer "no," or at least "not originally"—the psalmist was not thinking about Jesus when he wrote Psalm 23. Others say that the

---

4. Levenson, "Theological Consensus or Historicist Evasion?," 82–105. This endlessly quotable essay argues that "the historical-critical method compels its practitioners to bracket their traditional identities, and this renders its ability to enrich Judaism and Christianity problematic" (105). Bracketing, Levenson says, has value but also limitations.

New Testament requires one to go back and reread a text like Psalm 23 and to realize that it speaks the truth about Jesus, although that is as much about the rereading as the psalm itself. A third approach attempts to say that the psalm really is about Jesus, in the sense that its basic theological claims may rightly be seen fully in and through Christ, and while the New Testament may be a trigger of sorts to realizing it, what we realize is something that was always true about the psalm. I will forsake a theoretical discussion of these approaches and offer a brief comment on how they relate to Psalm 23.[5]

Readers will realize that I have not been persuaded that we can answer questions about who the author of Psalm 23 was, when and where they were writing, or why. An approach marked predominantly by such historicizing interests would more or less relegate the topic of "Psalm 23 for the life of the church" to a separate addendum by definition, so I will say no more about it here.

The second approach is more promising, since it lets the status of Psalm 23 as part of a two-testament Christian canon come into play. It is handed a range of ways to make Christian sense of the psalm because the New Testament picks up on "good shepherd" language in multiple places and claims it as referring to Christ. The most prominent example is in John 10:1–18, where Jesus says, "I am the good shepherd" (v. 11) in the midst of a discourse that draws heavily on shepherd imagery to describe the nature of Jesus's identity and in particular his ministry as compared to the leadership—or lack of it—exercised by other types of shepherd figures. At the heart of Jesus's claims in John 10 is that he lays down his life for his sheep (v. 11) and comes to bring them abundant life (v. 10). Bailey's study

---

5. Those aware of the literature will recognize the three approaches as modeled respectively by, for example, Barton, *Nature of Biblical Criticism*, 137–86 (esp. 158–64), locating Christian resonance at a secondary ("application") stage; Hays, *Echoes of Scripture in the Letters of Paul* and *Echoes of Scripture in the Gospels*, advocating adopting the New Testament's approach of rereading the Old Testament in christological focus (and admirably presented briefly in *Reading Backwards*); and Seitz, *Elder Testament*, seeking actual reference to Christ in Old Testament Scripture, albeit not named on the surface level of the text.

of the "good shepherd" image through Scripture charts an illuminating path that goes from Psalm 23 at root, through several texts, en
route to Jesus's appropriation of the imagery in John 10.[6] That the
leaders of Israel were failing in their duty to be good shepherds is
the focus of Jeremiah 23:1–8 and especially Ezekiel 34, which ends,
"You are my sheep, the sheep of my pasture, and I am your God, says
the Lord GOD" (Ezek. 34:31).[7] Bailey also picks up on the Synoptics'
use of the imagery in Luke 15:1–10 (and slightly differently in Matt.
18:10–14) and in Mark 6.[8] John 10 is thus bringing to fulfillment a way
of thinking about God's rule (or "kingdom," as traditional English
language has it) in shepherding imagery—imagery that has become
deeply embedded in Scripture and is hereby appropriated directly by
Jesus in describing himself.[9]

It makes sense to say that all this New Testament development
invites us as Christians to go back and reread Psalm 23 and see that
it is (also) about Jesus, the Good Shepherd. Straightforwardly this
might allow one to say that Jesus leads us by quiet waters (understood
now metaphorically) and restores our souls (lives). Likewise Jesus
guides us through the valley of the shadow of death, and armed with
a Christian understanding of resurrection focused on the resurrection
of Christ himself, this invites us to take the comfort of the psalm and
express it in terms of the comfort of the Christian life in the face of
death and in the hope of resurrection. All this seems entirely fair as a
Christian rereading of the text, and of course it overlaps a little with
the first approach, in that it is describing the promises and purposes

6. Bailey, *Good Shepherd*, studying relevant passages in three different prophets
and all four Gospels.

7. The NRSV follows the LXX here. The Hebrew adds an explanatory "you are
'ādām [people]" after "sheep of my pasture." "Lord GOD" here is 'ădōnāy yhwh
because the tetragram (YHWH) takes the pointing of 'ĕlohîm when it occurs after
'ădōnāy.

8. Bailey, *Good Shepherd*, also devotes chapters to Zech. 10 (noting that chap. 11
is also relevant) and 1 Pet. 5.

9. For the sake of this discussion, it makes little difference to note that it is John
who articulates the issues through the speaking Christ as encountered in his Gospel.

of Psalm 23 as appropriated in Christ.[10] The difference is that this second approach sees such a move not as a separate (optional) second stage, but as an attempt to read Psalm 23 at face value in its location as part of Christian Scripture.

Although it is not the core issue with Psalm 23, the other main difference that separates this approach from the first one is that it takes seriously the New Testament handling of the Old as a model of how to receive that Old Testament Scripture (i.e., the collection of holy books as it already was—more or less—by the time of Jesus). The concern would be to let New Testament readings of Psalm 23, and other texts, model for us how we might rightly handle Psalm 23. To illustrate, Psalm 22 is a major test case of the benefits and limitations of this approach, given the way that its opening words ("My God, my God, why have you forsaken me?") are appropriated by Jesus in the canonical Gospels (Matt. 27:46 // Mark 15:34). Is the meaning of Psalm 22 rightly understood in Christian theological terms without reference to Christ on the cross? No, says Richard Hays, and most Christian readers would probably agree with him, at least in outline.[11]

Psalm 23 is not quoted directly in the New Testament—at least according to the usual understanding of textual citation, which is nevertheless a little complex since we are asking about a Greek text quoting a Hebrew predecessor, most commonly via its Greek translation (LXX). Lists of such citations, as provided in Greek New Testaments, record no direct quotes.[12] Indeed Dale Allison notes that "the

10. Thus Craigie, *Psalms 1–50*, 208–9, whose approach might more naturally be the first one (i.e., exegesis + application), writes of this development that "it is the words of Jesus himself, amplified by the early church . . . which make possible a 'rereading' of Ps. 23 in the light of the gospel of redemption" (209).

11. Although on details it does get more complicated, of course. On Ps. 22 see Hays, *Echoes of Scripture in the Gospels*, 83–85 (on Mark), 161–62 (on Matthew), 235–36 (on Luke). Note also that Hays relates John 10 to Ezek. 34, not Ps. 23, though he is brief on this John passage (*Echoes*, 310). Several articles that interact helpfully with Hays's book (and a response from Hays) are collected in *Journal of Theological Interpretation* 11:1 (2017): 1–99.

12. The standard critical text (NA28) lists only allusions for v. 1 and 2ff. in Rev. 7:17, which we consider in a moment, and the echo of v. 5 in the language of "anoint[ing] my head with oil" in Luke 7:46.

psalm has left scarcely a trace in early Christian literature. It is, in fact, never quoted in the NT and is cited but once in the Apostolic Fathers."[13] But this is not the whole story, as Allison himself goes on to argue in a helpful, brief survey article that I draw on here.

The nearest direct use of Psalm 23 language in the New Testament is in Revelation 7:17, as John the Seer surveys the multitudes in worship awaiting the opening of the seventh seal: "The Lamb at the center of the throne will be their shepherd, and he will guide them to springs of the water of life." The previous verse in Revelation draws from Isaiah 49:10, but the vocabulary of 7:17 suggests that Psalm 23 also lies behind the text.[14] The account of the feeding of the five thousand in Mark 6 is also worth hearing clearly. Having noted that the large crowd was "like sheep without a shepherd" (6:34), Jesus orders them to "recline" on the "green grass" (6:39).[15] Bailey draws out how Jesus, in the presence of his enemies, makes the people lie down in green pastures and provides for them: "The voice of Psalm 23 can also be heard in the background."[16]

Allison suggests that underlying such appeals to Psalm 23 is an early Christian view that Jesus is the Davidic shepherd-king whose coming heralds the beginning of the end times and that his second coming would bring in fully the reign of the shepherd-king as imagined in Ezekiel 34. In short, Psalm 23 has been read eschatologically, pointing to the life of the world to come.[17] However, Allison's clear analysis pulls a Christian reader up short when he goes on to say, "The shepherd [in Rev. 7:17] is not the Lord God of the OT. He is

13. Allison, "Psalm 23 (22) in Early Christianity," 132–37, here 132.
14. See Allison, "Psalm 23 (22) in Early Christianity," 132–33.
15. The command is to "recline" (*anaklinō*; "sit [at table]," "recline"), almost always translated as "sit" but thereby losing a sense of the meal imagery. See Bailey, *Good Shepherd*, 170.
16. Bailey, *Good Shepherd*, 170.
17. Allison, "Psalm 23 (22) in Early Christianity," 135–36. He suggests that this accounts also for the sole reference in the Apostolic Fathers—the discussion of resurrection in 1 Clem. 24–27 that cites Ps. 23:4 as part of its scriptural support in 1 Clem. 26:2: "I lay down and slept; I rose up, for *you are with me*." Otherwise this psalm verse seems somewhat removed from concerns with resurrection.

rather the Lamb in the midst of the throne, Jesus Christ."[18] This nicely illustrates that the frame of reference for one's reading makes considerable difference, since the traditional Christian view would find this "not"/"rather" contrast misleading and see instead an identification here of Christ the Lamb *with* the Lord God of the Old Testament. This takes us on to our next approach.

The third category to be discussed here is the view that Psalm 23 is actually and really about Jesus. That the direct focus of the Old Testament text's "literal sense" (appropriately understood) is christological, or more broadly trinitarian, is the argument of Christopher Seitz in his striking book *The Elder Testament*: what we normally call the Old Testament "had and has its own providential role in articulating the doctrine of God toward which Trinitarian confession is calibrated."[19] In some ways Seitz seeks to rehabilitate older trinitarian models of reading, emphasizing that the reality of God found in the Old Testament is the same as the reality found in the New Testament. In this sense, the voice of the Old Testament (what Seitz calls its *"per se* voice"—its voice in itself) is already a voice of Christian theology, and it is not just as that voice is received and reread in the New Testament that the christological reference comes into play.[20] Again Psalm 23 is not a primary exhibit in Seitz's approach (Psalm 22 is more central),[21] though he does offer one sentence (not further explored) that is precisely relevant to our task here: "Who is 'the LORD is my shepherd' of Psalm 23 if not YHWH the triune God, the Lord Jesus, and the Holy Spirit who has given rise to the Psalm in the first place."[22] How then might a reading of

18. Allison, "Psalm 23 (22) in Early Christianity," 133.

19. Seitz, *Elder Testament*, 264. His book is carefully worded and appropriately guarded—more so than my brief summary can capture. A helpful précis of Seitz's case is his "Trinity in the Old Testament," 28–40. E.g., "It is the unique theological depiction of the Holy One of Israel that forces one to reflect dynamically and dogmatically on the triune life of God as true to that life in an ontological sense" (30).

20. On this see also Seitz, *Character of Christian Scripture*, especially 137–56.

21. E.g., Seitz, *Elder Testament*, 273–74; and "Trinity in the Old Testament," 33.

22. Seitz, *Elder Testament*, 199. The statement is intended rhetorically as a conclusion and thus has no question mark.

Psalm 23 proceed, informed by this account? I offer here a suggestion in outline.

The Lord (Yhwh) who is my shepherd in Psalm 23 is both the God who is God over the whole scene and the God who accompanies me in and through the whole scene. Thus Yhwh leads me beside quiet waters and along the right paths, and he invites me to sit and eat at the prepared "table." But Yhwh is also quietly present over the whole scenario, whether I lie down or rise, rest or struggle, eat in the presence of my enemies, or even sing Yhwh's praises in the temple—in this life or in whatever imagined future the psalm might leave open. Yhwh is not named as the creator God in Psalm 23, but the sense that creation is entirely within Yhwh's right ordering is manifest, including the sense that creation is to be enjoyed as a good and life-giving gift. Likewise the praise offered to Yhwh is left implied in the final verse's dwelling or returning to the temple "forever," but the God who inhabits that temple is of course the God of heaven and earth. Further, the goodness and mercy that pursue me in the final verse are, as *The Message* translation helpfully emphasizes, God's goodness and mercy. Divine attributes are imagined as actively at work in the creation, described in this verse in the standard form of idiom by which the Old Testament protects God's transcendent otherness while still managing to talk about divine action experienced in the world. Yhwh in Psalm 23 is rightly called by the church the God and Father of her Lord Jesus Christ.

Who then is the shepherd who walks with me in Yhwh's good creation and who invites me to stop and eat at his table? In addition to all that has just been said about the Father, the shepherd figure who accompanies me is God the Son: Christ the Good Shepherd, as he will be more fully known in due time. And thus Yhwh in Psalm 23 is rightly also called God the Son by the church. Furthermore, we noted in our exegesis of verse 4 how hard it is to pin down the sense of the language "you are with me" and how any attempt to ponder its reference to reality involves interpreters reflecting on how to articulate God's presence. Christian trinitarian language would most naturally meet this difficulty by saying that the God who is "with me" is known to the church as "God the Spirit," in light of which it becomes easier to see how the psalm's other references to divine leading and restoring and comforting may also be rightly attributed to God the Spirit.

Trinitarian language is notoriously difficult to handle well (and Old Testament scholars—even Christian Old Testament scholars—often get around this problem by not handling it at all). Emphasize any one aspect of the trinitarian language without the relevant checks and balances, and the result can sound awkward at best and misleading (and/or unorthodox) at worst. The reading just offered attempts to do justice to the fundamental conviction that YHWH language in the Old Testament fully engages the reality of the three-in-one-God of Christian confession. As Seitz insists, this is not about finding "threes" in the Old Testament that distribute reference to God into three independent categories, although I can imagine how my reading might be misunderstood that way.[23] For the sake of illustration, I tried to highlight from various aspects of the psalm the ways in which the portrait of YHWH in Psalm 23 is about God the Father, Son, and Holy Spirit, but this is absolutely not intended to suggest that God is the Father in verse 1, the Son in verses 2–3, the Spirit in verse 4, and so forth. Ideally one would go through the whole psalm three times over and show how it all relates to each person of the Trinity. The resulting reading would grow longer. Erasmus's "threefold exposition" of Psalm 22 (though not in fact trinitarian in its threefoldness in quite this imagined way) runs to seventy-five large pages in his *Collected Works* edition.[24] Once approached with due openness to its mysterious multiple literal senses, then like the remarkable time-traveling spaceship of the long-running UK TV show *Doctor Who*, Scripture is "bigger on the inside than the outside." The present book may be understood in part as an attempt to defend this point while

23. For his critique of finding "threes" as indicators of the Trinity, see Seitz, "Trinity in the Old Testament," 30–31.
24. Erasmus, "A Threefold Exposition of Psalm 22," 125–99.

also paying careful, critically trained attention to the specifics of the text. Which is exactly what Erasmus did, in fact.

This brings us to consider the other initial question we wished to explore in this chapter: How was Psalm 23 read by the early church and others who read prior to the modern era? The core point to understand here is that it was traditional to read the Psalms in a range of "voices," indeed, in different *personae*—to adopt the label we explored in chapter 2. Michael Fiedrowicz summarizes, "Augustine followed the pattern customary in early Christian exegesis, which interpreted the psalms either as a word to Christ . . . or as a word about Christ . . . or as a word spoken by Christ himself . . . or in an ecclesiological perspective as a word about the Church . . . or finally as a word spoken by the Church."[25] This will help us understand the range of ways that the church traditionally read Psalm 23 in dialogue with the claims of Christ, ways that have slowly been reappropriated in recent times as part of a *"ressourcement"* move toward learning from the older traditions.[26]

I do not intend to review or classify all the various ways that Psalm 23 has been read. The work has been done admirably by others, including Waltke and Houston in their fine compendium of "historical commentary."[27] I noted this work in our introduction and commented that it holds an uneasy balance between attending to the history of interpretation and reconstructing a reading of any given psalm based on close critical work with the Hebrew to find the author's intention. The latter project is problematic, as I have suggested, but the review of past interpretations is very well done, when not preoccupied with trying to match it up to modern-style exegesis. Waltke and Houston begin with Athanasius, referring readers of the psalm to baptism, chrism (i.e., with oil), and the Eucharist; then turning to Cyril of Alexandria, likewise linking it to the Eucharist; then discussing Theodore

25. Fiedrowicz, "General Introduction," 13–66, here 45.
26. On the Psalms in particular see Byassee, *Praise Seeking Understanding*, which opens with a review of what he calls the "return to allegory" movement (9–53). He does not discuss Ps. 23. See also his *Psalms 101–150*.
27. Waltke and Houston, *Psalms as Christian Worship*, 416–33.

of Cyrrhus, finding it a prophetic pronouncement of Israel's renewal; and going on to medieval, scholastic, and Reformation readings.[28] Their account reads Calvin as a kind of climactic summation of the tradition, revealing in the process that the Reformation pullback to reading the Psalms with reference to their human authors (though not exclusively) is their own preferred approach. Calvin's Psalms commentary is, they say, "perhaps the most remarkable ever composed," not least because his "long, central preoccupation" concerns reading David and other psalmists as "the exemplars of proper prayer, and of the issues and struggles of the Christian life."[29]

I am intrigued that amid all the renewed interest in the history of interpretation of the Psalms, little attention is paid to Erasmus's exposition, mentioned above, which is the longest I have found on Psalm 23. Perhaps this is because he does not fit neatly into any particular narrative of the development of interpretation, such as that discerned in Waltke and Houston's book.[30] I therefore conclude this section by offering the briefest of summaries of Erasmus's exposition.

The standout feature of Erasmus's reading is his eschewing of Psalm 23's literal sense and his deliberate move to offer three readings (a "triple exposition") of its allegorical sense (twice) and its tropological sense. He even acknowledges, "I know that it is rather awkward to refer this present psalm to Christ, in a way that abandons the physical sense, but nevertheless, with the Lord's favour, I shall attempt it."[31] In particular, his threefold reading of the psalm harks back to earlier models: as the voice of Christ, the voice of the church, and as the voice of the individual. The first reading is brief, running through the

---

28. Waltke and Houston, *Psalms as Christian Worship*. My summary includes some wording taken from their review of early Christian fathers (416–17). Source material for the fathers may also conveniently be found in Blaising and Hardin, *Psalms 1–50*, 177–83.

29. Waltke and Houston, *Psalms as Christian Worship*, 431.

30. They do discuss his readings of Pss. 1–4, found in his *Collected Works* vol. 63, and they like his reading of Ps. 3 but dismiss his reading of Ps. 4 in revealing terms as failing to "understand the Reformers' doctrine of justification *sola gratia*." Waltke and Houston, *Psalms as Christian Worship*, 219 (cf. 190–92 on Ps. 3).

31. Erasmus, "Threefold Exposition of Psalm 22," 127.

psalm as Christ's own words addressed to the Father. This reading understands the incarnation and redemption according to an outline of the Lord's leading in the words of the psalm: through death, via a triumphal feast, and to the eternal dwelling with the Father.[32] The second and much longer reading follows Augustine's lead of having the church speaking to Christ; Erasmus follows at length the details of the text as they pertain to the church being shepherded by Christ the Good Shepherd.[33] The third ("tropological") reading sees in the psalm the journey of the individual, led to salvation by recognizing one's status as a sheep, guided to the pastures of the church, and then fortified even to and beyond martyrdom—through the valley of the shadow of death—before finishing in God's presence.[34]

Some aspects of Erasmus's final reading feel rather like what might pass for contemporary spiritual reflection on the psalm today. The overall attention to textual detail is clear, although not in fact based on reading the Hebrew. The concern is to build upon the *assumption* that Psalm 23 is about Christ and the church and then let the details of the text shape the resultant convictions. Erasmus wrote his exposition in 1529–30. I do not wish to suggest that everything in his approach is a model to follow—indeed his own approach is not systematic enough to serve as a model anyway.[35] But in some respects, what follows in my present chapter is an attempt to work in a comparable manner with the living voice of Psalm 23 nearly five hundred years later. We turn therefore to four reflections on Psalm 23 in the life of the church today.

Restoration: Psalm 23 Confronts the Stresses of Life

Psalm 23 was not written to engage our modern concept of stress, obviously. But its opening section, especially verses 2–3, may serve as

---

32. Erasmus, "Threefold Exposition of Psalm 22," 128–31.
33. Erasmus, "Threefold Exposition of Psalm 22," 131–71.
34. Erasmus, "Threefold Exposition of Psalm 22," 171–99.
35. See further Heath, "Erasmus and the Psalms," 28–44: "Erasmus' exegetical method is informal and flexible, as the variety of his titles suggests" (32).

a powerful resource for considering life in ways that might helpfully address stress.[36] The logic of these verses is comparable to that of the Sabbath in that both seek to describe a bigger picture of life in all its fullness that helps to gain a wise and proper perspective on the work to be done or the trials to be endured. Even in the face of hardship—and in the exodus traditions, in the face of actual slavery—Israel is called to recognize the world as God's creation, with the result that one day in seven is to be set aside as holy, and no work is to be done. The countercultural appeal of such a claim has become increasingly clear in modern industrialized societies in the twentieth and twenty-first centuries, and theological responses have drawn well on Sabbath traditions in the Old Testament to make this point.[37]

Sabbath rest in the Old Testament is not fundamentally about self-denial and restraint. It is about celebrating instead the presence of God rather than the presence of work, other demands, or other people. More pointedly, it is celebrating the presence of God even while in the presence of enemies, of whatever sort. Of course, arguments about the observance of the Sabbath devolved over time into adjudication of what was and was not allowed: both in ancient Israel, as we find the arguments developed in the Mishnah and other traditions, and in the modern world, with churches making their demands of abstention on Sundays when the Sunday was consciously modeled on Sabbath ideas. I would like to suggest that Psalm 23 allows us to avoid such difficulties, partly because it is not a legal text and therefore operates in a different rhetorical style, and partly because of its generous focus on God's provision as the key to rest.

Recall that verse 1 of our psalm anchors its conviction about lacking nothing in the shepherd-provision of YHWH. YHWH looks out for us with generous care and attention. The name of YHWH is to be honored and further recognized via the fourfold recital of all that

36. The modern concept of stress is usually traced to the work of Hungarian-born medical scientist Selye, who first published *Stress of Life* in 1956.
37. See, e.g., Brueggemann, *Sabbath as Resistance* and Scarlata, *Sabbath Rest*. The Jewish classic that stands behind recent appeals is Heschel, *Sabbath*.

YHWH does and has done for me (vv. 2–3). He lets me lie down, leads me by quiet waters, restores my life, and leads me in the right direction. As I emphasized in chapter 3, what leading there is here is not primarily concerned with movement but with direction or oversight; it is focused on the opportunity to stop, rest, and be restored in body, mind, and spirit (which were all captured by the single Hebrew word *nepeš*).

First, notice the framing of this rest. It follows from the recognition of YHWH in verse 1 and precedes the switch in focus to the shadow of death in verse 4. It is surrounded by recognition of greater powers, in other words, and it recognizes its fourfold celebration of restoration as being all "for his name's sake" (v. 3). Obvious though it may be to say it, we do not obtain rest from weariness by focusing on rest. Restoration of the soul (the life, *nepeš*) is not achieved by focusing on restoring the soul. Rather, these are among the benefits that follow from focusing on God. Of course, this point would rightly be made from the Ten Commandments too, where the gift of Sabbath follows after the opening recognition that "I am the LORD your God" (Exod. 20:2 // Deut. 5:6).

Secondly, the poetic sweep of Psalm 23 operates in the manner of stopping to enjoy the sensory delights of God's provision: the green pastures and the quiet waters in particular. What is emphasized in the rest is precisely the opposite of absence: "I will not lack" (v. 1). Hence rest has been grasped as fullness and provision rather than abstention or denial. I have found helpful David Ford's way of articulating this in his extended meditation *The Shape of Living*.[38] Recognizing that modern life in particular is overwhelming in multiple ways, Ford reconceptualizes life as subject to a range of "overwhelmings," whether positive (joy; some kinds of desire) or negative (suffering; other kinds of desire). He then invites readers to cultivate and receive the positive overwhelmings, partly by rooting them in recognition of the presence and activity of God. This, he avers, is "the secret of the Psalms,"

38. Ford, *Shape of Living*.

which "have drawn generation after generation into the great over-whelmings" by God and by a huge range of experiences, emotions, and desires.[39] Psalm 23 does not feature in his book. But if it did, it would doubtless be by way of allowing us to let the life-restoring rest of verses 2–3 overwhelm us with the goodness of God's provision.

Thirdly, we return to the opening response to YHWH being my shepherd: "I will not lack." We discussed in chapter 3 the various ways in which this does and does not translate to provision: not provision of my every desire but rather the training of my desire to recognize YHWH as the one who provides for me. Unequivocally we must say that this is not something that works out straightforwardly in this life. The Psalms remain one of the strongest testimonies to that complex reality: think of Psalm 73's "as for me, my feet had almost stumbled. . . . For I was envious of the arrogant; I saw the prosperity of the wicked" (73:2–3). Satisfied statements of provision in the Psalms are to be read not as naive aspirations that all shall be well if we ignore enough evidence to the contrary. Rather they are images of the good life that we do experience in the present but only along-side equally real struggle and suffering. The very (lack of) thematic progression in the Psalter's jumbling of psalms of lament and praise is in part testimony to this point. While there are some discernible movements of theme and mood in the Psalter, as we saw in chapter 2, this does not overrule the obvious point that one can move from a psalm of longing to a psalm of rejoicing (and back) over and over again in the book of Psalms.

Consider then what might make for a wise response to any par-ticular psalm that affirms goodness in some more or less untroubled way. One can either criticize such a psalm for its apparent naivety—a criticism often accompanied by a confident claim that "we know better"—or one can entertain the possibility that the psalmist knew, too, that life is not as simple as a straightforward positive affirmation

39. Ford, *Shape of Living*, 40. Later editions have different page numbers. This is a section of chap. 2 entitled "Worship as the Shaping of Desire."

can make it sound, but had reasons for the positive affirmation anyway. Although writing about Proverbs rather than Psalms and thus addressing poetry about the moral life rather than more generally, Robert Alter makes this point with wisdom and precision: such positive claims are "very neat, but, we may ask, is that the way the world is? Obviously not—obvious, I think, not only to us but also to the poet . . . [who gives us] an underlying principle of moral causation that he believes to be present in reality but that he knows would never be so perspicuous in the untidiness of experience outside literature."[40] Part of the function of this sacred literature is precisely to point to the underlying reality, in full knowledge that it is not self-evident in daily experience. After all, if it were self-evident, why would anyone write a poem about it in the first place? In short, the psalmist is fully aware of what a counterintuitive claim he makes when he says, "I will not lack." It is *because* life is difficult, and so easily characterized by lack, that the psalmist makes this affirmation up front. Part of its purpose for us as readers is to cultivate the same reordering of perspectives and desires so that on many daily matters we too might understand our lives in terms of satisfaction rather than lack.

I have known Christian traditions that struggle to enjoy the affective and aesthetic dimensions of God's good gifts. They might rush past the greenness of the fields or the quietness of the waters, looking for theological depths of other kinds, unimpressed by the beauty of God's pastoral elegance. Psalm 23 *can* be used to reflect on death and resurrection and so forth, and I will do that in a moment. But Psalm 23 also invites us to a slowing of the pace of life and to a rest that might even get as far as stopping completely, laying down, and knowing that life will move on—even toward enemies and death (it will do so within this very psalm, no less)—but also rejoicing in the restoration that Yhwh the shepherd offers.

In light of this, we need to be clear that the enjoyment of God's good gifts is not the same as the sentimentalization of natural beauty

40. Alter, *Art of Biblical Poetry*, 169.

or pleasant experiences as self-sufficient good things, as ends in them-selves. The psalm does *not* end with "I will dwell in a lovely café at the end of the day." It is not sponsored by a local walking group. It is not even implicitly arguing that rural life is better than urban life—that is simply a conversation far from its own horizons. The psalm is not misty eyed about a life with no challenges, nor is it suggesting that we ignore the ones we do have. To appreciate this section on rest and restoration with full force, we need to consider alongside it the psalm's stance on death and our enemies. It is the whole picture that is lifegiving, not one extracted part of it.

I will talk directly of enemies below. But prompted by the observa-tion that God slows down the pilgrims of Psalm 23 and leads them to rest and to lying down, I offer one final thought on the issue of rest and stress. We discussed in the exegesis in chapter 3 that the traditional English translation "he makes me lie down" gives the image of God *insisting* that I stop, when the point of the verse is closer to saying that God offers or facilitates my stopping. Nevertheless, in reflecting more broadly on stress in life and the rhythms of grace that God seeks to have us inhabit, is it worth asking whether God may at times precisely *insist* that we stop? Might God sometimes bring us to unsought rest, slowing us to a moment of progress-free "dwelling," knowing that this is what we will need before the trials of life's darker moments to come? Could such dwelling in God's presence in these moments of interrup-tion in life even be understood as anticipating the final dwelling "in the house of the LORD" that Psalm 23 offers as our longer-term prospect?

Resurrection: Psalm 23 Confronts the Challenge of Death

In the exegesis in chapter 3 I argued that verse 4 can be rightly heard to say, "even though I walk through the valley of the shadow of death," de-spite frequent examples of modern translations that speak of a "dark-est valley." I also said that an appropriate understanding of death in the Old Testament allows us to recognize that death is seen as a force at work in this life too, so that the ill and suffering can be understood to be in the shadow of death. This understanding is especially prevalent in poetic texts that imagine death as the enemy, a force set against the force of life found in YHWH. I drew this understanding in particular from the work of Jon Levenson, whose core argument is that God in Jewish Scripture and faith is a God of life, so that any theology that takes this God seriously will not be able to allow death to have a final word.[41] Resurrection, he points out, is a key tenet of Rabbinic Judaism, and so it must in a sense be found in the Torah, mainly as an underlying assumption that makes sense of its promises. Passages like Ezekiel 37's resurrection of the army in the valley of dry bones, or the mention of resurrection in Daniel 12:2–3, are not late turns to a new understanding that gets allied either to Persian influence or to later Greco-Roman conceptions of immortality, relegating resurrection to a byproduct of thinking, "There must be more than this." On the contrary, such passages represent the conscious articulation of the conviction that YHWH triumphs over death by virtue of being the God of life.[42] In my judgment, Levenson's book more or less single-handedly overturns a general, older consensus among many Old Testament scholars that resurrection did not really loom that large on the horizon, a conviction that then allowed some New Testament readers to form the opinion that Jesus's resurrection is in a whole new category of its own, as if it were an unanticipated twist in the tale. In contrast, Levenson's approach shows that resurrection as a category was already fully available for the New Testament writers long before Jesus.[43]

The argument that death is at work as a power in this life, and is not solely to be understood as physical/medical death, has benefits

41. See Levenson, *Resurrection and the Restoration of Israel*. The two parts of this title ("resurrection" and "restoration of Israel") are two sides of the same coin according to Levenson, so all Jewish hope of restoration assumes and implies a commitment to resurrection.

42. On the Torah, Ezek. 37, and Dan. 12, see 23–34, 156–65, and 181–200 respectively in Levenson, *Resurrection and the Restoration of Israel*.

43. The Jewish-Christian aspects of Levenson's thesis are helpfully drawn out in Madigan and Levenson, *Resurrection*.

in the life of the church beyond the assessment of Hebrew poetry. It offers pastoral insight and blessing for the tasks of visiting and tending to the sick and elderly. It explains the experience many will have had of sitting with a dying person and recognizing that one is already in the presence of death; or of nursing someone through a long illness in which it seems appropriate to say that the battle with death is already raging. The modern clinical model of death has its obvious benefits: precision (up to a point), clarity (to a degree), and resolution of questions of liability (within limits). Despite the ever-present gray areas, these really are benefits. But there are also signs that the clinical model of death is starting to be rethought among medical and caring professionals under the strain of its inadequacy to present needs.[44]

In the twenty-first century Psalm 23 is a mainstay of funeral liturgy for churches that use set liturgy. Given that funerals often bring out more formal approaches to services, even in churches that generally eschew written liturgy, it is likely that Psalm 23 is also used regularly for funerals in churches that do not normally make use of formal liturgy. The continued popularity of sung versions of the psalm in contemporary musical idiom for worship also indicates the continued widespread appeal of its imagery. But how did Psalm 23 become such a standard for funeral ministry?

Here the fascinating study of William Holladay, appended to his book on the history of interpretation of the Psalms, makes a striking suggestion. He entitles his study "How the Twenty-Third Psalm Became an American Secular Icon."[45] The headline finding of this wonderful piece of historical detective work is that Psalm 23 was rarely, if ever, used in connection with death prior to the American Civil War. But by 1880 it was becoming commonly so used, and by the end of the nineteenth century, such use had become massively widespread. Three cultural and ecclesial shifts in this period suggest to Holladay that

44. For a thoughtful probing of these matters written by a doctor, see Gawande, *Being Mortal*.
45. Holladay, *Psalms through Three Thousand Years*, 359–71.

the psalm found fertile ground at this time: a move toward individual piety (whether evangelical or liberal); a move toward sentimentality in religious language, partly rooted in women's experiences including loss of loved ones in the war; and the rise of civil religion.[46] These shifts, combined with one or two very high-profile appeals to Psalm 23 that would have highlighted it for many ministers, help explain the sudden turn to the psalm in end-of-life contexts.[47] In light of this, the key characterization of Psalm 23 that Holladay makes is as follows: "It is short and therefore easily memorized. It is undemanding. It does not mention sin or suggest the appropriateness of participating in any ecclesial community. It simply seems to affirm that God (or, alternatively, Jesus) accompanies the speaker and takes care of him or her. . . . It is a psalm that could be used in public contexts, acceptable to both Jews and Christians and giving no offense to anyone."[48] I am no expert on late nineteenth-century American religious and cultural life, but Holladay seems to have made a strong case for locating the rise of this "secular icon" as a biblical text used almost as a badge of good citizenship in the face of death, rather than as a Jewish or Christian affirmation.

What I can add is that this fairly accurately characterizes the use of Psalm 23 in funeral ministry in my own experience in the Church of England. Although I write at a time when cultural standards are in turmoil in public life—indeed, who knows what the status of Christian funeral services may be before too long—it is certainly true that Psalm 23 works well in a context where grieving people want an acknowledgement of loss wrapped up in a low-key affirmation of hope. On a surface level Psalm 23 provides this admirably. One typically mixed blessing of civic religion—which is still officially alive and well in the UK even if it struggles in practice, and perhaps has been officially dispensed with in the US even if it flourishes in practice—is

46. Holladay, *Psalms through Three Thousand Years*, 365–69.
47. In particular Holladay mentions a widely influential piece on Ps. 23 by Henry Ward Beecher dating to 1856–58 (*Psalms through Three Thousand Years*, 362–64).
48. Holladay, *Psalms through Three Thousand Years*, 364.

that "the valley of the shadow of death" is now taken to represent a universal human experience rather than an aspect of the world to be negotiated under the shepherding oversight of YHWH. The blessings of civic religion are not to be despised, and there is much to treasure about the opportunity it affords to let those without faith engage in public—at funerals, for example—with a God who seems distant to them. Nevertheless, what might Psalm 23 say in the face of death to those whose pilgrimage is consciously under the oversight of God their shepherd?

The psalmist entertains the reflection on the shadow of death barely one line after celebrating the riches of peace and restoration in verses 2–3. Death is always potentially one step away. This was of course well known traditionally and then was obscured in the modern era by people's increasing ability to control their lives with respect to health and security. In the twenty-first century the unpredictability of life seems to be returning once more, amid increasing violence or disaster in various forms, whether international, national, or local, and this is loudly lamented by cultural commentators, often with good reason. But it should not obscure the more traditional under-lying truth that the good gift of life is precisely a gift, and that even if it is to be understood as a right in some sense, it is not an easily securable right.

How is one to respond to the potential ever-presence of death? "Without fear" would be the immediate response of the psalm. God's presence ("for you are with me") outweighs the shadow of death. The threat of death may be overwhelming, but the psalm's response is not to attempt to withdraw to a place where there is no overwhelming (to borrow that language once more). Such a place would reflect a very modern concept of peace, which is all about absence—the attempt to keep life's passions at arm's length. Psalm 23 knows better. The response to the overwhelming of death is the greater overwhelming of God's presence. The result can be a peace that embraces life's pas-sions rather than denying them. This is at the heart of what the Old

Testament idea of peace ("shalom," *šālôm*) is about: a rest rooted in the fullness of God's presence rather than the absence of troubles.

A second response is to allow the reality of death's presence. "I fear no evil, for you are with me" does not mean that I am invited to have confidence that I will not die (for the moment at least). Far from it. The open-ended poetry of Psalm 23 allows two equally affirming readings of its final two verses with respect to death. It may be that I am confidently accompanied through the valley of the shadow of death by God my shepherd—delivered from death's snares to resume my healthy pilgrimage through this life. In which case the meal that is provided in verse 5 and the longing to praise God in the presence of God and God's people (in the temple or whenever gathered for worship) is to be eagerly anticipated in this life. Or it may be that my life comes to an end, which I also need not fear, since God is with me. In this case the meal of verse 5 sounds more like the heavenly banquet, albeit with the reference to "enemies" perhaps referring to those who will have been left behind upon arriving at God's kingdom meal. On this view verse 6 suggests that I will truly dwell in God's house forevermore, in the life of the world to come (or arguably that I will return home to God). Each of these readings imagines a specificity of the meal and the dwelling (or returning) that the psalm does not determine one way or the other. In any case, God's goodness and mercy pursue me always; part of the point of verse 6 is that their pursuit of me is sure, irrespective of any particular outcome of my walking through the valley of the shadow of death.

I offer two other brief reflections on Psalm 23's comfort in the face of death. Recall the precise wording of verse 4: *lō'-'îrā' rā'*, which I translated "I will not fear evil." Our smoothed English translation shifts the negation to the evil rather than the fear—that is, "I will fear no evil" rather than "I will not fear evil." The slight nuance lost in such a move is the implied contrast between fearing evil (which I will not do) and whatever the alternatives are that we might fear instead (which I will do). Anyone reading the Psalms and reading wider in the Old Testament will know that one implied alternative is that I will instead embrace "the fear of the LORD."[49] In other words, I wonder if Psalm 23:4 invites readers to recognize that fearing evil is the life-denying opposite of fearing the LORD. This really requires us to remember that the core issue in "fearing" here is only inadequately captured in our modern English word. The modern mind is more likely to link experiences of fear and being afraid with terror or being scared—in this case perhaps scared of God and frightened of the consequences of wrongdoing that will incur God's anger. By contrast, fearing the LORD in the Old Testament is fundamentally about honoring YHWH and letting YHWH set the proper agenda for life (and be the one who determines the consequences). In short, I will not fear evil because YHWH is my shepherd—that is, I will fear YHWH instead. The "consequences" include being pursued by goodness and mercy. Fear is not the key issue. The object of the fear makes all the difference.[50]

Secondly, the core issue in not fearing death is not about focusing on death and not fearing it, in the same way as the issue with rest is not to focus on rest. Verse 4 is found amid the emphases on rest and the meal of verse 5, and this is part of how the psalm locates experiences of the valley of the shadow of death. Death is potentially ever present but not the focus. In practice it seems to me that it is the cultivation of thankfulness for God's good gifts that allows us the resilience to face death appropriately. God's guidance through our lives, symbolized in the rod and staff of verse 4 as well as the provision of the surrounding verses, includes accompaniment through the presence of death. One extraordinary ministerial privilege in which I have shared is sitting with the dying who are able to say, "I have had a good life, and I am not afraid of death." Thankfulness helps to create and to constitute the character to receive God's comfort at the moments of confronting death—our own or the death of those

49. In the Psalms, see Pss. 19:9; 34:11; 111:10. Of the many references in Proverbs note especially and programmatically 1:7 and 9:10; see also Job 28:28.

50. For a thoughtful approach to "the fear of the LORD," see the reading offered by Moberly, *Old Testament Theology*, 245 in the context of 243–77.

we love. The confident affirmation of verse 6 is relevant here too: goodness and mercy will surely pursue me "all the days of my life." In particular they will pursue me up to and including the last days of my life. Verse 6 expresses this as a forward-looking hope. From the perspective of imminent death, could it be appropriate to return the hope as thanksgiving? Such retrospective review allows one to acclaim: goodness and mercy *have* pursued me to the very end. Not, to reiterate, because there was no trouble or distress (or bluntly, evil) in life, but because it was also and always true that God's goodness and mercy pursued me. In life, as in Psalm 23, thanksgiving may have the final word.

In all these ways, Psalm 23 can be a word of supreme comfort for the dying and the bereaved. Holladay's study suggests what a broader perspective on the canon would also indicate; namely, Psalm 23 is never going to be the only or all-sufficient response to death. Holladay pointed to the psalm's light touch regarding some of the other elements of Judeo-Christian understanding: the nature of sin, for example, or the corporate implications for life and death. It would be strange (and unnecessary) to suggest that Psalm 23 can be the sole resource for a good response to all these issues. But as in the Old Testament, so in the life of the church today, Psalm 23 bears witness to the core claim that death does not have the final word.

Protection: Psalm 23 Confronts the Reality of Enemies

In verse 5 God sets a table in the presence of my enemies. I sometimes want to say in response, "Call me ungrateful, but I might rather have enjoyed a meal anywhere else." In the exegesis in chapter 3 I said that the assumed reasoning here is that there are no other options: there are always enemies, and while one need not (and does not) talk about them all the time, it can always be appropriate to remember that enemies are at hand. We should recall also the point that "enemies" are underdefined in the psalm, and indeed in the Old

Testament in general. They include foreign foes, but also any threats to life including those posed by the wicked, pursuers, or even wild animals, and including threats of death, illness, and disaster. In short, one's enemies are anyone or anything that poses a threat of some sort. This is yet one more issue for which the underdefined nature of any original reference to historic enemies serves the useful function of freeing us up as readers today to reapply the label to a range of potential candidates in our own experience. In some ways, the preceding discussion of death is one specific example of pondering the psalm's engagement with enemies.

In this section, I want to broaden the focus to look at the contribution that Psalm 23 makes to the lives we lead in our contested and antagonistic world. In my view, this is one of the most important contributions the psalm can make to the life of the church today. Perhaps surprisingly, that the meal of verse 5 is "in the presence of my enemies" often seems to be passed over with relatively little reflection on what that says about the nature of the world in which we live. Furthermore, those who do stop and consider the theme are not always positive about the psalm's point here.

One of the few discussions of this overall issue that I have found is offered in a tone of some frustration by Erich Zenger: "And who is not disappointed that the intimate Psalm 23 . . . evidently can only project its vision of a mystical communion with God in terms of the pride of victory over a hostile world, and in the knowledge of the fear-inspiring rod that lurks in the background."[51] Admittedly the tone of this quote may be due to its rhetorical function in Zenger's book. He is at the point of soliciting initial evidence of the Psalms' propensity for violent language, and this is the opening move in a book that will in due course go on to offer an eloquent defense of the Psalms' language as testimony to life-giving divine judgment. The overall case is well made, although obviously not indisputable. But

---

51. Zenger, *God of Vengeance?*, 10–11. He cites Ps. 23:4–5 at this point, before moving straight on to other texts.

in the process Psalm 23 is made to serve rather unhelpfully as a foil to the bigger argument.

I think Zenger assumes that his expressed frustration with Psalm 23 would be widely shared and that the psalm's claim is somewhat regrettable. To which one might say that twenty-first-century developments in our world make it look *more* like a hostile world than less so. Further, since the "pride" and "fear" that he mentions are by no means self-evident in the text, I find that my overall response to Zenger's question "Who is not disappointed?" is "Me! I am not disappointed." In fact, surely this is one of the psalm's key points: the world is full of enemies, in a general sense, and we need not (and perhaps should not) exert ourselves in defining or identifying them. Rather we should accept this picture of the world and sit and eat at the table prepared for us by our LORD, the Shepherd. Otherwise what on earth is God doing setting the meal in the presence of my enemies in the first place?

One particular and influential popular account of how to handle the issues of enemies (along with judgment and cursing) in the Psalms is C. S. Lewis's discussion in his little book *Reflections on the Psalms*.[52] He even chooses to begin the book by talking about judgment and cursing because he wants to get the hardest issues out of the way first. On close inspection it turns out that his (first) treatment of enemies in the Psalms in his book is not unlike Zenger's. In fact, overall, Lewis's *Reflections on the Psalms* offers a strange mixture of possibly incompatible interpretive approaches to Israel's poetry. It combines a quite startling range of material—from profound insight right through to somewhat problematic comparison between Jewish and Christian spiritualities in which certain types of psalms come off rather badly.[53] When Lewis gets going toward the end of

---

52. Lewis, *Reflections on the Psalms*.

53. The wider question of the divergences between Lewis's interesting handling of Scripture and his critically accomplished and interpretively acute scholarly work on English medieval and renaissance texts must be left for another day. It is true that the first sentence of his Psalms book is "This is not a work of scholarship" (followed

the book on "second meanings," derived from his awareness of how other great texts work and specifically allied to some reflections on the status of Scripture, it leads to a final chapter ("Second Meanings in the Psalms") that offers a second and altogether more successful argument about enemies. There he gives a powerful defense of allegorical reading regarding cursing and imprecation in the Psalms. In my judgment this is largely successful, though it is sometimes appropriated by readers as if it were the same as the first argument, when clearly it is not.

In the early chapters of the book, he tries to confront issues about judgment and cursing in the Psalms head-on and in the process develops an uncomfortably strong contrast between Christian thinking and what he sees as problematic Jewish thinking. For much of the opening three chapters, he effectively mines the Psalms for insights that can be shown to develop and deepen various New Testament and Christian themes. This is not in itself a problem unless and until it is allied to a corresponding negative thesis, that on occasion the Psalms fall short of such insights and then should be evaluated negatively. Sadly that negative thesis is fairly clear: references to "that typical Jewish prison of self-righteousness" and to the Psalms' cursings as "indeed devilish" highlight the difficulty.[54]

When we come to Psalm 23, we reach one of those moments where Lewis's analysis reveals more about a certain kind of twentieth-century British propriety than about the world of the scriptural text. Perhaps oddly, Lewis cites Psalm 23 from Moffatt's translation, in which verse 5 reads that the host "spreads a feast for me while my enemies have to look on." Possibly misled by this, Lewis comments: "The poet's enjoyment of his present prosperity [i.e., in v. 5's meal] would not be complete unless those horrid Joneses (who used to look

---

immediately by "I am no Hebraist"). A deeply unimpressed Jewish reader of the book suggests that it may reflect the zeal of Lewis's wife, Joy Davidman, at the time of writing, and her earlier conversion from Judaism to Christianity. See Rosenbaum, "Our Own Silly Faces," 486–89.

54. Lewis, *Reflections on the Psalms*, 15, 22.

down their noses at him) were watching it all and hating it." This may not be as "diabolical" as other psalms, says Lewis, but "the pettiness and vulgarity of it . . . are hard to endure."[55]

It is hard to avoid the conclusion that Psalm 23 is completely out of focus here, partly because of the specific translation to which Lewis appeals, but more likely because the framework operative at this stage in the book effectively rejects the Psalms' vision of an inevitable conflict between God's goodness and the intentions of one's "enemies."[56] Lewis understands mythological language very well, better probably than most commentators on the Psalms, and he is willing to face the difficulties of the text(s) when they engage violently with enemies. But at heart he thinks that we should move beyond the language of enemies, albeit perhaps drawing some comfort from the incidental psychological benefits of this language.[57]

In contrast, I think the tenor of Psalm 23:5 is worth taking straightforwardly and seriously, as a constructive model for how to understand whoever and whatever we call enemies in our daily lives. First, it is worth emphasizing the brevity of the mention of enemies. Although I have dwelt here on Zenger and Lewis's lengthy discussions of the issue, it is indeed a passing reference in verse 5. But as with the presence of death and its shadows in verse 4, what the passing reference does is acknowledge the reality of enemies while focusing attention elsewhere. The focus in verse 5 is on the host and gracious provision—specifically the oil and the overflowing cup. What might twenty-first-century life learn from letting the reality of enemies be left as a passing mention? The tone of public and private life would be very different indeed.

55. Lewis, *Reflections on the Psalms*, 18.

56. It is not that Lewis does not see that "the ferocious parts of the Psalms serve as a reminder that there is in the world such a thing as wickedness" (*Reflections on the Psalms*, 28) but rather that he thinks of this as a defensive move *in extremis* to rescue problematic texts.

57. Lewis, *Reflections on the Psalms*, 24–28. This last emphasis is independently taken up in the work of Walter Brueggemann on the Psalms, which is noted below. See various passing comments in *Message of the Psalms* and also "Costly Loss of Lament," 57–71. In my view, it is a useful practical point but not one that gets at the heart of the Psalms in question in their role as Scripture.

Secondly, the encouragement in the presence of enemies needs to be affirmed alongside the recognition that life experience very obviously works out differently for different people. It has long seemed to me that the dynamic at work here is the one encapsulated by the apostle Paul in his remarkable word in the letter to the Romans: "Rejoice with those who rejoice, weep with those who weep" (Rom. 12:15). In the context of Romans's attempt to bring about a mutual participation in one another's lives of Christ-centered faith (strong and weak; Jew and gentile), Paul juxtaposes these probing words of pastoral insight: one is to respond with joy to those who rejoice and with compassion to those who weep. Sometimes, as ministers will attest, one is called to do both at the same time. A verse like Psalm 23:5 can cut both ways. The table is set in the presence of my enemies. Will this be experienced as joy? Or will it be experienced as difficulty—a hard blessing to be wrestled with? Clearly the life contexts in which the verse is taken to heart can range from the celebratory to the troubled. The verse does not indicate that there will therefore be no hurt or trouble. But the opportunity for comfort is there, whether a comfort of exultant celebration, a comfort of tender consolation, or one of many forms of comfort somewhere between these two.

Thirdly, Christian reading of Psalm 23 will find here an irresistible invitation to understand the Eucharist as one particular and supreme exemplar of the provision imagined in verse 5. This is obviously not a point about original intention, but is rather more like Lewis's "Second Meaning": to take bread and wine at the celebration of the Eucharist is to experience the same reality that the psalmist is talking about in verse 5. The early church, as we have seen, saw this clearly. Modern concerns with the way that the early church may have expressed the point in relation to the text of Psalm 23 should not obscure the point itself.[58]

The average worshiper in church is indeed living a life surrounded by enemies of various sorts—as wide ranging and undefined as they

58. This is well handled by Charry, *Psalms 1–50*, 119–20.

were originally in the Psalms. Likewise, worshipers in church will be at a range of points on a spectrum from rejoicing to weeping. In any gathering of believers of any size, there will surely be the full range. As we explored in our exegesis of the passage, the note of overflowing joy in the setting of the table, in the anointing with oil, and in the cup overflowing finds full expression in the eucharistic worship of the church. The action of taking the bread and sharing the cup may be undertaken wordlessly by any particular worshiper (traditions vary), but in some ways that allows the emphasis to fall entirely on the overflowing hospitality that welcomes the worshiper to the table. While one may indeed walk out of the church service back into a world where enemies loom large, the image of the psalm reminds us that in taking the bread and the wine, the believer has been brought to dwell in God's presence.[59]

Perhaps it might even be fitting to use verse 6's affirmations as part of a postcommunion prayer that expresses a longing to be shepherded back by God's goodness and mercy to dwell and/or return to the LORD's house to worship again, and ultimately forever. Note how the language of dwelling and of returning both make perfect sense here. The reality of communion with God that is indicated in the meal in verse 5 is to overwhelm the reality of the presence of enemies. Those who worship in the life of the church experience that positive overwhelming in part, especially in and through the Eucharist, and they anticipate it in full in the house of the LORD forever.

Worship: Psalm 23 Gives Voice to Hope

This last reflection has brought us already to consider Psalm 23's contribution to the worshiping life of the church. To begin at the most basic level: it may be read; it may be sung; it may be prayed; it

---

59. This would be understood in various ways in different traditions but would be true for all but the most memorialist understandings of "the Lord's Supper." I have no stake in labeling the celebration as "the Eucharist," but decided to use one consistent label for simplicity.

may be preached. The preaching of Psalms is a much-neglected opportunity in some parts of the church, and in the final chapter I will offer some personal reflections on the preaching of Psalm 23, mindful of McCann's pointed emphasis that the Psalms were intended to function as torah (instruction) and therefore to teach, alongside all the other things they do.[60]

More expansively, I offer three considerations of Psalm 23's functions in the life of worship, drawing briefly on three rather wide-ranging traditions and scholarly discussions of the Psalms. I consider Psalm 23's contribution to our hope in dialogue with eschatology in the Psalms, with Walter Brueggemann's work on disorientation and reorientation in the Psalms, and with the use of the Psalms as a key element of what is often called "Celtic spirituality."

The first emphasis—that Psalm 23 has often been read eschatologically—draws together some elements noted throughout our study. By this is meant that the psalm looks ahead to "the end," anticipating a world that is yet to be—more specifically God's world as it will be.[61] It is sometimes suggested that the whole Psalter has an eschatological perspective: this has been a major (though contested) emphasis of recent scholarship. On some level it is clearly true. The specific debate centers on whether that eschatological hope looks for a restoration of the Davidic kingship or alternatively focuses on YHWH as king (with any human Davidic king as either irrelevant or incidental to the overall point).[62] The general point, however, is clear. In Childs's

60. See McCann, *Theological Introduction to the Book of Psalms.*
61. Karl Barth offers a one-page "eschatological" reading of Ps. 23 along these lines, full of joyous Barthian overstatement. ("Ps. 23 is a summary of the whole Psalter. . . . It is the self-documentation *in nuce* of the existence of the sinner justified by the gracious God.") See Barth, *Church Dogmatics* IV/1, 608. By contrast, Alter's Jewish perspective settles for the following: "The poem is in and of the here and now and is in no way eschatological." Alter, *Hebrew Bible,* 3:71.
62. Wilson's influential *Editing of the Hebrew Psalter* argues that the future perspective of the Psalter focused on YHWH's kingship, not on any hope for the restoration of Davidic kingship, interestingly taking a different view from Childs, under whom the thesis was originally written. A helpful untangling of the issues is Mitchell, "Lord, Remember David," 526–48.

words, "However one explains it, the final form of the Psalter is highly eschatological in nature. It looks forward to the future and passionately yearns for its arrival."[63] Since Psalm 23 opens with the acclamation that Yhwh is my shepherd (which we have noted suggests "shepherd-king"), one can see how Psalm 23 might get caught up in this discussion, tending toward a messianic hope for Yhwh to be king, rather than David. In practice, discussions of this issue seem to focus on Psalm 23 mainly with regard to whether its LXX translation leans toward an eschatological perspective, which seems to me to add only the lightest of emphases, if any at all.[64]

It is the general point that matters. As we noted in our discussion of death, Psalm 23 invites two merged readings regarding the hope of the final verse: on the one hand, the hope to return one day in the future to the particular experience of worship in the temple or to dwell in the temple in some undefined way; and on the other hand, the hope to enter into God's eternal rest beyond death and to dwell in the midst of praise and worship. We saw this aspect emphasized in Revelation 7:17 earlier in this chapter.

In his illuminating work on the destiny of the righteous in the Psalms, Jerome Creach makes a point that may assist us here. He shows that righteousness is not fundamentally a moral term in the Psalter, but "is essentially a relational term . . . [identifying] righteousness mainly as an aspect of God's character in which humans may participate."[65] As he goes on to say, "The main sign that the righteous are in right relationship to God is that they recognize that God is in control of the world, that 'the Lord reigns.'"[66] This points us to how worship allows the articulation of the core issue of Yhwh being Lord and thereby allows us to enter (already) into

63. Childs, *Introduction to the Old Testament*, 518.

64. The general case for (messianic) eschatology as a feature of the LXX Psalter is made by Schaper, *Eschatology in the Greek Psalter*. The case seems unlikely; note the rather devastating review by Albert Pietersma in *Bibliotheca Orientalis* 54 (1997): 185–90.

65. Creach, *Destiny of the Righteous in the Psalms*, 150.

66. Creach, *Destiny of the Righteous in the Psalms*, 151.

"righteousness," understood in this relational sense. Creach finds these ideas at the heart of Psalm 23: "The idea of being near God is really the subject of the entire psalm."[67] In particular Creach sees the essence of "I shall not want" and "I shall dwell" (in vv. 1, 6) as addressing being near God. The emphasis of his whole analysis is that this "destiny" is engaged already in this life in and through the Psalms, which is to say in their use and appropriation in the life of worship.

My impression is that Christian worshipers move easily and freely between the two contexts—now and the future—not least since worship can often facilitate a certain theological depth that is harder to explain analytically. Perhaps we speak most truly of God when we gather to worship, rather than when we engage in analytical theological investigation.[68] In any case, one of the reasons that the poetry of Psalm 23 provides hope for this life is precisely because a hope for life beyond death informs and permeates life on this side of death. Hope is not optimism: the aspiration that things might work out after all. Optimism tends to rely on a certain kind of positive thinking, a typically energetic can-do attitude, and to be fair, this often makes a better contribution to life than a contrasting pessimism. But Psalm 23 grounds hope in the shepherd-kingship of Yhwh, experienced through rest and recuperation in this life and confidently embraced even precisely when in the midst of the valley of the shadow of death. The rich lifting up experienced in the meal and the anointing in verse 5 sees the future hope of verse 6 *already* embraced. The reflection on the Eucharist in our previous section would point in precisely this direction: in celebrating the Eucharist, God's people experience now—albeit momentarily—the realities of the fullness of the kingdom to come. In the words of my own tradition, "As we eat and drink these holy gifts in the presence of your divine majesty, renew us by your Spirit, inspire us with your love, and unite us in the body of

---

67. Creach, *Destiny of the Righteous in the Psalms*, 43.
68. Though the present book seeks to model the point that analysis and worship are by no means mutually exclusive pursuits.

your Son, Jesus Christ our Lord."[69] Worshipers are then sent out "to live his risen life" and "give light to the world." Life now and life to come are seen as mutually informing. Our worship invites Christian hope to take root in our hearts for today and for the life everlasting, and to begin embracing already our destiny of dwelling with God.

A second note regarding the Psalms in the life of worship turns to consider the significant and helpful work of Walter Brueggemann on the Psalms. Probably no scholar has done more to mediate the riches of the Psalms for the wider worshiping life of the church, and his publications on the Psalms make a fine resource for thoughtful readers.[70] In what he now refers to as his "signature take on the Psalms," Brueggemann offers an influential approach to classifying the function of Psalms in terms of their way of engaging the reader in "orientation," "disorientation," and "new" or "reorientation."[71] His *Message of the Psalms* offers commentary on fifty-nine of the 150 Psalms under this rubric and locates Psalm 23 as a psalm of "Thanks and Confidence" in the "New Orientation" section of the book.[72] This helpfully recognizes that the overflowing trust of the psalm is not a freestanding presumption that all is well if we have faith. It is indeed part of the psalm's point that God is with us even when all is not well. The work of this claim is done in Brueggemann's location of the psalm in his scheme, rather than in the brief comments he makes on Psalm 23.

There is clearly something at work in this analysis that connects helpfully with students of the Psalms in recent years. Brueggemann's descriptions of how the Psalms both reflect our experiences of disorientation and lead us through them make sense to many readers. There is an interesting ambiguity, however, in what the classifying project (the "typology") seeks to achieve. It is rightly called a typology

69. The Church of England's *Common Worship* prayer A.
70. In addition to his *Message of the Psalms*, see also his helpfully practical works: *Praying the Psalms* and *From Whom No Secrets Are Hid*.
71. Brueggemann, "Psalms and the Life of Faith," originally in *JSOT* 17 (1980): 3–32 and reprinted in his *From Whom No Secrets Are Hid*, 149–75. The "signature take" claim is in his author's preface to the latter book (xii).
72. Brueggemann, *Message of the Psalms*, 154–56.

"of function"—in other words, of the functions the Psalms have. But it seems to me that it must therefore in part be about readers as much as the texts themselves. It is therefore slightly awkward to label psalms according to the category they belong to, a point made early on in a response by John Goldingay, who notes that any given psalm might lead a reader (and reflect the experience of an author) going through many or all stages of dis-/re-/orientation.[73] I suspect it is this more flexible approach that has become the understanding in recent Psalms studies, although it is interesting that the "signature take" is almost entirely absent in Brueggemann's own coauthored 2014 *Psalms* commentary.[74]

My own reflection is that one chief value of Brueggemann's emphasis on the dynamic functions of Psalms is in part a response to older forms of Psalms criticism that were somewhat sterile with regard to the appropriation of these texts in the life of faith, and that his work is illuminating and positive as a counterbalance to that problem. I do, however, wonder whether the result is an approach that is better at analyzing some types of problems in Anglo-American spirituality and church life than at capturing the plain sense of texts of praise, worship, and lament. The hope of Psalm 23 is only about "reorientation" for worshipers who have felt the pressures of disorientation. Note that all the psalm's points about confidence in the face of enemies and so forth were addressed in our exegesis in chapter 3 as a result of being features of the text, not with regard to whether they effected (or effect) reorientation. I have therefore avoided the "orientation" language in this book since I think it can let the emphasis fall in the wrong place.[75]

73. Goldingay, "Dynamic Cycle of Praise and Prayer in the Psalms," 85–90, with Brueggemann's agreement stated in his "Response to John Goldingay," 141–42.

74. Brueggemann and Bellinger, *Psalms*. It is unclear what role each author had. The book makes reference to "orientation" of any kind in the sense discussed here only twice in its over six hundred pages (with reference to Pss. 42–43 [p. 204] and Ps. 98 [p. 421]).

75. Brueggemann's own brief piece, "Psalms 22–23 in the Life of the Church" (*From Whom No Secrets Are Hid*, 100–105), fits entirely within the positive appeal to the text that I am describing and makes no mention of orientation either.

My own perspective is doubtless also colored by my participation in a church tradition that prays the Psalms every day, as part of
the Church of England's "Daily Office" of Morning and Evening
Prayer. One result of such a practice is that psalms of all orienta-
tions are encountered at random and without regard to one's own
daily spiritual experience. Hence such psalms function more to
map out a theological vision of the world in which we live—at all
points from "hallelujah" to "why have you forsaken me?" To use
the Psalms this way in worship frees us to let Psalm 23 talk straightforwardly of hope, whether we ourselves are experiencing a day
more like verses 2–3 or verse 4 or verse 5. As we have had cause to
note in this book, the experiences of joy and trouble may be only
a verse or a day away, and they fall in no predictable pattern. Our
worship refocuses our attention to the bigger vision, and therein
lies part of the hope.

Reference to my own context also leads me to a third and final
consideration of the Psalms in the life of worship, drawn from the
so-called Celtic traditions that are prominent in the North of England, where I live, surrounded by the heritage of great abbeys and
communities from Iona to Lindisfarne and beyond.[76] There is no
little debate about how far one can truly discern a separate Celtic
tradition in British (and other) Christianity. Like any broad-brush
picture, there is both general value and many specific problems with
the idea that Christianity came to Britain from the south via Roman
influence and from the north via Celtic influence, meeting at the
Synod of Whitby in 664 to work out how to hold the two traditions
together. There is, in any case, no need to locate Celtic Christianity
as a totally separate tradition. Recent studies have moderated overly
enthusiastic accounts of the matter.[77] What is worth noticing is some
of the typically Celtic influences that may be interwoven in all forms

---

76. A wonderful resource for exploring this is the two-volume prayer book produced by the Northumbria Community, *Celtic Daily Prayer*.

77. Most helpful here is Bradley, *Following the Celtic Way*, partly rebalancing
some of his own earlier writings.

of Christian spirituality, but which might be helpfully grasped afresh with reference to their prominence in Celtic traditions.

The one point I wish to draw out in particular is that Celtic Christianity was profoundly Psalm-centered. In his study of multiple characteristics of "the Celtic way," Ian Bradley puts second (after "Prayerful") that the tradition was "Psalm-Centered": "Chanted, recited, copied, studied and prayed, the psalms were central to the spiritual and devotional life of Irish monasteries," and detailed instructions regarding their use characterize most monastic rules.[78] This is arguably in part because the rich imagery drawn from natural life appealed to the Celtic imagination, although more simply, it easily resonated with daily experience. Perhaps this partly led to a Psalms focus rather than a Pauline focus—Bradley notes that Paul is almost absent in Celtic texts, and one may discern a slightly wistful note here that a Psalms focus is indeed all to the good.[79] Bradley also points out that singing unaccompanied psalms remains central to Free Church worship in many parts of the Scottish highlands and islands, often with the use of elegant and beautiful melodies. It is certainly interesting to reflect that there is a natural role for lament and consolation in Scottish spirituality that enables a relatively uncomplicated and thankful face-value use of such psalms in this tradition, in contrast to the sense one may have in reading Brueggemann—that lament tends to be oriented to protest.[80]

Bradley closes his account of *Following the Celtic Way* by reflecting on the central image of pilgrimage, sometimes undertaken physically and literally, but also of real significance metaphorically: "Pilgrimage

78. Bradley, *Following the Celtic Way*, 45–48, quotation from 45.
79. Bradley has paid particular attention to extant "Celtic texts" rather than general themes and impressions in his rebalancing account. On Paul, see Bradley, *Following the Celtic Way*, 136–37, noting Eph. 6:10–20 as one exception to this point.
80. This lies behind my earlier observation about the Anglo-American context of Brueggemann's work, by which phrase I intended to avoid reference to the Celtic traditions. I owe this point about Scottish spirituality to conversations with my friend John Chapman, a Scotsman ministering in Barcelona, after I spoke on the Psalms at a conference in Spain. He also pointed out that many Latin American traditions have a similar ability to embrace lament more naturally.

has much to offer an age such as ours where there is so much anxiety, yearning and seeking. It fits the needs of a restless generation—but perhaps restlessness is, in fact, part and parcel of the human condition."[81] This seems a wise comment with regard to an appropriate emphasis on provisionality and journey, not holding on too tightly to what one has but seeing life as movement forward. I suggest that it also chimes strongly with the reading of Psalm 23 that I have offered.

My approach to Psalm 23 in this book has resisted locating specific reference to king and cult in ancient Israel and has resisted separating out the supposed "sections" of the psalm into sections on the LORD as shepherd or host, as is so common in studies of the psalm. Instead I chose to focus on Psalm 23 as leading us along one continuous but multifaceted path through the ups and downs of life, emphasizing the unpredictability of what sorts of spiritual experience are likely to occur from one day to the next, but all en route to dwelling in worship in the house of the LORD. I now see that this reading fits naturally into a rubric such as "pilgrimage," particularly in the kind of metaphorical way that Bradley discusses. Such a reading of Psalm 23 envisages all of life as worship and invites us to orient our whole lives toward hope in the LORD as we travel onward.

81. Bradley, *Following the Celtic Way*, 153, and more generally 152–57.

5

Conclusion

Hearing and Preaching Psalm 23 Today

"The LORD is my Shepherd; I shall not want." What I have tried to do in this book is let the voice of Psalm 23 sound loud and clear in and for the life of the church. This has fundamentally been a task of attending to the text, and not of looking elsewhere—to history, to spiritual experience, or to other texts that get closer to something we would rather say instead. There is still much wisdom in C. S. Lewis's famous word about getting ourselves out of the way when attending to a text: the text will do its work if we let it. With not uncharacteristic exaggeration, Lewis imagines that our first move before any text worthy of being called a work of art is to "surrender": "The first demand any work of any art makes upon us is surrender. Look. Listen. Receive. Get yourself out of the way. (There is no good asking whether the work before you deserves such a surrender, for until you have surrendered you cannot possibly find out.)"[1] With some texts, I am not so sure this is great advice, but for canonical texts that have survived persistent scrutiny over centuries, it is a point worth noting.

---

1. Lewis, *Experiment in Criticism*, 19. Less widely noted, he later attributes more or less this advice to Matthew Arnold (*Experiment in Criticism*, 120).

It will be helpful to stick with Lewis's argument here a little longer. The quote in question comes from his final and still markedly underrated work of literary theory, *An Experiment in Criticism*.[2] The experiment reverses the usual order of things. Instead of trying directly to assess the merits of a text, he proposes distinguishing between different, varying types of reading. He defines a good text as one that sustains certain (good) practices of reading and a bad text as one that only supports other kinds of reading. Lewis was particularly interested in the power of poetic, literary, and mythical texts to remake the reader by way of a reading that could not be equated to such pursuits as reading the newspaper or children's comics.[3] As such, his work lends a largely untapped depth to various notions of literary reading which, in biblical studies at least, have grown considerably more prominent in the intervening years.[4] However, the point I wish to highlight here is that at the root of such literary reading, for Lewis, is the imaginary figure of Professor Dryasdust. Dryasdust was the expert on details—precisely the kinds of details that we have explored at length in this book regarding the words and phrases of Psalm 23. He is seen as the most valuable of all critics: "At the top comes Dryasdust. Obviously I have owed, and must continue to owe, far more to editors, textual critics, commentators, and lexicographers than to anyone else. Find out what the author actually wrote and what the hard words meant and what the allusions were to, and you have done far more for me than a hundred new interpretations or assessments could ever do."[5] Arguably the critical hierarchy was the way it was for Lewis because he was more than capable of working

2. I have discussed *Experiment in Criticism* also in "How to Do Things with Meaning," 143–60, from which this paragraph is partly drawn.

3. A strikingly similar argument would be made in due course by Umberto Eco, who distinguishes between "open" and "closed" texts along much the same lines, in *Role of the Reader*, 3–43 especially.

4. The only piece I know that makes sustained use of this book in biblical studies is the fine and thought-provoking article of Wright, "Experiment in Biblical Criticism," 240–67.

5. Lewis, *Experiment in Criticism*, 121.

toward his own imaginative interpretations once fueled by sufficient grasp of the details of the text before him. Clearly this is not a gift shared by all readers. But to affirm that detailed work with the text needs to go hand in hand with questions of broader poetic and theological imagination—that is an affirmation about careful theological reading of Scripture worth holding on to.

Good preaching must do no less. Too much literature on preaching is concerned with technique and rhetorical elements, which do indeed have their place. Too many sermons spend their time talking about something other than what the text says. But the key virtue of good preaching, stripped down to the essentials, is once again to focus on what the text says and to make the text clear to the congregation so that they, too, may hear what it says. The point is well made by Gerhard von Rad in the wonderful reflection that serves as the introduction to a posthumous collection of his sermons. This short address, "About Exegesis and Preaching," was offered to his students in a 1965–66 class on preaching:

> The great discovery which all of you must make in preaching is that the texts themselves actually speak (Deutero-Isaiah must have experienced something like a panting and groaning on God's part when he was silent for a while! [Isa. 42:14]). The best sermons are those in which one notes the preacher's own surprise that—and how—the text suddenly began to speak. . . . I give you about ten to twenty beginners' sermons, in which you will repeat what you have learned. Then you will have preached yourselves out. Then if you do not make the discovery that every text wants to speak for itself, you are lost. We are dealing with that word that is sharper than a two-edged sword.[6]

I still remember a student coming back to visit after his first couple of years in church ministry and pondering this quote with me one more time. His main reflection was that von Rad's figure of "ten to

6. Von Rad, *Biblical Interpretations in Preaching*, 11–18, here 17–18. The German original was published in 1973, two years after von Rad's death.

twenty beginners' sermons" was generous. He suggested that the figure was more like three. It took him very little time to discover for himself in ministry that the preacher is called to get out of the way and let the text speak.[7]

When preachers do this, then all those present are invited to a feast, a veritable theological event in which God addresses those gathered around the word. It does not have to be clever or flashy—indeed it most likely will not be—because that would precisely not be "getting out of the way." My own journey through preaching has included many experiences of being in the way or of losing my nerve and substituting an amusing story, a moral lesson, or an insight from some other passage in place of the warp and woof of the scriptural text in front of us. On occasion, even so, the word of life breaks through.

I therefore wish to close my account of Psalm 23 by reflecting on my own unexpected but joyful experience of seeing the word of life connect congregations to the world imagined by Psalm 23. I have had the opportunity to preach the psalm in various places in God's world. This has been a blessing but also a considerable challenge, and I have been fortified by the issue we have explored in this book: this psalm with a minimally defined background has a maximally effective reach into new and different contexts. This does not mean that all points of cultural resonance work well or that I have not sometimes failed to be clear in letting the text speak. But as throughout this book, it is the points of theological resonance that I want to bring to the foreground, as they have emerged in and through the cultural interpretive issues.

I first preached from Psalm 23 in a beautiful English parish church, in a village in the rural Durham countryside in North East England. The context almost seemed to invite gentle pastoral reflection and

7. I am not trying to offer a theoretical account of preaching, but let me take the opportunity to recommend one book in particular to preachers who wish to explore further the vision of preaching outlined here: Davis, *Preaching the Luminous Word*. Note especially her worth-the-price-of-admission opening three pages, "On Not Worrying About Sermon Illustrations" (xxii–xxiv).

to build toward that most English of blessings—a nice cup of tea after the service. As I worked on the sermon, set in the Church of England's readings for the week before Easter that year, I began to realize that Psalm 23 was interested in something more piercing than warm thoughts. That despite the beauty of the setting, the lives that people were leading were of course more complicated and challenging. Below the surface image of England's green and pleasant land, Psalm 23 was interested in offering life in the face of enemies. Indeed, preaching that sermon sowed the initial seeds for this present book.

The second time I preached from Psalm 23, I was in Sri Lanka, visiting Colombo Theological Seminary for ten days to teach a course on hermeneutics. The students were kind enough to say that they benefited from the course, but the privilege was all mine as I learned (a little) what Scripture looked like through (some) South Asian eyes. I was asked to preach in the weekly chapel service and chose Psalm 23. It was double translated as we went, so I spoke and then it was offered also in Tamil and then in Sinhala. That gave me plenty of time to think about two things: I wondered exactly what sermons the Tamil and Sinhalese speaking members of the student body were hearing; and I wondered how I had ever thought I would be able to comment on Psalm 23's Davidic wisdom in post-civil-war Sri Lanka, where rich tropical rain forests and beautiful sunny beaches did their best to distract from harsh political realities. The hard edges of life were closer to the surface than in my English parish church. The quiet waters and green pastures resonated strangely with a very different landscape, but the table before the enemies was a strong and powerful claim about divine presence in the midst of it all. "The LORD is my shepherd . . ." How is that heard by a Sri Lankan Christian? With my one week of experience there, I did not think it was up to me to say, but I could still be faithful in laying before them the voice of the psalm in all its theological boldness. I could also easily see that I was not equal to all that God might yet do through this short scriptural text.

The third time I preached from Psalm 23, I was in Prague, and thereby hangs a more complex tale. I was speaking at a conference on the Old Testament in the life of the church, and I learned just before I spoke that in Czech the Old Testament is called the "Starý Zákon," the "Old Law." How Christians should relate to the Old Law (of Moses?) is an interesting question, but was not quite the focus of my talks. Context played its part once more. The conference went well, and the discussions were enriching.

How much more did context play a role as I stayed on for the Sunday, when I had been invited to preach, and discovered that the date was a special one. It was November 17, a date marked in the history of the Czech Republic as the anniversary of the Velvet Revolution, the beginning of the nonviolent removal of communist rule that had begun on November 17, 1989. I made some opening comments about the importance of freedom in specific contexts—the Czech context, other cultural contexts, the ancient Israelite context—and then sought to bring God's word of life from Psalm 23 to the assembled Czech congregation, mindful once more that Psalm 23's relative lack of context would surely allow it to speak afresh if I could give a faithful account of what it says.

The sermon I preached then, which was not unrelated to the sermons on the previous two occasions, included many of the theological emphases that I have written about in chapter 4 of this book, albeit a little more briefly. All went well until I came to the section of my script that rehearsed the issues of enemies and God's countermanding pursuit through goodness and mercy. As I had written, so I said: "What God's goodness and covenant love will do is not so much follow us, as *pursue* us, come running after us, track us down. Whatever is crowding in on your life, God's goodness and mercy will find you. They know where you live." Even as I said it, I realized that this language of "knowing where you live" and "tracking you down" was at best a very awkward image to use on a day of celebration of the end of the Czech Republic's Cold War occupation. Had I been remarkably insensitive, or perhaps even offensive? Lacking the courage to address this issue, I pressed on. My sense was that overall the sermon had been well received. Perhaps it was only me, a self-critical preacher, who was aware of the hermeneutical bridge on which I had so suddenly slipped as I spoke?

Not so. It seemed that everyone had noticed it. But in general, as far as I would be able to discover, they had found the point helpful. One English-speaking member of the congregation sought me out and relayed their perspective: "We knew exactly what it was to have someone track us down and knock on our doors in the middle of the night, and it was never good—but the psalm's image showed us that it is instead God who will seek and find us, and that was exactly the good news we needed in our church service today, of all days."

I am still not sure it is quite how I would phrase the point again in the same context. However, what my listener heard that day was indeed what Psalm 23 wants to say to those of us who live in a world characterized by the presence of enemies, which is to say all of us, in some way or other. The shepherding oversight of the LORD provides for us all, in and through the valley of the shadow of death. We are called beyond our present difficulties to a vision of peace that outlasts our present darkness. Psalm 23 continues to train the lives and imaginations of those in the church, wherever in God's world they may be. The more we study the psalm, the more it may shape us as readers who embody its convictions.

Here is how my sermon ended on that occasion in the Czech Republic, a variation on the ending that I have used whenever I have preached from this psalm:

> This is how we know that God may be trusted: not because everything works out for us, or we find ourselves mysteriously delivered from all our troubles, or that we have discovered a way to organize our society that will ensure peace and justice for all, but precisely because in the very midst of our difficulties, God is good and reaches out to us with good things—connecting us with rest, with restoration, with the table that he sets before us . . . He is our shepherd, in fact. May this psalm sustain us, through this week, this year, and every year—until the LORD himself returns—and we dwell in the house of the LORD, all our days.

I should say that I have gone on to preach from Psalm 23 on several occasions in the routines of weekly church ministry in England. The psalm is ever and always a word for today, as long as it is called "today." It invites us to restoration, to resurrection, to comfort, and to hope. Against such things there is no law.

If preachers reading this book are encouraged to hold their nerve in the face of this text and to let their congregations hear its words and its message, then I will have succeeded in one of my goals for this study. I have wanted to model the conviction that we know no better wisdom than that found in the scriptural texts, which has implications for how we address the world in which we live in the light of a text like Psalm 23. Our primary job as readers and preachers of the text is not to supplement it or replace it with other worthy and true things, but to attend to the simple art of hearing what Scripture says. That involves both attending carefully to what it does say, and also not dwelling too much on what it does not say.

This "simple" art is too little practiced in the academy when we turn instead to look for background information and matters of historical and authorial context. It is too little practiced in popular spirituality, when we turn instead to stories and illustrations from the reader's present context that seek to package up the point of Psalm 23 and replace the text with the substituted story, fascinating and edifying as such stories may often be. The practices involved in hearing what the text of Scripture says are profound, character forming, and life changing. They thus take time. I hope that everything I have written in this book will serve that work of attending to the text.

As and when we do succeed in hearing Psalm 23, our task is then to point other people to seeing and hearing what it says. And then we stand back and watch what life-giving work God might do: by quiet waters, in the valley of the shadow of death, at the table that God sets before us, and—forevermore—as we dwell in the house of the LORD.

That is Psalm 23 for the life of the church. *Tolle, lege*; take and read.

Appendix

Notes on Psalm 23 in Hebrew

Notes here relate to points discussed in the exegesis in chapter 3, marked with an * in the text. They are provided for the benefit of those with some knowledge of Hebrew, who may wonder how what is being described in chapter 3 fits with the traditional categories of Hebrew grammar.

Verse 1

- *rōʿeh* is the participle of *rāʿāh* used (as is common) as a noun—thus, one who shepherds.
- *ʾeḥsār* is a Qal impf 1cs of *ḥāsēr*, "to lack/be lacking," described by Muraoka as a "future of potential modality"[1]—on which see the discussion of "will/shall" in chapter 3.

1. Muraoka, *Biblical Hebrew Reader*, 125, cf. 61.

■ Verse 2

- *bin'ôt* incorporates a fem plural construct of *nāwâ*.
- *yarbîṣēnî* is a Hiphil impf 3ms of *rābaṣ*, "to stretch/lie down," with a 1cs suffix.
- *mê mənuḥôt* is the masc plural construct form *mê* (from *mayîm*; dual, "water[s]"), hence "waters of," linked in a construct of purpose to the fem plural of *mənuḥâ*, "resting place; rest." The plural form *mənuḥôt* here may be to agree with the dual form of *mayîm*,[2] or it could be intensive (so GKC 124e), a reading favored by Goldingay, who thus renders the phrase "by completely restful waters."[3]
- *yənahălēnî* is a Piel impf 3ms of *nāhal*, "to lead, guide, cause to rest" (with a 1cs suffix), but the Piel is not marked as an intensive form.

■ Verse 3

- *yəšôbēb* is a Polel impf 3ms of *šûb*, to "turn back" or "return" (the Polel being the Piel stem for biconsonantal verbs).

■ Verse 4

- *'îrā'* is a Qal impf 1cs of *yārē'*, "to fear."
- *'immādî* is equivalent to *'immî*, "with me."
- *yənahămunî* is a Piel impf 3mp of *niham*, "to comfort," with a 1cs suffix.

---

2. So Muraoka, *Biblical Hebrew Reader*, 126.
3. Goldingay, *Psalms*, 1:344.

▦ Verse 5

- *ṣōrərāy* is a pausal form for *ṣōrəray*, a Qal participle of *ṣārar*, "to be hostile," with the *–ay* 1cs suffix ("my"), hence "my enemies."
- *diššantā* is a Piel perf 2ms of *dāšēn*, "to anoint," derived from the Qal, meaning "to be/grow fat."

▦ Verse 6

- *yirdəpûnî* is a Qal impf 3mp of *rādap*, "to pursue," with a 1cs pronominal suffix.
- *ḥayāy* (in a pausal form) uses a plural by convention in Hebrew and means "my life"—it is *ḥayîm* with a 1cs pronominal suffix *–ay*.
- *wəšabtî*, as vocalized in MT, is a Qal waw-consecutive perf 1cs of *šûb* ("to return"). *šûb* is a biconsonantal (or "hollow") verb that would be *šabtî* ("I returned") as a Qal perf 1cs.
- Repointed to *wəšibtî*, it becomes a Qal inf construct of *yāšab*, "to dwell, remain," with 1cs suffix and preceded by a conjunction. The inf construct of *yāšab* is *šebet*, dropping the initial *y* (as is common for inf constructs), but the pronominal suffix then changes the form to *šibtî*.

Bibliography

Abernethy, Andrew T. "'Right Paths' and/or 'Paths of Righteousness'? Examining Psalm 23.3b within the Psalter." *JSOT* 39 (2015): 299–318.

Allison, Dale C., Jr. "Psalm 23 (22) in Early Christianity: A Suggestion." *Irish Biblical Studies* 5 (1983): 132–37.

Alter, Robert. *The Art of Biblical Poetry*. Edinburgh: T&T Clark, 1985.

———. *The Hebrew Bible: A Translation with Commentary*. 3 vols. New York: Norton, 2019.

Arterbury, Andrew E., and William H. Bellinger Jr. "'Returning to the Hospitality of the Lord': A Reconsideration of Psalm 23, 5–6." *Biblica* 86 (2005): 387–95.

Augustine. *Expositions of the Psalms*. Vol. 1. Translated by Maria Boulding. Hyde Park, NY: New City, 2000.

Bailey, Kenneth E. *The Good Shepherd. A Thousand-Year Journey from Psalm 23 to the New Testament*. London: SPCK, 2015.

Barré, Michael L. "The Formulaic Pair חסד(ו)טוב in the Psalter." *Zeitschrift für die Alttestamentliche Wissenschaft* 98 (1986): 100–105.

Barth, Karl. *Church Dogmatics* II/1. Edinburgh: T&T Clark, 1957.

———. *Church Dogmatics* IV/1. Edinburgh: T&T Clark, 1956.

Barton, John. *The Nature of Biblical Criticism*. Louisville: Westminster John Knox, 2007.

Birkeland, Harris. *The Evildoers in the Book of Psalms*. Oslo: J. Dybwad, 1955.

Blaising, Craig A., and Carmen S. Hardin, eds. *Psalms 1–50*. Ancient Christian Commentary on Scripture, OT 7. Downers Grove, IL: InterVarsity, 2008.

Blenkinsopp, Joseph. *Sage, Priest, Prophet: Religious and Intellectual Leadership in Ancient Israel*. Louisville: Westminster John Knox, 1995.

Bono. Introduction to *The Book of Psalms*, vii–xii. Edinburgh: Canongate, 1999. Reprinted in *Revelations: Personal Responses to the Books of the Bible*, 135–40. Edinburgh: Canongate, 2005.

Bosma, Carl J. "Discerning the Voices in the Psalms: A Discussion of Two Problems in Psalmic Interpretation (Part I)." *Calvin Theological Journal* 43 (2008): 183–212.

———. "Discerning the Voices in the Psalms: A Discussion of Two Problems in Psalmic Interpretation (Part II)." *Calvin Theological Journal* 44 (2009): 127–70.

Bradley, Ian. *Following the Celtic Way: A New Assessment of Celtic Christianity*. London: Darton, Longman & Todd, 2018.

Briggs, Charles, and Emilie Briggs. *A Critical and Exegetical Commentary on the Book of Psalms*. 2 vols. International Critical Commentary. Edinburgh: T&T Clark, 1906–7.

Briggs, Richard S. "Biblical Hermeneutics and Practical Theology: Method and Truth in Context." *Anglican Theological Review* 97 (2015): 201–17.

———. "How to Do Things with Meaning in Biblical Interpretation." *Southeastern Theological Review* 2 (2011): 143–60.

———. *Jesus for Life: Spiritual Readings in John's Gospel*. Eugene, OR: Cascade Books, 2019.

———. *The Virtuous Reader: Old Testament Narrative and Interpretive Virtue*. Studies in Theological Interpretation. Grand Rapids: Baker Academic, 2010.

Brown, William P., ed. *The Oxford Handbook of the Psalms*. Oxford: Oxford University Press, 2014.

———. *Psalms*. Interpreting Biblical Texts. Nashville: Abingdon, 2010.

———. "The Psalms and 'I': The Dialogical Self and the Disappearing Psalmist." In *Diachronic and Synchronic: Reading the Psalms in Real Time; Proceedings of the Baylor Symposium on the Book of Psalms*, edited by Joel S. Burnett, W. H. Bellinger Jr., and W. Dennis Tucker Jr., 26–44. LHBOTS 488. London: T&T Clark, 2007.

Broyles, Craig C. *Psalms*. New International Biblical Commentary. Peabody, MA: Hendrickson, 1999.

Brueggemann, Walter. *Cadences of Home: Preaching among Exiles*. Louisville: Westminster John Knox, 1998.

———. "The Costly Loss of Lament." *JSOT* 36 (1986): 57–71.

———. *Finally Comes the Poet: Daring Speech for Proclamation*. Minneapolis: Fortress, 1989.

———. *From Whom No Secrets Are Hid: Introducing the Psalms*. Edited by Brent A. Strawn. Louisville: Westminster John Knox, 2014.

———. *The Message of the Psalms: A Theological Commentary*. Minneapolis: Augsburg, 1984.

———. *Praying the Psalms: Engaging Scripture and the Life of the Spirit*. 2nd ed. Milton Keynes, UK: Paternoster, 2007.

———. "The Psalms and the Life of Faith: A Suggested Typology of Function." *JSOT* 17 (1980): 3–32.

———. "Response to John Goldingay." *JSOT* 22 (1982): 141–42.

———. *Sabbath as Resistance: Saying No to the Culture of Now*. Louisville: Westminster John Knox, 2014.

Brueggemann, Walter, and W. H. Bellinger Jr. *Psalms*. New Cambridge Bible Commentary. Cambridge: Cambridge University Press, 2014.

Byassee, Jason. *Praise Seeking Understanding: Reading the Psalms with Augustine*. Radical Traditions. Grand Rapids: Eerdmans, 2007.

———. *Psalms 101–150*. Brazos Theological Commentary on the Bible. Grand Rapids: Brazos, 2018.

Calvin, John. *Commentary on the Psalms*. Translated by James Anderson. Grand Rapids: Eerdmans, 1949.

Carr, David M. *Writing on the Tablet of the Heart: Origins of Scripture and Literature*. New York: Oxford University Press, 2005.

Chapman, Stephen B. "Reclaiming Inspiration for the Bible." In *Canon and Biblical Interpretation*, edited by Craig Bartholomew, Scott Hahn, Robin Parry, Christopher Seitz, and Al Wolters, 167–206. SHS 7. Carlisle, PA: Paternoster, 2006.

Charry, Ellen T. *Psalms 1–50*. Brazos Theological Commentary on the Bible. Grand Rapids: Brazos, 2015.

Childs, Brevard S. *Introduction to the Old Testament as Scripture*. London: SCM, 1979.

———. "Psalm Titles and Midrashic Exegesis." *Journal of Semitic Studies* 16, no. 2 (1971): 137–50.

Clines, David J. A. "Translating Psalm 23." In *Reflection and Refraction: Studies in Biblical Historiography in Honour of A. Graeme Auld*, edited by Robert Rezetko, Timothy H. Lim, and W. Brian Aucker, 67–80. VTSup 113. Leiden: Brill, 2007.

Common Worship: Daily Prayer. London: Church House, 2005.

Cook, Edward M. "The Psalms Targum: An English Translation." NTCS: The Newsletter for Targumic and Cognate Studies, 2001. http://targum.info/pss/ps1.htm.

Cooper, Alan. "Some Aspects of Traditional Jewish Psalms Interpretation." In Brown, *Oxford Handbook of the Psalms*, 253–68.

———. "Structure, Midrash and Meaning: The Case of Psalm 23." In *Proceedings of the Ninth World Congress of Jewish Studies, Jerusalem, August 4–12, 1985*, 107–14. Jerusalem: World Union of Jewish Studies, 1986.

Craigie, Peter C. *Psalms 1–50*. Word Biblical Commentary 19. Waco: Word, 1983.

Creach, Jerome F. D. *The Destiny of the Righteous in the Psalms*. St. Louis: Chalice, 2008.

Croatto, J. Severino. "Psalm 23:1–6: A Latin-American Perspective." In Levison and Pope-Levison, *Return to Babel*, 57–62.

Croft, Steven J. L. *The Identity of the Individual in the Psalms*. JSOTSup 44. Sheffield: JSOT Press, 1987.

Dahood, S. J. Mitchell. *Psalms*. 3 vols. Anchor Bible. Garden City, NY: Doubleday, 1966–70.

———. *Psalms 1–50*. Anchor Bible. Garden City, NY: Doubleday, 1966.

Davis, Ellen F., with Austin McIver Dennis. *Preaching the Luminous Word: Biblical Sermons and Homiletical Essays*. Grand Rapids: Eerdmans, 2016.

Dawes, Stephen. *The Psalms*. SCM Study Guide. London: SCM, 2010.

DeClaissé-Walford, Nancy L. "An Intertextual Reading of Psalms 22, 23, and 24." In *The Book of Psalms: Composition and Reception*, edited by Peter W. Flint and Patrick D. Miller, 139–52. VTSup 94. FIOTL 4. Leiden: Brill, 2005.

———. *Introduction to the Psalms: A Song from Ancient Israel*. St. Louis: Chalice, 2004.

————. "On Translating the Poetry of the Psalms." In *Jewish and Christian Approaches to the Psalms: Conflict and Convergence*, edited by Susan Gillingham, 190–203. Oxford: Oxford University Press, 2013.

————, ed. *The Shape and Shaping of the Book of Psalms: The Current State of Scholarship*. Atlanta: SBL Press, 2014.

DeClaissé-Walford, Nancy L., Rolf A. Jacobson, and Beth LaNeel Tanner. *The Book of Psalms*. NICOT. Grand Rapids: Eerdmans, 2014.

Di Vito, Robert A. "Old Testament Anthropology and the Construction of Personal Identity." *Catholic Biblical Quarterly* 61 (1999): 217–38.

Eaton, John. *The Psalms: A Historical and Spiritual Commentary with an Introduction and New Translation*. London: T&T Clark, 2003.

Eco, Umberto. *The Role of the Reader: Explorations in the Semiotics of Texts*. Bloomington: Indiana University Press, 1984.

Erasmus. "A Threefold Exposition of Psalm 22." In *Collected Works of Erasmus*, Vol. 64, *Expositions of the Psalms*, 119–99. Toronto: University of Toronto Press, 2005.

Fiedrowicz, Michael. "General Introduction." In Augustine, *Expositions of the Psalms*, 13–66.

Firth, David G. *Hear, O Lord: A Spirituality of the Psalms*. Calver, UK: Cliff College Publishing, 2005.

————. *Surrendering Retribution in the Psalms: Responses to Violence in the Individual Complaints*. Paternoster Biblical Monographs. Milton Keynes, UK: Paternoster, 2005.

Flint, Peter W., and Patrick D. Miller, eds. *The Book of Psalms: Composition and Reception*. VTSup 94. FIOTL 4. Leiden: Brill, 2005.

Fokkelman, J. P. *The Psalms in Form: The Hebrew Psalter in its Poetic Shape*. Tools for Biblical Study 4. Leiden: Deo, 2002.

Ford, David F. *The Shape of Living*. London: Fount, 1997.

Frei, Hans W. *The Eclipse of Biblical Narrative: A Study in Eighteenth and Nineteenth Century Hermeneutics*. New Haven: Yale University Press, 1974.

Gadamer, Hans-Georg. *Truth and Method*. Translated and revised by Joel Wensheimer and Donald G. Marshall. London: Sheed and Ward, 1989.

Gawande, Atul. *Being Mortal: Illness, Medicine, and What Matters in the End*. London: Profile Books/Wellcome Collection, 2014.

Gillingham, Susan. *The Image, the Depths and the Surface: Multivalent Approaches to Biblical Study*. JSOTSup 354. Sheffield: Sheffield Academic, 2002.

———. "In and Out of the Sheepfold: Multivalent Readings in Psalm 23." In *Image, the Depths and the Surface*, 45–78.

———, ed. *Jewish and Christian Approaches to the Psalms: Conflict and Convergence*. Oxford: Oxford University Press, 2013.

———. *Psalms through the Centuries*. 3 vols. Wiley Blackwell Bible Commentaries. Oxford: Wiley Blackwell, 2008–.

Goins, Scott. "Jerome's Psalters." In Brown, *Oxford Handbook of the Psalms*, 185–98.

Goldingay, John. "The Dynamic Cycle of Praise and Prayer in the Psalms." *JSOT* 20 (1981): 85–90.

———. *Psalms*. 3 vols. Baker Commentary on the Old Testament Wisdom and Psalms. Grand Rapids: Baker Academic, 2006–8.

Green, Joel B. *Body, Soul, and Human Life: The Nature of Humanity in the Bible*. Studies in Theological Interpretation. Grand Rapids: Baker Academic, 2008.

Gunkel, Hermann. *Introduction to Psalms: The Genres of the Religious Lyric of Israel*. Completed by Joachim Begrich. Translated by James D. Nogalski. Macon, GA: Mercer University Press, 1998. German original published in 1933.

Hamlin, Hannibal. *Psalm Culture and Early Modern English Literature*. Cambridge: Cambridge University Press, 2004.

Hays, Richard B. *Echoes of Scripture in the Gospels*. Waco: Baylor University Press, 2016.

———. *Echoes of Scripture in the Letters of Paul*. New Haven: Yale University Press, 1989.

———. *Reading Backwards: Figural Christology and the Fourfold Gospel Witness*. Waco: Baylor University Press, 2014.

Heath, Michael J. "Erasmus and the Psalms." In *The Bible in the Renaissance: Essays on Biblical Commentary and Translation in the Fifteenth and Sixteenth Centuries*, edited by Richard Griffiths, 28–44. Burlington, VT: Ashgate, 2001.

Heschel, Abraham Joshua. *The Sabbath: Its Meaning for Modern Man*. New York: Farrar, Strauss & Giroux, 1951.

Hobbs, T. R., and P. K. Jackson. "The Enemy in the Psalms." *Biblical Theology Bulletin* 21 (1991): 22–29.

Holladay, William L. *The Psalms through Three Thousand Years: Prayerbook of a Cloud of Witnesses*. Minneapolis: Fortress, 1993.

Hunter, Alastair G. *An Introduction to the Psalms*. T&T Clark Approaches to Biblical Studies. London: T&T Clark, 2008.

Jacobson, Karl N. "Through the Pistol Smoke Dimly: Psalm 23 in Contemporary Film and Fiction." SBL Forum Archive. Accessed October 22, 2019. https://www.sbl-site.org/publications/article.aspx?Article Id=796.

Jacobson, Rolf A., and Karl N. Jacobson. *Invitation to the Psalms: A Reader's Guide for Discovery and Engagement*. Grand Rapids: Baker Academic, 2013.

Janzen, J. Gerald. "Revisiting 'Forever' in Psalm 23:6." In *When Prayer Takes Place: Forays into a Biblical World*, edited by Brent A. Strawn and Patrick D. Miller, 188–208. Eugene, OR: Cascade Books, 2012.

Johnson, Nathan C. "Living, Active, Elusive: Toward a Theology of Textual Criticism." *Journal of Reformed Theology* 12 (2018): 83–102.

Johnston, Philip S., and David G. Firth, eds. *Interpreting the Psalms: Issues and Approaches*. Leicester, UK: Apollos, 2005.

Keel, Othmar. *The Symbolism of the Biblical World: Ancient Near Eastern Iconography and the Book of Psalms*. Winona Lake, IN: Eisenbrauns, 1997. Originally published in 1972.

Keller, W. Phillip. *A Shepherd Looks at Psalm 23*. Grand Rapids: Zondervan, 1970.

Kinoti, Hannah W. "Psalm 23:1–6: An African Perspective." In Levison and Pope-Levison, *Return to Babel*, 63–68.

Knauf, Ernst A. "Psalm xxiii 6." *Vetus Testamentum* 51 (2001): 556.

The Koren Siddur. Hebrew/English edition. Jerusalem: Koren, 2013.

Kraus, Hans-Joachim. *Theology of the Psalms*. Translated by Keith Crim. Minneapolis: Augsburg, 1986.

Kreitzer, Larry. *The New Testament in Fiction and Film: On Reversing the Hermeneutical Flow*. Biblical Seminar 17. Sheffield: Sheffield Academic, 1993.

———. *The Old Testament in Fiction and Film: On Reversing the Hermeneutical Flow*. Biblical Seminar 24. Sheffield: Sheffield Academic, 1994.

Kriegshauser, Laurence. *Praying the Psalms in Christ*. Reading the Scriptures. Notre Dame: University of Notre Dame Press, 2009.

Kushner, Harold S. *The Lord Is My Shepherd: Healing Wisdom of the Twenty-Third Psalm*. New York: Random House, 2003.

Lamb, John Alexander. *The Psalms in Christian Worship*. London: Faith, 1962.

Lash, Nicholas. "What Might Martyrdom Mean?" In *Theology on the Way to Emmaus*, 75–92. London: SCM, 1986.

Levenson, Jon D. *Resurrection and the Restoration of Israel: The Ultimate Victory of the God of Life*. New Haven: Yale University Press, 2006.

———. "Theological Consensus or Historicist Evasion? Jews and Christians in Biblical Study." In *The Hebrew Bible, the Old Testament, and Historical Criticism*, 82–105. Louisville: Westminster John Knox, 1993.

Levison, John R., and Priscilla Pope-Levison, eds. *Return to Babel: Global Perspectives on the Bible*. Louisville: Westminster John Knox, 1999.

Lewis, C. S. *An Experiment in Criticism*. Cambridge: Cambridge University Press, 1961.

———. *Reflections on the Psalms*. London: Fontana, 1958.

MacDonald, M. C. A. "Literacy in Oral Environments." In *Writing and Ancient Near Eastern Society: Papers in Honour of Alan R. Millard*, edited by Piotr Bienkowski, Christopher Mee, and Elizabeth Slater, 49–118. LHBOTS 426. London: T&T Clark, 2005.

Madigan, Kevin J., and Jon D. Levenson. *Resurrection: The Power of God for Christians and Jews*. New Haven: Yale University Press, 2008.

Magonet, Jonathan. *A Rabbi Reads the Psalms*. 2nd ed. London: SCM, 2004.

Marlowe, W. Creighton. "David's I-Thou Discourse: Verbal Chiastic Patterns in Psalm 23." *Scandinavian Journal of the Old Testament* 25, no. 1 (2011): 105–15.

Maxwell, Nathan Dean. "The Psalmist in the Psalm: A Persona-Critical Reading of Book IV of the Psalter." PhD diss., Baylor University, 2007.

Mays, James Luther. *Psalms*. Interpretation. Louisville: John Knox, 1994.

———. "A Question of Identity: The Threefold Hermeneutics of Psalmody." In *The Lord Reigns: A Theological Handbook to the Psalms*, 46–54. Louisville: Westminster John Knox, 1994.

———. "The Self in the Psalms and the Image of God." In *Preaching and Teaching the Psalms*, 51–67. Louisville: Westminster John Knox, 2006.

McCann, J. Clinton. "The Shape of Book I of the Psalter and the Shape of Human Happiness." In *The Book of Psalms: Composition and Reception*, edited by Peter W. Flint and Patrick D. Miller, 340–48. VTSup 94. FIOTL 4. Leiden: Brill, 2005.

———. *A Theological Introduction to the Book of Psalms: The Psalms as Torah*. Nashville: Abingdon, 1993.

———. "'The Way of the Righteous' in the Psalms: Character Formation and Cultural Crisis." In *Character & Scripture: Moral Formation, Community, and Biblical Interpretation*, edited by William P. Brown, 135–49. Grand Rapids: Eerdmans, 2002.

Miller, Patrick D. "The Sinful and Trusting Creature: The Anthropology of the Psalter II." In *Way of the Lord*, 237–49.

———. *The Way of the Lord: Essays in Old Testament Theology*. Grand Rapids: Eerdmans, 2007.

———. "What Is a Human Being? The Anthropology of the Psalter I." In *Way of the Lord*, 226–36.

Mitchell, David C. "Lord, Remember David: G. H. Wilson and the Message of the Psalter." *Vetus Testamentum* 56 (2006): 526–48.

Moberly, Walter. *Old Testament Theology: Reading the Hebrew Bible as Christian Scripture*. Grand Rapids: Baker Academic, 2013.

———. *The Theology of the Book of Genesis*. Old Testament Theology. Cambridge: Cambridge University Press, 2009.

Moon, Cyris Heesuk. "Psalm 23:1–6: An Asian Perspective." In Levison and Pope-Levison, *Return to Babel*, 69–72. Louisville: Westminster John Knox, 1999.

Muraoka, Takamitsu. *A Biblical Hebrew Reader with an Outline Grammar*. Leuven: Peeters, 2017.

Nasuti, Harry P. *Defining the Sacred Songs: Genre, Tradition and the Postcritical Interpretation of the Psalms*. JSOTSup 218. Sheffield: Sheffield Academic, 1999.

Neale, J. M., and R. F. Littledale. *A Commentary on the Psalms from Primitive and Mediaeval Writers*. 4 vols. London: Masters, 1869–74.

Nel, Philip J. "Yahweh Is a Shepherd: Conceptual Metaphor in Psalm 23." *Horizons in Biblical Theology* 27, no. 2 (2005): 79–103.

Northumbria Community. *Celtic Daily Prayer: Book One; The Journey Begins*. London: William Collins, 2002.

————. *Celtic Daily Prayer: Book Two; Farther Up and Farther In*. London: William Collins, 2015.

Oesterley, W. O. E. *The Psalms in the Jewish Church*. London: Skeffington & Son, 1910.

Parkander, Dorothy J. "'Exalted Manna': The Psalms as Literature." *Word and World 5*, no. 2 (1985): 122–31.

Parris, David Paul. *Reading the Bible with Giants: How 2000 Years of Biblical Interpretation Can Shed New Light on Old Texts*. 2nd ed. Eugene, OR: Cascade Books, 2015.

Parrish, V. Steven. *A Story of the Psalms: Conversation, Canon, and Congregation*. Collegeville, MN: Liturgical Press, 2003.

Pietersma, Albert. Review of *Eschatology in the Greek Psalter*, by Joachim Schaper. *Bibliotheca Orientalis* 54 (1997): 185–90.

Polk, Timothy. *The Prophetic Persona: Jeremiah and the Language of the Self*. JSOTSup 32. Sheffield: JSOT Press, 1984.

Prothero, Rowland E. *The Psalms in Human Life*. London: John Murray, 1903.

Pyper, Hugh S. "The Triumph of the Lamb: Psalm 23 and Textual Fitness." *Biblical Interpretation* 9 (2001): 384–92.

Reardon, Patrick Henry. *Christ in the Psalms*. Ben Lomond, CA: Conciliar Press, 2000.

Roncace, Mark. "Psalm 23 as Cultural Icon." SBL's *Bible Odyssey*. Accessed October 21, 2019. https://www.bibleodyssey.org/en/passages/related-articles/psalm-23-as-cultural-icon.

————. "Psalm 23 and Modern Worldviews." In *Teaching the Bible: Practical Strategies for Classroom Instruction*, edited by Mark Roncace and Patrick Gray, 205–6. Atlanta: Society of Biblical Literature, 2005.

Rosenbaum, Stanley N. "Our Own Silly Faces: C. S. Lewis on Psalms." *Christian Century* 100 (1983): 486–89.

Sakenfeld, Katharine Doob. *Faithfulness in Action: Loyalty in Biblical Perspective*. Overtures to Biblical Theology. Philadelphia: Fortress, 1985.

Sawyer, John F. A. "The Psalms in Judaism and Christianity: A Reception History Perspective." In *Jewish and Christian Approaches to the Psalms: Conflict and Convergence*, edited by Susan Gillingham, 134–43. Oxford: Oxford University Press, 2013.

Scarlata, Mark. *Sabbath Rest: The Beauty of God's Rhythm for a Digital Age*. London: SCM, 2019.

Schaper, Joachim. *Eschatology in the Greek Psalter.* Wissenschaftliche Untersuchungen zum Neuen Testament 2/76. Tübingen: Mohr Siebeck, 2016.

Seitz, Christopher R. *The Character of Christian Scripture: The Significance of a Two-Testament Bible.* Studies in Theological Interpretation. Grand Rapids: Baker Academic, 2011.

———. *The Elder Testament: Canon, Theology, Trinity.* Waco: Baylor University Press, 2018.

———. "The Trinity in the Old Testament." In *The Oxford Handbook of the Trinity,* edited by Giles Emery and Matthew Levering, 28–40. Oxford: Oxford University Press, 2011.

Selderhuis, Herman J. *Calvin's Theology of the Psalms.* Texts and Studies in Reformation and Post-Reformation Thought. Grand Rapids: Baker Academic, 2007.

Selye, Hans. *The Stress of Life.* New York: McGraw-Hill, 1956.

Stec, David M. *The Targum of Psalms: Translated, with a Critical Introduction, Apparatus, and Notes.* Aramaic Bible 16. London: T&T Clark, 2004.

Strange, K. H., and R. G. E. Sandbach, eds. *Psalm 23: An Anthology.* Edinburgh: St. Andrews Press, 1987.

Strawn, Brent A. *The Old Testament Is Dying: A Diagnosis and Recommended Treatment.* Grand Rapids: Baker Academic, 2017.

Sumpter, Philip. "The Coherence of Psalms 15–24." *Biblica* 94 (2013): 186–209.

Sylva, Dennis D. "The Changing of Images in Ps. 23.5, 6." *Zeitschrift für die Alttestamentliche Wissenschaft* 102 (1990): 111–16.

Tanner, Beth L. "King Yahweh as the Good Shepherd: Taking Another Look at the Image of God in Psalm 23." In *David and Zion: Biblical Studies in Honor of J. J. M. Roberts,* edited by Bernard F. Batto and Kathryn L. Roberts, 267–84. Winona Lake, IN: Eisenbrauns, 2004.

Terrien, Samuel. *The Elusive Presence: Toward a New Biblical Theology.* New York: Harper & Row, 1978.

———. *The Psalms: Strophic Structure and Theological Commentary.* Eerdmans Critical Commentary. Grand Rapids: Eerdmans, 2003.

Treves, M. *The Dates of the Psalms: History and Poetry in Ancient Israel.* Pisa, Italy: Giardini Editori e Stampatori in Pisa, 1988.

Varhaug, Jørn. "The Decline of the Shepherd Metaphor as Royal Self-Expression." *Scandinavian Journal of the Old Testament* 33, no. 1 (2019): 16–23.

von Rad, Gerhard. *Biblical Interpretations in Preaching*. Translated by John E. Seely. Nashville: Abingdon, 1977.

———. *Old Testament Theology*. New York: Harper & Row, 1962.

Wallace, Mark I. *The Second Naiveté: Barth, Ricoeur, and the New Yale Theology*. 2nd ed. Studies in American Biblical Hermeneutics 6. Macon, GA: Mercer University Press, 1995.

Waltke, Bruce K., and James M. Houston, with Erika Moore. *The Psalms as Christian Lament*. Grand Rapids: Eerdmans, 2014.

———. *The Psalms as Christian Praise*. Grand Rapids: Eerdmans, 2019.

———. *The Psalms as Christian Worship*. Grand Rapids: Eerdmans, 2010.

Wenham, Gordon J. *Psalms as Torah: Reading Biblical Song Ethically*. Studies in Theological Interpretation. Grand Rapids: Baker Academic, 2012.

Whitman, Walt. *Leaves of Grass*. In *The Complete Poems*. London: Penguin, 2004.

Willgren, David. *The Formation of the 'Book' of Psalms*. Forschungen zum Alten Testament 2/88. Tübingen: Mohr Siebeck, 2016.

Wilson, Gerald H. *The Editing of the Hebrew Psalter*. Society of Biblical Literature Dissertation Series 76. Chico, CA: Scholars Press, 1985.

———. "The Structure of the Psalter." In *Interpreting the Psalms: Issues and Approaches*, edited by Philip S. Johnston and David G. Firth, 229–46. Leicester, UK: Apollos, 2005.

Wiseman, Matthew David. "Thou With Me: A Study in the Structure of Psalm 23." *Scandinavian Journal of the Old Testament* 30, no. 2 (2016): 280–93.

Wright, Stephen I. "An Experiment in Biblical Criticism: Aesthetic Encounter in Reading and Preaching Scripture." In *Renewing Biblical Interpretation*, edited by Craig Bartholomew, Colin Greene, and Karl Möller, 240–67. SHS 1. Grand Rapids: Zondervan, 2000.

Zenger, Erich. *A God of Vengeance? Understanding the Psalms of Divine Wrath*. Louisville: Westminster John Knox, 1996.

Scripture Index

Major discussions of Ps. 23 are given in bold.

Old Testament

Genesis

1 75–76
1:11 76
1:12 76
2:9 96
2:17 96
2:24 27n11
3:6 31
6:5 96
28:21 118n108
40 109
41 96
44 109
48:15 132n1

Exodus

15:13 79, 83
16:18 72
20:2 146
23:19 123n115

25 103
34:26 123n115
37 103
40 103
40:4 103

Deuteronomy

in toto 33
5:6 146
23:18 123n115

Joshua

6:24 123n115
8:16 115
8:17 115
8:20 115
8:24 115

Judges

19:18 123n115

Ruth

2:8–9 101
2:13 101

1 Samuel

1:7 123n115
1:24 123n115
3:15 123n115
9:9 27n11
13:14 68
16–17 56n81

2 Samuel

7:4–14 44n53, 123
12:20 44n53, 123n115

1 Kings

2:7 103
4:27 103
6–8 123

7:48 103
10:5 103

2 Kings

4:10 103
5:21 115

Job

24:17 90
28:28 156n49

Psalms

1 24
1–4 143n30
1–89 125n117
1:1 93n55
2 24
2:9 100
3 143n30
3:1 29
4 143n30
7 29n17
8 70n11
8:1 70n11
9–10 56
10 24
15 60
15–24 58–60, 62
16 59
16:4 88n43
16:5 60n92
17:8 88
19 59–60
19:8 60
19:9 156n49
20–21 59n90
22 61, 61n96, 137, 137n11,
   139, 141
22 title 24
22–24 61–62
23 title 6, **28–35**

23:1 24, 60, **67–74**, 76,
   137n12, 141, 145, 146,
   165
23:1–3 80
23:1–4 102
23:2 55, **74–79**, 80, 83,
   137n12
23:2–3 76n24, 86, 96, 141,
   144, 146, 147, 153, 168
23:3 75, **79–85**, 112, 146
23:4 55, 76n24, 80,
   85–102, 106, 124, 140,
   141, 146, 149, 154, 155,
   160, 168
23:5 46, 60n92, 96, 97,
   102–12, 137n12, 154,
   155, 156, 157, 159, 160,
   161, 165, 168
23:6 6–7, 44n53, 45n56,
   46, 46n59, 97, **112–28**,
   154, 156, 165
24 59–61, 61n96
24 title (LXX) 61n96
24:1 29n14
27:4 119–22, 125n117
30 title 44n53
31:3 79
32:7 98
33 24
33:2 29
34:11 156n49
34:14 115
36:8 125n117
40:1 29n14
40:3 30
41:11 98
42:4 125n117
43 24
46 29n17
47:6 29
52:8 125n117

60 title 24
68:1 29n14
69:16 115n103
71 24
72:20 30
73 147
73:2–3 147
73:23–24 98
78:70–72 100n71
80:1 68
81:2 29
84:10 125n117
92:13 125n117
93–97 24
95:7 68
98:5 29
100:3 68
101:1 29n14
109:1 29n14
109:21 115n103
110 33
110:1 29n14
111–113 24
111:10 156n49
114–116 56n82
116:3–4 95
116:8 95
116:19 125n117
118:14 29
118:26 125n117
122:1 125n117
122:9 125n117
132:8 78
132:14 78
134:1 125n117
135:2 125n117
139:1 29n14
147 56
150:3 30n18
151 (LXX) 56n81
151:4 56n81

Proverbs

1:7 156n49
2 83
2:9 83
2:15 83
2:18 83
9:10 156n49
15:30 108
141:5 108

Isaiah

7:14 98
9:2 90
40:1 101
40:11 79
44 68
44:24 68
44:28 68
45:1 70
49:10 79, 138
51:17 109

Jeremiah

23:1–8 136

Ezekiel

34 136, 137n11, 138
34:31 136, 136n7
37 150, 150n42

Daniel

12 150n42
12:2–3 150

Hosea

12:6 121n110

Micah

1:10–15 93n55
6:8 115n103

Zechariah

10 136n8
11 136n8

New Testament

Matthew

1:23 98
18:10–14 136
27:46 137

Mark

6 136, 138
6:34 138
6:39 138
12:36–37 33
15:34 137

Luke

7:46 137n12
15:1–10 136

John

10 135–36, 137n11
10:1–18 135
10:10 135
10:11 135

Romans

5–6 94n58
12:15 161

Ephesians

6:10–20 169n79

1 Peter

5 136n8

Revelation

7:17 137n12, 138, 164

Subject Index

Abernethy, Andrew T., 84n35
Allison, Dale C., Jr., 137–38, 138n17
Alter, Robert, 147, 163n61
ancient literacy, 31–32
anointing, 107–12, 137n12
application, 15–18
Arterbury, Andrew E., 117
Athanasius, 39, 142
attentive reading, 54, 171, 178
Augustine, 11, 11n17, 61n96, 122n114, 142, 144

Bailey, Kenneth E., 54–55, 100, 108n88, 135–36, 138, 138n15
Barth, Karl, 73n20, 163n61
Barton, John, 135n5
Bellinger, William H., Jr., 117, 124n116, 167n74
Birkeland, Harris, 105n81
blessing, 111
Bono, 34
Book of Common Prayer, 22, 25, 28, 73, 74, 92
book of Psalms, 55–62
  Book 1, 29, 58, 61n95
  Books 1–3, 56n80, 120, 125n117
  Book 2, 30, 58, 125n117
  Book 3, 58

Book 4, 42, 56n80, 58, 125n117
Book 5, 56n80, 125n117
canonical reading, 57–58
editorial arrangement, 57
Bosma, Carl J., 38–39, 40n40
Bradley, Ian, 168–70, 169n79
Brown, William P., 42n44, 59, 59nn89–91
Broyles, Craig C., 45, 46n59, 117–18
Brueggemann, Walter, 124n116, 160n57, 166–67, 167nn74–75

Calvin, John, 40, 61n96, 143
Carr, David M., 32n21
Celtic spirituality, 168–70
character, 16–17, 178
Chapman, Stephen B., 66n2
Childs, Brevard S., 27–28, 57n83, 163–64
Christ. *See* Jesus
Church of England, 168
Clines, David J. A., 67, 85, 85n37, 87n41, 89n46, 93–94, 113, 115n104
Common Worship, 25n7, 28
Coolio, 8
Cooper, Alan, 118n108
Coverdale, Myles, 22, 70n11, 92, 92n53, 113n98
Craigie, Peter C., 106n85, 137n10
Creach, Jerome F. D., 164–65

"Crimond" (hymn), 7
Croft, Steven J. L., 35–37, 105n80
cult, the, 39
"cup," 109–11
Cyril of Alexandria, 142
Cyrus, 70

Dahood, Mitchell, 76n24, 87n41, 88–89
daily office, 168
darkness. *See* shadow of death
David, King, 19, 84, 100, 123
  as author of Psalm 23, 6, 23, 31–34, 49
Davis, Ellen F., 174n7
Dead Sea Scrolls, 56n80
death, 89, 91–92, 94–95, 101–2, 107, 127,
  150–56
Death Valley, 93
DeClaissé-Walford, Nancy L., 58nn86–87,
  61, 61n95, 81n28
divine presence, 97–98, 140–41
Di Vito, Robert A., 81n29
Doctor Who (TV show), 141
Driver, G. R., 25n9
"dwell," 117–22

Eaton, John, 37, 100n72
Eco, Umberto, 172n3
editorial additions, 26–27
enemies, 20, 46, 104–7, 112, 154, 156–62,
  175
Erasmus, 10, 141–44
Eucharist, 110, 142, 161–62, 166–67
evil, 95–97, 106–7
exegesis, xi–xii, 5, 15–18, 19–20, 51, 65–67,
  173
Experiment in Criticism, An (Lewis), 172

Fiedrowicz, Michael, 142
first/third person. *See* "I-You."
Firth, David G., 65, 106, 106n84
Fokkelman, Jan, 66

follow. *See* pursue
Ford, David F., 146
forever, 106, 125–27
Frei, Hans W., 55n79
funerals, 20, 151–56

Gadamer, Hans-Georg, 16
"Gangsta's Paradise" (Coolio), 8, 10n11
Gawande, Atul, 151n44
Gillingham, Susan, 8, 12–13, 43–45,
  59n89, 60–61, 70n10
Goldingay, John, 57n84, 78–79, 89, 91, 96,
  96n60, 106n85, 121, 167, 180
Goodall, Howard, 8
goodness, 113–15, 115n103, 176
Gunkel, Hermann, 36, 38–39, 105

Hays, Richard B., 135n5, 137, 137n11
Heath, Michael J., 144n35
Hebrew tense, 72
Herbert, George, 41n42
hermeneutics, 4, 15–18
ḥesed, 114, 114n101. *See also* mercy
historical reconstruction, 2, 19, 27, 38–39,
  43–46, 48–49
Hobbs, T. R., 105n81
Holladay, William, 11, 56n80, 58n88,
  151–52, 152n47
Holy Spirit, 134, 141
hope, 164, 165–66
hospitality, 102–3
house of the LORD, 44–45, 112, 117–18,
  120, 122–25
Houston, James, 13, 70n12, 142–43,
  143nn28–30

"In Heavenly Love Abiding" (Waring), 73
interpretation
  canonical, 136–37
  christological, 110, 110n95, 139–44

critical, 4, 90–91, 172
historical-critical, 37–38
imaginative, 2–3, 18, 173
Jewish, 18n30, 131–32, 132nn2–3, 150
literary, 40–41, 60–62, 159, 172
metaphorical, 52–53
theological, 4, 39–40, 173
trinitarian, 140–41
tropological, 143
See also application; exegesis;
     hermeneutics
"I-You," 97, 97n63

Jackson, P. K., 105n81
Jacobson, Karl N., 42
Jacobson, Rolf A., 34n23, 42, 47n60, 103
Janzen, J. Gerald, 127, 127n121
Jerome, 21, 21n2, 25, 70–71, 82, 92, 110,
     116n105
Jesus, 33, 132–44
   as Good Shepherd, 135–36, 144
"Jesus Walks" (Kanye West), 8
Johnson, Nathan C., 122n114

Keller, W. Phillip, 50–54
king(ship), 70–71, 163, 163n62. *See also*
     royal psalms
King James Version, 22, 25, 30n18
Kraus, Hans-Joachim, 45–46, 46n58, 106
Kreitzer, Larry, 17n29
Kushner, Harold, 132

Lamb, John Alexander, 11
Lash, Nicholas, 17n29
Leaves of Grass (Whitman), 35n26
Levenson, Jon D., 94–95, 127n121, 133–
     34, 134n4, 150, 150n41
Lewis, C. S., 158–60, 160n56, 171, 171n1,
     172–73
literacy, 31–32

literal sense, 139, 143
"The Lord Is My Shepherd" (hymn), 75,
     75n23, 77–78
"Love Rescue Me" (U2), 9
LXX, 21, 29, 56, 82, 91, 108–10, 116,
     118–19, 121–22, 137, 164

MacDonald, M. C. A., 31
Magonet, Jonathan, 74n21
Masoretic Text/vocalization, 88, 91–92,
     118, 181
Maxwell, Nathan Dean, 42
Mays, James Luther, 41, 47, 100n72
McCann, J. Clinton, 58n87, 83n31, 163
mercy, 113–15, 115n103, 176
Message, The (Peterson), 71, 76, 84, 93, 109
midrash, 27, 55n78, 72, 72n15
Miller, Patrick D., 41
ministry, xi, 20, 152, 155
Moberly, Walter, 3n1, 155n50
Mowinckel, Sigmund, 36
Muraoka, Takamitsu, 99n68, 103, 115n104,
     179

Nasuti, Harry P., 40n39
Nel, Philip J., 47n60
New English Bible, 25, 25n8

Oesterley, W. O. E., 11, 11n15
oil, 51–52
overwhelming, 146–47

Parkander, Dorothy J., 41, 41n42
pastures, 75–76
peace, 153–54
persona, 35–48
Peterson, Eugene, 71, 76, 84, 93, 109,
     112n97, 113, 116
pilgrimage, 169–70
Pink Floyd, 8–9

plain-sense reading, 2, 4–5
Polk, Timothy, 41, 41n41
praise, 29–30
preaching, 18, 20, 163, 173–78
Presley, Elvis, 34
Prothero, Rowland E., 11, 11nn16–17
"psalm," 28–31
Psalm 23
  authorship, 6, 19, 23–35, 49
  background information, lack of, 63,
    106, 157
  canonical location, 55–62, 136–37
  and "Crimond," 7
  devotional readings, 13–15, 55
  global perspectives, 20n33
  historical-critical approaches, 10, 19
  history of interpretation, 3, 5, 7–15
  and the king. See Psalm 23: as royal
    psalm
  literary interpretation of, 12
  liturgical use, 11
  persona of, 43–48
  poetic structure of, 75, 77, 80, 97
  as poetry, 67, 73, 127
  popular readings, 13–15, 55
  postmodern approaches, 12–13
  reception history, 9–13
  as royal psalm, 46–48, 70–71, 100, 138,
    163–64
  and shepherding, 14, 19, 43–44, 48–55,
    76, 100n69, 102n73
  title, 24, 28–35
  translation, 128–29
  translations of, 21–22, 67
psalms
  anonymous, 32
  authorship, 36–37
  and the individual, 35–37
  as poetry, 31
  as praises, 29–30
  as prayers, 30

titles of, 23–28
  omission of, 25
  verse numbering, 24
Psalms, book of. See book of Psalms
Psalms as Christian Worship, The (Waltke
    and Houston), 13
pursue, 115–16, 154, 176
Pyper, Hugh S., 63

rest, 146–48
resurrection, 138n17, 149–56
return. See "dwell"
Revised English Bible, 25n8
Ricoeur, Paul, 4n2, 18n31
right(eous)ness, 83–84, 84n33, 164–65
rivers, 78
Rosenbaum, Stanley M., 159n53
royal psalms, 35–37, 46–48, 70–71

Sabbath, 145
second naivete, 4
Seitz, Christopher R., 135n5, 139, 139n19,
    141, 141n23
Septuagint. See LXX
shadow of death, 87–95, 153
shall/will, 73, 95, 119
Shape of Living, The (Ford), 146
"Sheep" (Pink Floyd), 8–9
shepherd, 68–71, 99–101
shepherding, 14, 19, 48–55, 76, 99–101,
    136
Shepherd Looks at Psalm 23, A (Keller),
    50–54
Sheriffs, Deryck, 74n22
song. See "psalm"
soul, 40, 81–82, 146
spiritual reading, 4, 14–15, 49–50
stress, 144–49
Sumpter, Philip, 59n91
superscriptions. See psalms: titles of

"table," 103–4
targum, 71–72, 91, 91n52, 93, 98, 98n66, 109n90
temple. *See* house of the LORD
tense, 72
Terrien, Samuel, 98, 98n64, 104, 104nn77–78, 109
textual emendation, 88–91
textual variants, 121, 122n114
Theodore of Cyrrhus, 142–43
Titanic (film), 9
Townend, Stuart, 7–8
Trinity, the, 134, 139–42
trust, 1

U2, 9, 34

valley of the shadow of death, 87–95, 153
Varhaug, Jørn, 47n60
Velvet Revolution, 176
verse numbering, 24
Vicar of Dibley, The (TV show), 8
voice. *See* persona
von Rad, Gerhard, 37, 37n31, 39, 39nn33–34, 43, 45, 173
Vulgate, 21, 25n6, 70–71, 82, 92, 108n89

Wadi Qelt, 87
Waltke, Bruce, 13, 70n12, 142–43, 143nn28–30
water, 78–79
Wenham, Gordon J., 84n33
West, Kanye, 8
Whitman, Walt, 35n26
Willgren, David, 24n4, 57n85
will/shall, 73, 95, 119
Wilson, Gerald H., 57n83, 163n62
wisdom, 16, 133, 178
wise reading. *See* wisdom
world
   behind the text, 18–19, 21–63
   in front of the text, 18–20, 131–70
   in the text, 18–20, 65–129
worlds behind, in, and in front of text, inseparability of, 19, 35
worship, 162–70
Wright, Stephen I., 172n4
Wycliffe Bible, 25

YHWH (divine name), 67–68

Zenger, Erich, 157–58, 160